TE

International Library of Criminology

Delinquency and Deviant Social Behaviour

Editors:

EDWARD GLOVER · HERMANN MANNHEIM

EMANUEL MILLER

No. 17: Schools for Young Offenders

PUBLISHED UNDER THE AUSPICES OF THE INSTITUTE
FOR THE STUDY AND TREATMENT OF DELINQUENCY

Schools
for Young Offenders

GORDON ROSE

TAVISTOCK PUBLICATIONS

PUBLISHED UNDER THE AUSPICES OF THE INSTITUTE
FOR THE STUDY AND TREATMENT OF DELINQUENCY

First published in 1967
by Tavistock Publications Limited
11 New Fetter Lane, London EC4
and printed in Great Britain
in 10 pt Plantin, 1¼ pts leaded
by Cox and Wyman Ltd
Fakenham, Norfolk

Distributed in the United States of America
by Barnes & Noble, Inc.

Contents

v

Preface

In this book my aim has been, first, to offer a brief descriptive account of the approved school system in England and Wales and, second, to discuss some of the problems of this form of training. I would certainly not claim to have dealt comprehensively with all aspects of this subject, though most have been touched upon, and attention is concentrated mainly on organizational questions and matters of principle. The fact that there is no detailed discussion of the teaching process, of leisure-time activities, casework, and so on is partly owing to limitations of space and largely owing to limitations in the author. My primary concerns have been to provide basic information that will enable people who wish to do so to get to know something about the schools, and to examine what appear to me to be some fundamental problems which, despite the Committee on Children and Young Persons (Ingleby Committee) and the debates on the Criminal Justice Bill, 1961, have not received adequate consideration.

Since this manuscript was written the Home Office White Paper *The child, the family and the young offender* (1965; Cmnd. 2742) has appeared. It is possible as a result of its recommendations that approved schools will disappear, senior schools being merged with borstals to create a system of 'youth training centres', and junior and intermediate schools being handed over to local authority children's departments. The original manuscript had envisaged this possibility and the arguments in Part II remain relevant, although some modifications have been made to take into account the proposals in the White Paper. If the approved school system as such is to be discontinued it is, of course, all the more valuable to try to collect together what is known about it, and about similar systems elsewhere.

The White Paper envisages also a change of name for juvenile courts and some change in their functions. They would become 'family courts' and would deal with all those under 16 years of age; young offenders' courts would handle the 16–21 age-group. Presumably there would be no direct committal to a residential training school under the age of 16; rather, the court would make an order similar to the present fit person order, after which the children's department would take the appropriate steps. The White Paper further proposes the establishment of 'family councils', to be appointed by children's departments; they would take any action agreed to by the parent, thus forestalling reference to the court, and it would be within the range of agreement to send to a residential school. In cases where this was not feasible, or where the arrangement broke down, the family court would need to consider making an order. For those over 16, the committal procedure would probably be very similar to the present one in respect of borstal training.

Some of the information that is presented as current practice in Part I may soon, therefore, become a matter of historical record. Though it will not be invalidated on this account, it may be wise to issue a warning to the reader, especially the overseas reader, to keep in mind the possibility of radical change.

I am heavily indebted to the Home Office for a great deal of help in assembling the facts, and to many people associated with individual schools who talked freely and frankly to me, and gave generously of their time. I need hardly say, however, that responsibility for the accuracy of the information and for the opinions expressed is entirely my own.

The very large number of approved schools in the country precludes anyone, except, perhaps, a few of the Home Office inspectors, from knowing what is happening in all of them, or even from visiting the majority of them. I have therefore thought it best not to try to single out particular schools by name. Also, it has proved rather difficult to talk comprehensively about training in establishments of this kind, or about those committed to them, without getting involved in tortuous or official phraseology. In an attempt to overcome this problem I have used the word 'institution' quite freely, and it is not intended to carry any derogatory overtones. Terms such as 'boy', 'girl', and 'child' are employed somewhat loosely to cover age-groups under 21, and, in conformity with the statutes, 'boy' often includes 'girl'. The context will, it is hoped, make clear what is meant in any particular case.

Publication of this book was held up for some time because new Approved School Rules were being prepared, and it was hoped to take account of these in the text and to include them as an Appendix. They now appear to have been superseded by the proposals of the White Paper mentioned above, and the old Rules remain in force until a decision is taken upon the future of the system. Suggestions put forward in the text regarding changes in the Rules have, in the circumstances, been left as they were, pending this decision.

GORDON ROSE

Acknowledgements

Thanks are due to the following for permission to reproduce material from published work: the Trustees of The Carnegie United Kingdom Trust in respect of *Delinquency and human nature* by D. H. Stott; the Controller of Her Majesty's Stationery Office in respect of *Approved school boys* by J. Gittins, and *The sentence of the court*; the Editor of the *British Journal of Preventive and Social Medicine* and Z. A. Stein and M. W. Susser in respect of 'A socio-medical study of enuresis among delinquent boys'.

PART ONE

Mainly Informative

I

Reformatory and industrial schools

'That part of the community which we are to consider consists of those
who have not yet fallen into actual crime, but who are almost certain
from their ignorance, destitution, and the circumstances in which they
are growing up, to do so, if a helping hand be not extended to raise
them; – these form the *perishing classes*:— and of those who have
already received the prison brand, or, if the mark has not been yet
visibly set upon them, are notoriously living by plunder, – who un-
blushingly acknowledge that they can gain more for the support of
themselves and their parents by stealing than working, – whose hand
is against every man, for they know not that any man is their brother;
– these form the *dangerous classes*. Look at them in the streets, where,
to the eye of the worldly man, they all appear the scum of the populace,
fit only to be swept as vermin from the face of the earth; see them in
their homes, if such they have, squalid, filthy, vicious, or pining and
wretched with none to help, destined only, it would seem, to be
carried off by some beneficent pestilence; – and you have no hesitation
in acknowledging that these are indeed dangerous and perishing
classes. Behold them when the hand of wisdom and of love has shown
them a better way, and purified and softened their outward demeanour
and their inner spirit, in schools well adapted to themselves, and you
hardly believe them to be separated by any distinct boundary from the
children who frequent the National and British Schools. Yet there is,
and will long be, a very strongly defined line of separation between
them, and which requires perfectly distinct machinery and modes of
operation in dealing with them' (Carpenter, 1851, pp. 2–3).

In these few sentences, one of the founders of the system of reformatory
and industrial schools, Mary Carpenter, summed up the springs of the
movement. With the immense compassion of the Victorian reformers
was linked their belief in education and industry as a means of reclaiming
the lower classes. The biblical phrasing that they employed points to
the essentially religious basis of their thought. Mary Carpenter's work
in this field, the facts and figures she presents in her book, offer a
practical approach to the problem and common-sense solutions – the
'machinery and modes of operation in dealing with them'.

She believed that three kinds of provision were needed. First, free day schools for the destitute and all those who were unable to obtain education in the existing establishments. This was really a plea for the further extension of primary education, but laying stress upon those who were unable to pay towards the cost. There already were a number of day ragged schools, and she wanted the system further extended, and very much improved in quality. Second, she proposed industrial feeding schools for those we should now think of as 'care or protection' cases. These would provide for those children who did not go to the free day schools, when it would be necessary for the court to exercise its powers to ensure their attendance at school. And, third, she wanted penal reformatory schools as a substitute for imprisonment where children had been convicted of crime.

We are primarily concerned here with the second and third of these proposals. When they were propounded in 1851 they were not new. Mary Carpenter's book marks the beginning of the transition from pioneering to a national system under statute. Industrial schools are, in fact, as old as the poor law; indeed, workhouses were originally industrial schools, mainly for grown-ups but also for children, and the principle of putting the poor of all ages to work was well accepted, though not often efficiently carried out, by the early part of the eighteenth century. Various efforts to make workhouses live up to their name, and to generalize the system, were ineffective, and institutional care for paupers was in decline over a considerable part of Britain in the last years of the eighteenth and early years of the nineteenth century, to be re-established with vigour by the 1834 Poor Law Amendment Act. Subsequent to this, at the instigation of James Kay, later Sir James Kay-Shuttleworth, a pioneer of English education, Boards of Guardians were empowered to set up district schools, but these, though humane in intention, still bore the poor-law stigma; they were also few in number, often poorly organized, and too large. Other important developments were a successful industrial school in 1840, and a 'child's asylum' in 1846, in Aberdeen. The latter was for children found wandering or begging, who, by a slight bending of the law, could be committed by the magistrates.

Much more significant influences, serving as an inspiration for both industrial and reformatory schools, came from abroad. In Germany there was the Rauhe Haus, founded in 1833: an industrial colony for children, based upon what we should now describe as the cottage-home system, each family of twelve having a superintendent discharging the duty of house father. In France there was Mettray, founded in 1839; it followed the example of the Rauhe Haus, but was on a larger scale, having eight houses with forty children in each. A Belgian law of 1848 established reformatory schools, and in the same year an institution was started at Ruysselede. W. Suringar, a Dutch reformer, established a 'Dutch Mettray' in 1850 at Zutphon. By this time a great many similar institutions had been founded in various Continental countries,[1] and a few in England.

By far the most important influence was Mettray, however, presumably because of its proximity. Both Sidney Turner, Chaplain to the Philanthropic Society founded in 1788 to help criminal and destitute children, who visited it in 1845, and Matthew Davenport Hill, the reforming Recorder of Birmingham, who visited it in 1848, were exceedingly impressed, and the Philanthropic Society as a consequence started Redhill School in 1849, with Sidney Turner as headmaster.[2]

The time was thus ripe for a reforming spirit and Mary Carpenter was that spirit. In 1851, in conjunction with M. D. Hill, she convened a national conference which endorsed the conclusions of her book that free day schools, day industrial schools, and reformatory schools should be set up, with State assistance. The conference led to the Select Committee on Criminal and Destitute Children, which in 1853 reported in favour of reformatory schools; the report recommended that State grants should be made available, although parents should continue to be financially responsible for their children, and that power should be given to the courts to commit to such schools in lieu of committal to prison. The outcome of the Select Committee was the Youthful Offenders Act, 1854 (usually referred to as the Reformatory Schools Act).

The 1854 Act gave the courts authority to send anyone under 16 years of age to a reformatory school at the expiration of his sentence, which must be of at least fourteen days; i.e. it was a 'dual track' system: sentence first and reformatory school after. The offender could be kept for two to five years in the school, but the Home Secretary could order his discharge at any time and could also transfer offenders from one school to another. The State was empowered to make a *per capita* grant to schools inspected and certified by one of H.M. Inspectors of Prisons (there had been Inspectors of Prisons since 1835). Absconding or refractory conduct could be punished by a sentence of up to three months.

---

[1] Joseph Fletcher, the most influential of the early H.M. Inspectors of Schools, read a paper on 'The farm-school system of the Continent and its applicability to the preventive and reformatory education of paupers and criminal children in England and Wales' to the Statistical Society of London in 1852 (Appendix 1, Report of the Select Committee on Criminal and Destitute Children, XXIII, Home Office, 1852–53).

[2] See the report on Mettray by Sidney Turner (ibid., Appendix 8).

Parents were compelled to contribute, if they were able, up to five shillings a week. This latter provision was strengthened by an Act of 1855 which, in cases of failure to pay, gave the courts power to summons parents, to make an order for payment, and to distrain upon the goods of the parents or commit them to prison if necessary.

The Act thus laid the foundation of the system of voluntarily managed, State-aided schools which has survived to the present day. Inevitably it provided a strong impetus to found such schools and a number of well-known schools were added to the few existing schools in this period.[1] In 1857 the Act was amended to allow local authorities to contribute both to the establishment of reformatories and to the upkeep of children in them; and the power to license, after half the period of detention, was added.

This legislation did not cover industrial schools in England, although an Act had been passed in 1854 dealing with these schools in Scotland. The first English Act was passed in 1857; it provided a similar system, but with some significant differences. The schools were to be certified not by the Home Secretary but by the Committee of the Privy Council on Education, that is to say, they were attached to the central control of the education system, such as it was, not the penal system, and were to be inspected by the education staff. Conviction for vagrancy was to be the initial step, and the justices could make an order only if the parent was unable to find surety for the child's good behaviour. Children between the ages of 7 and 14 could be committed and, whatever the age of committal, could be retained until the age of 15, but the justices could discharge a child at any time on the application of the parents or the managers of the school, and the managers could board him out. On the financial side there was no provision for aid from the Treasury, but parents could be made liable. Boards of Guardians could contract to send children to the schools, but were not liable to maintain them otherwise.

Thus industrial schools started off on a distinctly different track from reformatory schools, with a much more educational bias. But administrative convenience soon intervened: in 1860 the responsibility for industrial schools was transferred from the Committee of Education, at its request,[2] to the Home Secretary, and in 1861 a consolidating Act gave the Treasury power to provide financial assistance, and set the limit for parental contributions at the same level as for reformatory schools, viz. five shillings.

[1] Mary Carpenter herself founded Kingswood (for boys) in Bristol in 1852, and Red Lodge (for girls) in 1855.

[2] See Appendix XXXII, Report of the Committee on Reformatories and Industrial Schools, C. 8204 (Home Office, 1896).

In the meanwhile, however, the first Home Office inspector had been appointed (1857) in the person of Sidney Turner of Redhill.

In 1866 these and other amending Acts were consolidated in two measures applicable to the whole of Great Britain, and these two Acts remained the main statutory basis of the system until the Children Act of 1908. The Home Office could withdraw a certificate on six months' notice, and any substantial modification or addition to the school buildings was to be submitted for approval, as were the school rules and any proposed change in them. Thus the Home Office, working through its chief inspector, already had considerable powers over the running of the schools. There were various other modifications: in particular, the minimum age for reformatory schools was fixed at 10 years, and the classes of children who could be sent to industrial schools were extended so that they now covered those found begging, wandering, or destitute, or frequenting the company of reputed thieves; all those under 12 years of age who were convicted of offences; and all under 14 who were found, on the application of the parent, to be beyond control. The maximum age of detention for industrial schools was now 16. Prison authorities, that is to say counties and county boroughs by and large, could contribute to the upkeep or building of the schools.

Thus the basis of the system was laid and worked out in the twelve years between 1854 and 1866. At the same time, the number of schools and of children committed to them expanded steadily, and by the end of 1865 there were sixty-five reformatory and fifty industrial schools in Great Britain, accommodating 4,915 and 2,062 children respectively. Ten years later the number of industrial schools had risen to 117, whereas the number of reformatory schools remained the same. The number of industrial schools continued to rise fairly steadily, and there were over 15,000 children in such establishments in 1880. In contrast, the number of reformatory schools declined slightly, their population remaining around 5,000 to 6,000.

A notable factor in the development of the system was the foundation of the Reformatory and Refuge Union in 1856 as an offshoot of the series of conferences which had followed the original meeting in Birmingham in 1851. The Union provided a point of contact and a forum for exchange of views and expression of opinion, especially through its *Journal*, started in 1861. It was also concerned with 'rescue' work, with alcoholics, and with Discharged Prisoners' Aid Societies. In 1881 it was joined by a professional organization, the National Association of Certified Reformatory and Industrial Schools, a representative body of managers, superintendents, and heads of schools, and the two worked side by side until their formal amalgamation in 1898.

B

Both bodies exercised considerable influence on the legislation of the period.

Problems soon began to arise. The first and most important so far as the government was concerned was the rising cost, which the system of *per capita* State contribution did nothing to abate. If there were more children in industrial schools there was more expenditure, and the number of children sent to the schools depended not upon the Home Office but upon the courts.

Furthermore, in all cases of any seriousness the courts had a choice between imprisonment and committal to a school, but there was no other alternative. Although the idea of probation was known in England from about 1880 onwards (the work of the Church of England Temperance Society started in 1876, but the concept of probation as we know it really came from America), it was thought of as largely applying to adults, and came to fruition as a measure to rehabilitate children only as a result of the juvenile court movement in the 1900s. Corporal punishment could not be administered to anyone under 14 years of age, and there remained only the lesser penalties of fines and binding over, neither of them very useful for the types of case involved. It was not surprising, therefore, that despite a general decline in criminality in the 1880s (attributed variously to the efforts of the courts, the industrial and reformatory schools, and the prisons, according to the bias of the writer) the numbers in the schools did not fall off.

But this trend, in so far as it was due to the rise in numbers committed to industrial schools, was also related to another general trend, that of treating children more humanely. The names of Benjamin Waugh, Florence Davenport Hill, Dr Barnardo, T. B. Stephenson, Louisa Twining, and Henrietta Barnett are among those who, in various spheres, attempted to ameliorate the lot of unwanted and ill-treated children, and the feeling that had given rise to the schools in the first place steadily gained ground – that children should be cared for, not punished, and that they should not be allowed to fall victim either to the poverty or viciousness of their parents, or to the deficiencies of the general mixed workhouse. This attitude showed itself not only in a readiness to use industrial schools, but also in a growing volume of criticism of the schools as providing a régime which did not sufficiently take into account the individual needs of children. To a considerable extent the schools' deficiencies could be explained by problems of finance, since poverty in many cases meant a poor standard of staff and a tendency towards profitable industry rather than training.

There were also a number of lesser, but equally intractable, problems. Who was to inspect the educational work of the schools: the Home

Office or the Board of Education? And, if both, how were the dangers of dual inspection to be avoided? Should the period of imprisonment preceding committal to reformatory be continued, or was it undesirable? (This issue produced an extremely sharp division of opinion.) Could some form of classification be introduced so that those who were minor offenders would be segregated from the more serious offenders? How should the career prospects of the teachers be linked with those of ordinary teaching?

These were only some of the matters that gave rise to lively debate, and they led to two government committees, one of which reported in 1884 and the other in 1896. (The Home Office papers also contain an unpublished report of an internal committee of 1881.[1]) In 1906 there was an Interdepartmental Committee on the Provision of Funds for Reformatory and Industrial Schools. A number of changes were made in the Children Act, 1908, and in various minor Acts; and there was yet another committee, which reported in 1913.

This string of government inquiries points to an insoluble problem and the problem was that of control. The financial aspects were the most difficult: on the one hand, the Treasury complained of increasing expenditure; on the other, the schools found themselves in a series of financial crises. But behind these difficulties was the ever-present problem of how to provide a satisfactory service of high quality through a series of semi-independent units imperfectly controlled from the centre. The committee of 1896, which distinguished itself by producing no fewer than nine minority reports (four of them signed by the chairman!), split upon the fundamental questions of whether the treatment was appropriate and whether the schools should be managed by the Home Office or the Education Department. There is, incidentally, an underlying critical note, which runs through the whole report and is strongly expressed in the first minority report signed by the chairman and three of the nine members, stressing the disadvantages of the penal school and making a plea for fewer committals to industrial schools and more boarding out.

On one or two of the lesser problems, however, there was some advance. The period of preliminary imprisonment prior to reformatory school was abolished, after prolonged argument, in 1899. Further, some move was made towards classification by the setting up of truant schools and day industrial schools under an Act of 1876. The former, of which

---

[1] Public Record Office Paper HO45/9607. There are, in addition, a number of papers on the action resulting from the committees: see, in particular, HO45/A13312 on the 1884 committee.

there were fifteen in 1896, dealt with the less serious school-attendance cases, and the latter (twenty-three in 1896) were a kind of ragged school for the very poor, rather nearer in fact to Mary Carpenter's original conception of day feeding schools. Classification proper had to wait, however, until the Children Act, 1908, under which the law relating to the schools was again consolidated. Anyone between 12 and 16 years of age could be sent to a reformatory school if convicted of an offence punishable in an adult with imprisonment or penal servitude, and could be kept there from three to five years but not beyond the age of 19. Any child under 14 could be sent to an industrial school if found to be begging, wandering, or destitute; in the care of parents of criminal or drunken habits; the daughter of a father convicted of sexual assault upon her; frequenting the company of thieves or prostitutes, or living in a house of prostitution; failing to attend school, refractory in the workhouse, or beyond control. Once there, a child could be detained as long as the court directed, but not beyond the age of 16. Reformatory school-leavers remained under supervision until 19 years of age, and industrial school-leavers to 18. The managers could license children after they had been eighteen months in a school. Most of these, and other detailed provisions, merely reiterated what was already the situation.

The general standard of staff remained low. Teachers were eventually brought into the superannuation scheme for elementary school teachers, but there was still no superannuation scheme for other staff levels in 1913. The committee of 1913 compared the position at that time in 176 schools with the situation in 1896, and found that the number of certificated teachers had risen from 151 to 228, but there were still forty-seven schools at the later date without such teachers.

Furthermore, the inspection problem remained unsolved, and the various committees of inquiry recommended conflicting courses of action, with the result that inspection stayed with the Home Office and was very inadequately done; there was one single inspector for most of the period up to 1913, although the number of schools was increasing steadily year by year over much of this time. Another problem that remained unsolved was that of adequate aftercare, since the schools either did their own, within the very limited time at the disposal of the superintendents, or used any agency or person they thought suitable.

Despite all these difficulties the results were encouraging. Right from the start figures were kept of the proportion of successes, but like so many nineteenth-century returns they are open to criticism, and in fact came under heavy fire from the committee of 1896. Nevertheless, it seems likely that two-thirds to three-quarters of the children going through the schools might be reasonably claimed as successes, and this is no mean achievement, even if much of it is attributable to the fact that the schools removed children from an adverse environment and allowed them to grow up in a more favourable one.

Thus the First World War found the schools with their fundamental problems of control and finance unsolved. The government grant was revised in 1914 following the recommendations of the committee, but rising costs led once more to the familiar round of increased government grants and shortage of money in the schools. Local authorities had also been complaining for a long time that the fees charged at different schools varied immensely. In 1919 some unknown financial genius found the answer, and it was very simple. In future, there would be a flat rate per child, calculated upon the total estimated cost, and half of this would be paid by the local authority responsible for the child, and half by the Home Office. The rate would be adjusted each year to take into account deficiencies or surpluses in previous years. In addition, there were special grants for various purposes and a fund from which grants could be made at discretion. This is substantially the present financial basis, and it works well in that, in effect, it provides a grant based upon an estimate of cost for every school.

The 1913 committee also recommended that there should be a special branch at the Home Office to deal with these schools, with probation, and with other matters concerning children, and this was created in 1914.

Things, however, were changing in other respects. The appointment of C. E. B. Russell as chief inspector in 1913 represented a victory for those who, like Henrietta Barnett's State Children's Society, had been campaigning for fundamental changes in the way the schools were run, and Russell's first reports were extremely critical. He was very outspoken indeed as regards those regulations that militated against individual treatment and deadened self-respect and initiative among the children: uniforms, silence at meals, an over-organized curriculum, and regimentation in general.

The gradual growth of the probation service, which was put on a national basis by the Criminal Justice Act of 1925, together with the general decline in juvenile delinquency, led to a contraction in reformatory and industrial schools and to a change in attitudes towards them. In the nineteenth century they had been generally admired as a constructive alternative to prison; but in the twentieth century the growth of the feeling, not only that young people ought never to be sent to prison, but that they should not be committed to any institution if this was avoidable, made the schools appear in the light of an undesirable last resort, and this impression was strengthened by their failure to solve some of the fundamental problems of their existence. In 1922 Sir Edward Troup, a senior Home Office official lately retired, was already writing to *The Times*, appealing to magistrates to use reformatories more and referring to the wrong impression gained from attacks in some newspapers. The schools had by then fallen in number to thirty-one reformatory and ninety-nine industrial, with a total population of some 10,000, as against a wartime peak of 19,000 in 1915, and 17,000 in 1919.

The next event of note was the publication of the Report of the Departmental Committee on Young Offenders, 1927, one of the most significant committees in the history of methods of dealing with these classes of offender. The committee made numerous recommendations covering the whole field, and among them were: the abolition of the distinction between reformatory and industrial schools, and of the terms themselves, the schools to be described as 'approved by the Secretary of State'; the raising of the minimum age of committal to 10, and of the maximum, with certain exceptions, to 17 (this followed the recommended change in the age range covered by the juvenile courts from 7 to 16 years to 8 to 17); a general 'care or protection' provision; better classification; a maximum period of detention of three years, except that children of school age should be kept either for three years or to the end of the school period, whichever was the longer, the maximum for older offenders remaining at 19 (this represented a general reduction in the period of detention); the court to commit for three years in all cases, and the Home Office and the managers to decide the actual period; supervision up to 18 years of age, or, where the period of detention expired after the age of 15, up to 21; and some other minor changes. All these were embodied, virtually unchanged, in the Children and Young Persons Act, 1932, which was consolidated into the Children and Young Persons Act, 1933, the present statutory basis of the system.

In the 1930s the incidence of offences among juveniles began to rise, and the approved school population rose with it (by this time the majority sent to the schools were offenders, this being the result of improved educational and other social services, and of the success of the probation service). This rise, as we shall see, continued steadily through the war period, accelerating to a peak population of just over 11,000 in 1945; but, despite the continued post-war rise in the number of juvenile offenders, the proportion sent to approved schools has declined and the absolute figures have remained in the region of 8,000 to 10,000. We shall have more to say about this and about other aspects of the post-war situation in later chapters, but first it is necessary to examine more closely the present-day legal basis and organization of the schools.

2

The schools today

Approved schools are those certified by the Home Secretary 'for the education and training of persons to be sent there in pursuance of this Act' (the Children and Young Persons Act, 1933, s. 79).[1] Not only has the Home Secretary power to certify, but he may also withdraw a certificate either because he is dissatisfied with the condition and management of a school or because he considers its continuance as an approved school unnecessary, e.g. because committals are falling; or he can, without withdrawing the certificate of approval, prohibit admission to a school for a specified period or indefinitely. Under the Criminal Justice Act, 1961, he may give directions to the managers of a school if he thinks that the premises or equipment of the school, the number or grades of the staff employed, or the education, training, and welfare of those under the care of the managers (not merely in the school) are inadequate or unsuitable; and if the managers do not comply with his instructions he can withdraw the school's certificate or take the action outlined above (section 18). He also has powers under the same Act to regulate the constitution and proceedings of the managers, and to make additional appointments to the board of managers of a voluntary, but not a local authority, school (section 19).

Under the 1933 Act a local authority, or a combination of local authorities, may set up a school if the Home Secretary approves. The Act also lays a duty upon 'every local authority concerned' to remedy a deficiency of places. The intention is plainly to attempt to ensure that someone will take action in this event, but it is obviously unenforceable; indeed, it is very unclear who 'the local authority concerned' would be. Is it the authority financially responsible for the majority of those who can only be found places with difficulty, or are all local authorities 'concerned' in this situation?

In 1966 there were 123 schools, of which 93 were run by voluntary agencies and 30 by local authorities. Of these, 90 were for boys and 33 for girls. In them at 31 December 1965 there were 7,126 boys and 1,060

---

[1] Unless otherwise stated, references below to 'the Act' are to the Children and Young Persons Act, 1933.

girls, a total of 8,186.[1] (The figures are slightly higher in June than in December, and at 30 June 1965 there were 7,434 boys and 1,123 girls, making a total of 8,557.)

TYPES OF SCHOOL

The Home Secretary has power under the Act to classify schools according to age, religion, the character of the education and training given, 'and otherwise as he thinks best calculated to secure that a person sent to an approved school is sent to a school appropriate to his case, or as may be necessary for the purpose of this Act'. In other words, he can classify as he wishes and the managers must accept his classification,

TABLE 1 *Approved schools classified by age of intake*
(1966)

Type of school		Age on admission
BOYS		
Classifying	4	Up to 17th birthday
Senior	24	Between 15th and 17th birthdays
Intermediate	28	Between 13th and 15th birthdays
Intermediate/Junior	3	Between 12th and 14th birthdays
Junior (secondary)	14	From 10½ years up to 13th birthday
Junior (combined primary and secondary)	9	Up to 13th birthday
Junior (primary)	4	Up to 10½ years
Total	86	
GIRLS		
Classifying	Nil	
Senior	19	Between 14th and 17th birthdays
Intermediate	7	Between 14th and 16th birthdays
Intermediate/Junior	1	Up to 16th birthday
Junior	6	Up to 15th birthday
Total	33	
Grand total	119	

[1] Figures and other data presented here will inevitably become increasingly out of date, but the salient facts can easily be revised by reference to the Annual Statistics published by the Home Office and to the periodic Reports of the Children's Department (see Bibliography, pp. 235, 237).

with certain specified exceptions. There is, however, a proviso that, wherever practicable, a boy or girl committed to an approved school must be allocated to one catering for his or her religious persuasion. This has mainly affected Roman Catholic children, since Catholic schools have been outside the general system of classification and Catholic children have been allocated to schools by the vacancies section of the Home Office. (At the time of writing, it appears that they will be brought within the general scheme.) In the ordinary way, a child is, on committal, sent to one of the regional classifying schools. With regard to approved schools for boys, other than Roman Catholics, England and Wales are divided into four areas (a fifth area may be created), each with a classifying school attached to a training school. (In addition, the London area has a classifying centre in a remand home.) For girls there is no classifying school, and the work is partly carried out by remand homes.

All schools, with the exception of four (for boys) which take special classes, are classified by age of intake, as shown in *Table 1*.

Table 2 shows the sizes of the various types of school in 1966. It will be noted that the girls' schools are much smaller than the boys': over half of them accommodated fewer than 40 girls, whereas most of the boys' schools took over 80, and twenty of them over 120. The provision for Roman Catholic children is included in *Table 2*, and is also shown separately in *Table 17* (p. 47 below).

OUTLINE OF THE SYSTEM

In the succeeding chapters the structure of the schools will be considered in detail, but a brief outline of the system may be useful at this point. The schools are run by committees of managers of two main types. The majority are subcommittees of voluntary bodies or *ad hoc* committees of local people, often descended by appointment from the small group who got together originally to found the school. The minority of the schools are run directly by local authorities under their children's committees; in these cases the managers are a subcommittee of the children's committee and thus consist of councillors; there is, however, power to co-opt, which is sometimes exercised. The managers appoint their own chairman and treasurer, and a 'correspondent' who acts as their secretary.[1]

The managers are legally responsible for running the school, and the children in it are in their legal care. They are also directly responsible

[1] The Rules governing approved schools are embodied in a Statutory Instrument, currently the Approved School Rules 1933 (S.R. & O. 1933/774) as amended by S.I. 1949/2052 and S.I. 1963/1056.

TABLE 2 *Certified accommodation and type of school*
(excluding the 4 boys' classifying schools)
(1966)

Certified accommodation	Senior	Intermediate	Junior	Total
BOYS				
Under 40	—	—	4[a]	4[a]
40–59	2	2	6	10
60–79	4	—	5	9
80–99	9	7	4	20
100–119	7	10	6	23
120–139	5	8	4	17
140 and over	—	2[b]	1[b]	3[b]
Total	27	29	30	86
GIRLS				
20–29	7	1[a]	—	8[a]
30–39	6	4	1	11
40–49	2	2	2	6
50–59	1	1	1	3
60–69	2	—	—	2
70–79	—	—	—	—
80 and over	1[c]	—	2[cd]	3
Total	19	8	6	33

[a] New schools whose numbers are still growing: two junior boys and one intermediate girls.
[b] Intermediate schools of 147 and 160, and a junior school of 146.
[c] The senior school takes 84 girls. The two junior schools of 90 and 80 are both built on the cottage system.
[d] One of these schools also takes 32 intermediate girls.

for the release of each child at the appropriate time and for his subsequent supervision. In fact, however, most of their actions are closely controlled by the Home Office regional inspectorate which has, under the Rules, very wide powers to supervise the schools' activities; the actual work is, of course, largely carried out by the headmaster or headmistress and the other members of staff. This system of management gives rise to certain points of difficulty which will be discussed later. The managers appoint and dismiss staff, but the head's appointment has to have the approval of the Home Office, and in practice the regional inspectors tend to advise or sit in on the more important appointments.

Money is provided against estimates by the Home Office, but there is an arrangement whereby the local authority from whose area the child comes and the Treasury share the cost equally. Capital expenditure is strictly controlled by the Home Office.

The most important person in the school is, of course, the head. In boys' schools his wife usually acts as matron, a post that does not exist in girls' schools. The head is responsible to the managers for the running of the school, and is in constant touch directly with the regional inspectors and the Home Office. In a school of any size there is also a deputy head, and in most schools a third in charge. These posts apart, the two major grades of staff are those of teacher and housemaster, the latter likely to come from a background of social work, if indeed his previous experience is relevant in any way, rather than from schoolmastering.

Housemasters are almost exclusively a post-war phenomenon and the qualified teacher remains the mainstay of most schools, partly from tradition and partly because full-time education is provided for all children in the junior schools, and for some children in intermediate schools; there is some formal education in all schools, and the teacher is thus doubly useful. For those above school-leaving age formal education gives way to vocational training and useful work in a great variety of trades and employment, and instructors are employed to supervise these older children.

An approved school order under the Act of 1933 (s. 71 as amended by s. 71 of the Criminal Justice Act, 1948) covers a period of approximately three years' detention in a school (details are given below, p. 24). In actual fact, most children are released from a school not later than about two years after they enter it. Under the 1933 Act this form of release was called 'licence' (now 'supervision'), and it was not permissible to license anyone who had been less than one year at a school without Home Office consent; the 1961 Act has reduced this period to six months (section 14). The child is then under the supervision of someone acting for the managers of the school he has left.

Under the 1933 Act supervision lasted, if the child was under 15 at the end of the statutory period of detention, until he was 18, and, if he was over 15, for three years or until he was 21. In the Criminal Justice Act, 1961, these provisions have been altered (section 14 and Second Schedule) and the period of supervision now runs for two years or until the age of 21, whichever is the earlier, whatever the age of the child at the time of release. The 1961 Act adds the possibility of a further year under voluntary supervision if it is requested by the young person himself. The new Act also alters the provisions regarding recall. Previously a child could be recalled for three months, or up to six months with Home

Office consent; the period of recall now runs for the remainder of the period of detention or for six months from the date of a child's return, whichever is the longer. Both the 1933 and the 1961 Acts state that no one over 19 years of age can be recalled without the consent of the Home Secretary, and there is no provision for the recall of a person over 21.

Approved schools are open institutions without walls, though not always without locked doors at night. The buildings vary enormously, from collections of 'houses' to barrack blocks of the worst nineteenth-century type, and the activities carried out vary equally. Although formal education is the central theme in all schools containing children under school-leaving age, it is usually education in small classes and with special attention to problems of backwardness; in this respect approved schools are akin to the schools for special categories of pupils (those who are physically handicapped in various ways, educationally subnormal, or maladjusted) run by education authorities.

Like all boarding establishments, approved schools run many extra-curricular activities catering for the varied interests and needs of their charges. They also commonly operate a mark system under which there may be good marks for particularly good behaviour or work, or bad for the reverse, or both. Punishments may be awarded only as laid down in the Rules. Pocket money is paid according to scales agreed with the Home Office. The managers must, under the Rules, review each child's work and conduct with a view to his discharge under supervision towards the end of the first six months, and quarterly thereafter, and reports are produced for these occasions. These reports, together with the initial information from the classifying school or elsewhere and notes on any important events during the period of school life, form the basis of an individual record, which after release is continued by reports from the aftercare agent.

These brief notes are intended only as a preliminary sketch to give the reader who is not familiar with the system some orientation. All these points are discussed at greater length below.

THE APPROVED SCHOOL ORDER

Categories eligible for committal

The following classes of children and young persons (under 17) can be sent to an approved school:

1. Those found guilty of an offence punishable in the case of an adult with imprisonment (section 57 of the 1933 Act).

2. Those found to be in need of care, protection, or control (section 62 (1), sections 2 and 3 of the Children and Young Persons Act, 1963). They include, among others:

3. Those against whom any of the offences detailed in the First Schedule of the Act have been committed. These include any offence involving bodily injury, and a number of others ranging from incest to neglect, procuring, allowing persons under 16 to be in brothels, begging, exposing to risk of burning, or to danger in public performances, all of which are covered by the Act itself. The same applied, up to 1963, to section 10 of the Act (which relates to vagrants and children found wandering). All of these cases can be remitted to the juvenile court and the juveniles concerned may be sent to an approved school (section 63 (1)). (See below, p. 21.)

4. A child in the care of the children's department of the local authority, where the latter, inheriting the powers of the poor-law authority, satisfies the court that he is refractory and that it is expedient to send him to an approved school (section 65, as amended by section 7 (1) of the 1963 Act).

5. A child or young person who has been placed under the supervision of a probation officer, and whom the officer brings back to court as unsatisfactory (section 66 (1) and section 6 (1) of the 1963 Act). This provision now applies up to the age of 18 (1963 Act, s. 6 (2)).

6. A child or young person who is in the care of the local authority as a 'fit person', where the authority thinks he should be sent to a school and the court agrees (section 84 (8) and section 7 (2) of the 1963 Act), or a child who runs away from the care of a 'fit person' (section 85 (1)).

7. Those who have been brought to court for failure to attend school. The parent can be prosecuted and the child or young person remitted to the juvenile court to be treated as in need of care and protection, or the child himself may be brought before the court by the education authority (section 40, Education Act, 1944, and section 11, Education (Miscellaneous Provisions) Act, 1953).

The Home Secretary has power to transfer to an approved school any person under 18 who is in borstal, or detained at Her Majesty's pleasure (equivalent for the under 18s to sentence of death); certain juveniles detained in lieu of long sentences; and any young person (14–17) who has been sent to prison and pardoned on condition he undergoes training in a school (section 58 of the 1933 Act). The Home Secretary has no direct power to effect transfers in the opposite direction, but a young person in an approved school can be brought before the court for absconding or for serious misconduct, in which case a magistrates' court may send him direct to borstal (section 82 and paragraph 8 of the Fourth Schedule, 1933 Act, and section 72, Criminal Justice Act, 1948). Or he may be removed to borstal, again by a magistrates' court, under section 16 of the 1961 Act, if he is over 15, detained in a school as an offender, and the managers are of the opinion – and the Home Secretary and the court concur – that 'his continued detention in an approved school would be ineffective for the purposes of his own reformation or would be detrimental to the training or welfare of other persons therein', and the court considers that borstal training would be in his own interest. In 1963 two boys and two girls were sent to borstal for serious misconduct, sixteen boys and two girls for absconding, and six boys under section 16. In 1962 the corresponding figures were five and two, sixteen and five, and thirteen. The 1961 Act also provides that those of a like age who are 'seriously unruly and subversive' may be temporarily removed by the police on a Justice's warrant to another school, remand centre, or remand home for up to twenty-eight days, and there is further provision for an individual's immediate removal and detention in a police station for up to forty-eight hours (section 15). In 1963 seventeen boys and seven girls were so dealt with, and in 1962 seven boys and six girls.

Courts must not order a child of under 10 to be sent to an approved school unless they are satisfied he cannot be dealt with otherwise (section 44 (2) of the Act). The section specifically cites 'want of a fit person of his own religious persuasion' as a reason for committal in these circumstances.

Care, protection, or control

Care or protection is defined in the Children and Young Persons Act, 1963, s. 2, as follows:

1. A child or young person is in need of care, protection or control within the meaning of this Act if:

    (a) any of the conditions mentioned in subsection 2 of this section is satisfied with respect to him, and he is not receiving such care, protection and guidance as a good parent may reasonably be expected to give; or

    (b) he is beyond the control of his parent or guardian.

2. The conditions referred to in subsection 1 (a) of this section are that:

(a) he is falling into bad associations or is exposed to moral danger; or

(b) the lack of care, protection or guidance is likely to cause him unnecessary suffering or seriously to affect his health or proper development; or

(c) any of the offences mentioned in Schedule 1 to the principal Act[1] has been committed in respect of him or in respect of a child or young person who is a member of the same household; or

(d) he is a member of the same household as a person who has been convicted of such an offence in respect of a child or young person; or

(e) the child or young person is a female member of a household a member of which has committed or attempted to commit an offence under section 10 of the Sexual Offences Act, 1956.

The major part of subsection 1 (and both subsections have to be proved before the court) is thus put in more definite form than before in the light of what a good parent may reasonably be expected to do rather than in terms of the parent or guardian being unfit or not exercising proper care. Subsection 2 (b) refers also to 'proper development'. Whether these provisions will be interpreted as an extension of powers depends on the courts.

It is important to note that under section 3 of this Act the parent or guardian no longer has power to bring the child before the court as beyond control, as was the case under the previous legislation, unless a local authority refuses to do so (in which case the issue before the court becomes the complaint by the parent against the local authority, and is not directly against the child).

It is, of course, of great importance that there should be wide powers to bring a child before the court, and these are given, in section 62 (2) of the 1933 Act, to any local authority, constable, or authorized person 'having reasonable grounds' for believing that the child or young person is in need of care or protection. The 1952 Act goes further and makes it a duty for the local authority to investigate if it receives any information suggesting that this might be the case. The only authorized persons are the officers of the National Society for the Prevention of Cruelty to Children. Although the Ingleby Committee recommended, with one dissentient, that their special power should be withdrawn, this has not been done, but now the NSPCC consults the local children's department, except in emergencies, before starting a prosecution.

[1] See 3 above, p. 19.

Other provisions

It will be noted that the court makes an approved school order; it does not, as, for instance, in the case of borstal training, pass sentence. The same thing is true of a probation order, or 'fit person' arrangements. A good deal is often made of this distinction on the grounds that it demonstrates that an order is not a punishment but a form of training or re-education. On a similar point, there was much argument at the time of the passing of the 1948 Criminal Justice Act about whether the court should proceed to a conviction before making a probation order. There was rather more justification here, since the possibility of some curtailment of civil liberties is always present with a conviction, and the eventual change in this direction in the 1948 Act was hedged around with safeguards. In practice, however, there seems little distinction between a finding of guilt and a conviction, or between an order and a sentence. Borstal training is no less training because it is a sentence, and approved school orders appear on the records of previous convictions as regularly as any other measures used by the courts.

An approved school order may take effect immediately or its operation may be postponed by the courts pending reception arrangements. It must state the age and religion of the child, and the local authority in whose area he lives. (Since the local authority becomes responsible for a payment of approximately half the cost, this is an important point, and there are sometimes prolonged arguments over 'residence'. If residence cannot be established, the authority for the area in which the offence was committed becomes responsible.) The order does not name the school to which the child is to go, which is for decision by the Home Secretary; he is normally sent to a classifying school or centre, if applicable, and otherwise direct to a training school. The order also provides for any waiting period before dispatch to a school: this period may be spent, according to circumstances, in a remand home, or in a special reception centre in the care of a fit person, or, if a child is unruly, in a remand centre.

Under section 81 of the Act the managers of a school may refuse to accept a child if he is of another religious persuasion; or if the school belongs to a local authority not liable to contribute (the point presumably being that a local authority can in the last resort refuse to take in another authority's dirty washing, although this seems anomalous as against the voluntary schools); or if the managers satisfy the Home Office that their school is full (the Home Office says how many they can take in any case).

A fit person order is suspended while the child is under an approved school order, and it may be revoked by the authority of the Home

TABLE 3 Length of stay in approved schools of boys and girls released for the first time in 1963

Length of stay in months	BOYS' SCHOOLS				GIRLS' SCHOOLS			
	Senior (N=1,572)	Inter-mediate (N=1,554)	Junior (N=800)	Total (N=3,926)	Senior (N=421)	Inter-mediate (N=119)	Junior (N=172)	Total (N=712)
	%	%	%	%	%	%	%	%
6 and under	1	(0·5)	(0·1)	1	3	—	1	2
Over 6 and up to 12	23	7	1	13	19	11	3	14
Over 12 and up to 18	52	29	13	34	48	34	33	43
Over 18 and up to 24	21	43	20	30	24	45	29	28
Over 24 and up to 30	3	16	28	13	5	8	19	6
Over 30 and up to 36	(0·4)	5	19	6	1	1	9	3
Over 36 and up to 42	(0·1)	(0·3)	10	2	—	1	6	1
Over 42 and up to 48	—	—	5	1	—	—	—	—
Over 48 and up to 54	—	—	2	(0·3)	—	—	—	—
Over 54 and up to 60	—	—	1	(0·2)	—	—	—	—
Over 60	—	—	1	(0·1)	—	—	—	—
Average length of stay	15	20	27	20	16	18	22	18

Note: The length of stay is calculated as the period from admission to first school (including classifying school) until the first release. Data for 1963 are given here; the figures have varied little from 1961 to 1965.

c

Secretary; otherwise it comes into force again subsequently. A child (up to the age of 18) who ceases to be in the care of a local authority during the period of the approved school order may continue to be visited and befriended by the authority so long as he is in the school (section 15, 1963 Act).

A boy or girl under the age of 12 years and 4 months at the date of committal may be kept in an approved school until the age of 15 years and 4 months. A boy or girl who has reached the age of 12 years and 4 months at the date of committal may be kept in a school until the expiry of three years from that date, or until reaching the age of 19, whichever is the shorter period. Detention can be extended by a further six months (and up to $19\frac{1}{2}$ where necessary) either by order of the court in the case of misconduct or absconding; or by the managers, with the Home Secretary's consent, where they think further training is necessary and no suitable employment is available (section 73, 1933 Act). The average length of stay is, however, considerably shorter, as *Table 3* shows.

3

The intake and the classifying process

Up to 1916 there was a great deal of detailed information about the schools and the children in them in the annual reports of the Chief Inspector of Industrial and Reformatory Schools. There then ensued a period of considerable paucity during which the Home Office published only the Reports of the Children's Department, at intervals which, for various reasons, grew longer and longer. It is only recently that the procedure for collecting statistics has been revised and the Home Office has begun to collate the basic statistical information in a revised and improved form. Now, under section 25 of the Act of 1961, the Home Office publishes an annual statistical statement on approved schools, remand homes, and attendance centres in England and Wales; and, as from 1964, it is publishing, every four years, a report on these forms of treatment. The figures given here are intended only to provide an impression of the order of the data, and some historical perspective, and the relevant publications should be consulted for the most recent figures.

Furthermore, very little research has been done in approved schools.[1] There are, in fact, no major studies between that by Mary Barnett in 1913 and D. H. Stott's *Delinquency and human nature* (1950), and the latter is much more a study of crime causation than of the schools themselves.

Thus there is very little information available other than that from official sources, of which by far the most useful publication is John Gittins's *Approved school boys* (1952), a major study in itself. In order, however, to present some picture of the boys and girls who are sent to approved schools I have collected material from several sources, and what follows is based mainly on Gittins, on the Home Office statistics, and upon information provided by classifying schools for their review meetings at Red Bank (north-west – boys), Kingswood (south-west –

[1] Since this was originally written several studies have been started by the Home Office, and Dr Howard Jones (University of Keele) has also carried out a study. Projects in train at Kingswood School are summarized in the *Approved Schools Gazette* for August 1966. No results were available when this book went to press.

boys), and the Magdalen (southern half of the country – girls).[1] It should be remembered that the material from the boys' classifying schools does not cover Roman Catholic children, and that the Magdalen is concerned only with girls of 14 or over and does not include Roman Catholics.

The number of committals to approved schools, which in 1938 stood at 3,913 (3,256 boys and 657 girls), rose throughout the period of the Second World War to a peak of 5,658 (4,464 and 1,194 girls) in 1945. The total then decreased to 4,141 in 1949, rose to 4,427 in 1952, and declined again to a low point of 3,200 in 1955 (2,621 boys and 579 girls). Admissions have since been rising again, and the total number in 1963 was 5,412 (4,644 boys and 768 girls); it was slightly less in 1964 and 1965.

Rather more significant than the number of committals is the number of persons resident. This figure is given as at 31 December of each year up to 1954, and thereafter as at 30 June and 31 December. The total is often higher in summer; but the additional information mainly shows the trend more clearly. In 1938 there were 8,764 resident (7,268 boys and 1,496 girls), and the total rose to a peak of 11,150 in 1944 (9,086 and 2,064). The number resident then declined fairly steadily, with a slight rise in 1952, until the end of 1956 when the figure stood at 6,667 (5,531 girls and 1,136 boys). Subsequently there has been a rise: the total at 30 June 1960 was 8,084 (6,884 and 1,200), and at 30 June 1965 it stood at 8,557 (7,434 and 1,123).

During this period there have been some interesting changes in the distribution of the population between various types of school. These, of course, have important consequences upon the types of school provided. The proportions of both boys and girls in junior schools have declined. In 1938, 41·5 per cent of boys and 60·5 per cent of girls were in junior schools. The proportion did not change radically for boys until the 1950s, but it has since declined (27 per cent in June 1965). The proportion of girls in junior schools has been falling fairly steadily, and is now below 25 per cent (23 per cent in June 1965). There have been corresponding increases in the proportions of children in intermediate and senior schools: in June 1965 intermediate and senior schools held 38 per cent and 31 per cent of the boys respectively, and 22 per cent and 51 per cent of the girls. The increase in the proportion of girls in senior schools has been of the order of 10 per cent since 1938; for boys the proportion in senior schools rose from 1956, following a fall in the post-war period. (At any one time in the post-war years a small proportion

---

[1] I am indebted to the Home Office and to the schools concerned for making this information available. The Magdalen School has since closed.

are in classifying schools, but this does not affect the trends.) Information about actual age distribution is given in the separate sections on boys and girls below.

Further data on admissions to approved schools are presented in the *Criminal statistics*. Of children found guilty at magistrates' courts, the proportion of under 14s who were sent to approved schools declined from 8 per cent in 1938 to 5 per cent in 1962, and that of the 14–17 age-group from 12·6 per cent to 7·8 per cent. The decline has been slow with considerable periods of stability, but the trend is very clear. The figures for non-offenders, and thus for most girls, are not given in the same form since in these cases orders are made by the court and there is no finding of guilt; the above percentages must therefore be taken to refer primarily to boys.

Grünhut's *Juvenile offenders before the courts* (1956) examines committal to approved schools by the courts in an analysis of the figures for 1948–50. He found that 6·6 per cent of boys aged 8–13 and 11·1 per cent of those aged 14–17 were sent to approved schools; the corresponding figures for girls were 5·7 and 8·2 per cent. The overall figure for committals of 8·4 per cent compares with 41·4 per cent put on probation and 14·6 per cent fined. There were, however, considerable differences in the frequency with which approved schools were used between one police district and another, and a small number were markedly different from the average. A more detailed analysis of five areas showed a slightly higher use of approved schools in two rural as compared with three industrial districts, but it appeared that the differing rates were related to the number of adverse factors in the delinquents' environment. Courts were much more concerned with the delinquents' personal background than with the gravity of their offences. Moreover, the actual proportions allotted the usual modes of treatment may well be affected by the number of police cautions given; thus an area with a high police-cautioning rate may have a lower rate of cautioning or fining by the court, and hence will appear to have a higher rate of disposal to the approved school.

BOYS

Age

In 1965 new admissions (excluding readmissions and recalls) were distributed as shown in *Table 4*. In the north-west in 1959 the average ages on admission to receiving schools after classification were: seniors, 16·0 years; intermediates, 14·3 years; and juniors, 11·11 years.

Table 5 presents the ages of all those in approved schools (including classifying schools) at 30 June 1965. It is clear from the table that there

TABLE 4 *New admissions classified by age – boys*
(1965)

Age	Number	Per cent
Under 13	732	15·8
13–14	1,878	40·5
15	1,036	22·4
16 and over	987	21·3
Total	4,633	100·0

is a distinct emphasis on the upper age-groups. This tends to shift the emphasis from school to work, and also means that boys are introduced at an age when they are often more difficult to handle.

TABLE 5 *Approved school population by age – boys*
(June 1965)

Age	Number	Per cent
8 and under 13	763	10·3
13 and under 15	2,644	35·6
15	1,724	23·2
16 and over	2,303	31·0
Total	7,434	100·0

Reasons for committal

The offence for which a child is sent to an approved school tells one very little. As might be expected, the great majority of boys, about 80 per cent of the offenders, are committed for stealing in some form or other. Only about 2 per cent come in for offences of violence, and the same proportion for sexual offences. Among the non-offenders, the largest groups tend to be those under section 62 (1) – care or protection cases; and under section 66 – breach of probation; and, before the 1963 Act, under section 64 – beyond control; but none of these categories amounts to more than 30 per cent of the non-offenders. Very few boys come in under section 63 – as a consequence of a crime committed by an adult, or under section 85 (1) – escape from fit person. About one-eighth of the non-offenders are committed under the Education Act, 1944, for truanting.

Previous careers

The only recently published study to examine this aspect in any detail is that of Stott, to which reference will be made presently. There is, however, some information available from the classifying schools, particularly from a survey of 1,000 admissions to Red Bank in 1955–56. The picture is very much what would be expected. There is a heavy incidence of broken homes; at Red Bank only 57 per cent of those admitted had been living with both parents. From 1950 to 1952 Kingswood recorded the incidence of 'disruption' in the family background – that is to say, death of one or both parents, separation or divorce of parents, or evacuation away from parents – and this occurred in about 50 per cent of admissions in each six-monthly period. In 1951 and 1952 the age at which the disruption first occurred was recorded, and in a third of the cases it had taken place when the child was under 3 years of age.

The recording of fathers' occupations has too large a category of 'not known' or 'miscellaneous' to be reliable, but it seems to show the usual picture of a preponderance of unskilled work. In the Red Bank survey, most of the mothers were at home, but in about 100 of the 1,000 cases they appeared to be in full-time work, and the same number were in part-time work. In both Kingswood and Red Bank classifying schools the large majority of boys, about 80 per cent, had come from secondary modern schools, but very few had been in schools for the educationally subnormal or the maladjusted; special schools have, however, recently become more prominent and, in Kingswood by 1960, 10 per cent of the intake had come from this type of school.

TABLE 6 *Previous treatments of admissions to Kingswood classifying school (Boys—1959–62)*

	Year of admission to Kingswood			
Type of treatment	*1959*	*1960*	*1961*	*1962*
	%	%	%	%
Probation	65·0	69·0	72·0	78·0
Child guidance clinic for treatment	28·5	28·2	23·8	19·8
Children's home	12·3	12·6	14·2	9·0
Approved school	12·8	10·0	10·7	9·9
Fit person order	8·7	8·0	2·8	3·0
School for maladjusted: residential	5·8	6·0	4·3	4·1
Attendance centre	5·5	6·9	7·3	8·7
Supervision order	5·9	4·9	3·0	7·0
Detention centre	1·3	2·6	3·5	0·7
Detention in remand home (up to 28 days)	7·0	7·8	5·3	8·4
Probation hostel	2·2	0·62	0·6	1·0
School for ESN:				
Day pupil	2·0	2·3	3·6	1·9
Resident	2·2	1·3	1·7	1·9
Mental hospital	0·13	0·12	0·47	0·4

Table 6 shows the proportions of boys admitted to Kingswood classifying school in the years 1959–62, who had previously experienced other forms of treatment (not mutually exclusive). It is interesting that the proportion previously on probation has risen over the period, whereas the proportion previously treated at a child guidance clinic has declined. It may also be noted that the punishment of detention in a remand home has a higher incidence among the 1962 admissions (and the same is true of the years before 1959). The percentage of admissions who had been previously in an approved school remained fairly constant, at around 10 per cent. It must be remembered that these figures may be affected to a considerable extent by changes in the age composition of the intake; although this factor is not taken into account here, it is unlikely that there would be any significant alteration over the period considered.

At Red Bank the data are broken down further. They show, as would be expected, that previous committal to an approved school is more frequent with age, and is about 15 per cent for seniors.

Table 7 shows the number of previous periods of probation for Red Bank boys admitted in 1959. One senior boy had been on probation no fewer than eight times, and two seniors and two intermediates had been put on probation six times each. There may have been special circumstances in these cases, but one wonders what they were.

TABLE 7 *Previous periods of probation among Red Bank boys (1959)*

Previous periods of probation	Seniors		Inter- mediates		Juniors		Total	
	No.	%	No.	%	No.	%	No.	%
None	63	24·2	50	19·8	27	20·9	140	21·8
1	119	45·8	91	36·1	57	44·2	267	41·7
2–3	67	25·8	99	39·3	45	34·9	211	32·9
4 or more	11	4·2	12	4·8	nil	—	23	3·6
Total	260	100·0	252	100·0	129	100·0	641	100·0

There does not seem to be any general information available about the incidence of previous findings of guilt or appearances in court among those admitted to approved schools, but the Home Office aftercare statistics, summarized in *Table 8*, show the position among those placed out in 1959.

TABLE 8 *Previous findings of guilt or appearances in court*
(Boys placed out in 1959)

Record prior to admission to approved school	Seniors No.	%	Inter-mediates No.	%	Juniors No.	%	Total No.	%
Offenders with previous proved offence	1,034	85·3	862	84·6	699	88·6	2,595	85·9
Offenders without previous proved offence	97	8·0	89	8·7	50	6·3	236	7·8
Non-offenders with previous proved offence	52	4·3	47	4·6	26	3·3	125	4·2
Non-offenders without previous proved offence	29	2·4	21	2·1	14	1·8	64	2·1
Total	1,212	100	1,019	100	789	100	3,020	100
Included above Those previously in an approved school	183		40		4		227	
Those previously in a detention centre	22		2		1		25	

D. H. Stott's 'Delinquency and human nature'

Although Stott's book (1950) is primarily a study in the causation of delinquency, it proceeds by means of a detailed examination of the personalities and backgrounds of 102 boys aged 15–18 in an approved school 'somewhere in England', and we may therefore take his findings as indicative of the nature of at least the upper end of the approved school population. They are presented in great detail and we cannot do more than summarize them here. Stott has his own system of classification and of psychological analysis (a fact which has not endeared him to the adherents of any of the psychological and psychiatric schools of thought).

The cases are classified according to the major cause of the delinquency and its results in the behaviour of the child. Thus we have:

		No. of cases
1.	Anxieties over parents' health	7
2.	Parental quarrels	10
3.	Desertion threats and inferiority	10
4.	Estrangement from parents	8
5.	Estrangement from parents after evacuation	5
6.	Feared desertion of parent	5
7.	Emotional difficulties following loss of parent	13
8.	Unwanted or abandoned in childhood	9
9.	Unwanted or discriminated against during childhood	8
10.	Unsatisfactory parents – complete family unit	12
11.	Unsatisfactory parents – separated or remarried	8
12.	Unsatisfactory parents – neurotic, hysterical, etc.	7
	Total	102

The behaviour reactions are grouped as follows:

1. Avoidance-excitement (avoidance is 'the urgent, yet unconscious effort to prevent the mind dwelling on a distressing anxiety or memory' (p. 25), and this leads to a constant search for excitement). Present in fifty-three cases.

2. Resentment against parents ('the delinquency was directed as an act of spite, retaliation and resentment against the parents' (p. 356)). Present in forty-two cases.

3. Delinquent-attention (testing out of parents, resulting in crime). 'Identified positively in twenty cases, but almost certainly present in more' (p. 356).

4. Inferiority-compensation (leading to acts of bravado). Present in twenty-one cases.

5. Removal from home (the boy wishes to be out of an intolerable home situation, although he will often not admit it to himself). Present in fifty-five cases.

6. Delinquency encouraged or condoned by the parent. Present in five cases.

7. Intolerance of people, near-psychotic violence. Present in five cases.

8. Miscellaneous, specific or unclassified motives. Present in eight cases.

These symptoms exist, of course, in various combinations in each case, and it is necessary to read the book to see how they work out. 'Delinquent-attention', for instance, is said to be closely allied to 'resentment against parents' and sometimes to merge with it, and 'inferiority-compensation' 'was not found as a sole motive' (p. 357).

It may be added, however, that it is somewhat difficult to relate the above divisions to the classification of behaviour reactions and other influences given in detail as a matrix in the statistical summary at the end of the book; and if the 1, 2, 3 assessment of how strongly the factor is present (3 being the strongest) is used as a pointing system it appears that the most important group of reactions are those somewhat vaguely described as 'demonstrative reaction', those under the heading of 'avoidance reaction' taking decidedly second place. However, some items that include avoidance are given under other headings also. It is interesting to note that, from the first list, 'anxieties over parents' health' and 'parental quarrels' taken together, and 'unsatisfactory parents – complete family unit' score highest in terms of the presence of all the various symptoms.

It is hardly necessary to add that the above are judgements, and obviously heavily overlapping judgements, made by Stott without any check from an outside source, and the sample is fairly small. These are common difficulties in psychological and psychiatric studies of this kind, however, and the Stott classifications of behaviour, many of them closely allied to previous classifications, are not necessarily invalid because he gives them his own names and fails to discuss them in the light of previous work of this type. As a statement of delinquency causation, however, the study should be read in conjunction with other works of this kind.[1]

Gittins's classification

In *Approved school boys* Gittins categorized 2,100 boys entering the classifying school at Aycliffe as follows (Gittins, 1952, p. 37 *et seq.*):

A. Positive. This describes a boy who tends to make his own decisions. They may be good or bad but he moves, as it were, under his own steam.

B. Confused. Many of the boys lack stability or direction and their efforts to achieve their goals (which may or may not be socially or morally desirable) are not tenacious.

[1] For example: Burt (1925) *The young delinquent* (the 4th edition, 1944, has a useful Appendix on subsequent developments and methodology); Healy (1915) *The individual delinquent*; Friedlander (1947) *The psycho-analytic approach to juvenile delinquency.*

C. Apathetic. Many of the boys seem to be totally lacking (or nearly so) in drive, interests, or initiative.

D. Psychopathic. This term is not used in its strict psychological meaning but describes those boys many of whose actions seem to be outside the power of their conscious control. They need special therapy.

These notes are obviously intended to be a working guide to the type of training required rather than personality analyses, but nevertheless it is of interest to see in what proportions the four groups are found among the boys. *Table 9* presents this information per 1,000 boys. The number in the 'positive' group is surprising, since one would have expected that the other three types put together would predominate to a considerable extent, and would certainly account for more than half of the boys. If the categories and their distribution are valid, one may wonder how far they explain the comparatively high success rates still enjoyed by the schools in the period around 1950 when this information was collected. It is also of interest that the proportion in the D group is high in the seniors. The categories were the consequence of discussion among staff members and the classification was jointly carried out, but Gittins notes that variations are discernible between groups of assessors (there were three), and that there was probably some haloing; he does not pursue these points.

TABLE 9 *Personality types in Gittins's sample*

Personality type	Seniors No.	Seniors %	Inter-mediate No.	Inter-mediate %	Junior Secondary No.	Junior Secondary %	Junior Primary No.	Junior Primary %	Total No.	Total %
A. Positive	146	49·7	172	46·7	141	54·9	46	56·8	505	50·5
B. Confused	79	26·9	106	28·8	73	28.4	18	22·2	276	27·6
C. Apathetic	53	18·0	82	22·3	40	15·5	15	18·5	190	19·0
D. Psycho-pathic	16	5·4	8	2·2	3	1·2	2	2·5	29	2·9
Total	294	100	368	100	257	100	81	100	1,000	100

Source: Gittins (1952).

Mental health

A small number of boys and girls are transferred to psychiatric hospitals on account of mental disorder. This used to be done by an order under section 9 of the Mental Deficiency Act, 1913, but since January 1958 it has become possible to admit to the relevant hospitals on an informal basis (following a reinterpretation of the law). The Mental Health Act, 1959, changed practice into law by making informal admission the normal thing for most cases of mental disorder of any kind, but the Secretary of State has power under the Act to transfer a person in an approved school to hospital or place him under guardianship (sections 72 and 79).

At Kingswood the proportion of all admissions who were referred for psychiatric treatment in each of the years 1959 to 1962 was about 5 per cent – but the number of referrals may well depend upon known availability of resources. Gittins reports an investigation of 212 boys referred to the psychiatrist from Aycliffe over a period of five years. Of the aetiological factors found, it is not surprising that 'faulty parental or familial patterns' and 'evidence of severe emotional stress' rank high, and the list covers a number of other well-known factors in the causation of delinquency. The cases were also divided into the following categories:

1. Simple reactive delinquency (15 per cent) – a reaction to stress from various causes without strong evidence of a fixed antisocial pattern.
2. Psychoneurotic delinquency (19 per cent) – delinquency apparently due to a profound conflict deep in the boy himself.
3. Defective delinquents (28 per cent) – the main feature seemed to be feeblemindedness, but half of these boys had been subjected to severe emotional stresses.
4. Organic reaction types (10 per cent) – some organic problems such as epilepsy, head injuries. These boys were frequently liable to explosive outbreaks.
5. Psychopathic personalities (15 per cent) – the kind of case in which the features described above are not present, but there is an intense egocentricity, lack of feeling for the rights of others, a lack of real remorse, and a general failure in adaptation.
6. Psychotic episodes and pre-psychotic states (12 per cent) – these boys showed signs of recognized mental illness.

EEGs were carried out in twenty-eight cases, and marked departure from normal patterns was noted in seventeen cases. This is a lower proportion than that reported in a special study made in 1949–50 of 100 boys admitted to Kingswood classifying school (ages between 10 and 17, average 14·3), in which only sixteen were found to be in the normal category. It is, however, difficult to know how far the two studies are comparable. On the basis of a comparison of various features in the boys' histories it was suggested that the common factor was 'ductility', which implies 'rather a tendency to be easily drawn out than easily beaten into shape', and which is intended to summarize qualities described as 'likely to be helped, submissive, dependent, docile, easily influenced, childlike, babyish, nice, easy to get on with, sociable, companionable, affectionate, weak, easily led, malleable' (Hodge, Walter & Walter, 1953). Such a view does not seem to accord easily with other findings about delinquents.

Intelligence

So far as intelligence is concerned, about 70 per cent of approved school boys fall below IQ 100, about 10 per cent are between 70 and 80, and some 5 per cent below 70. The Kingswood figures for 1950 show 80 per cent under IQ 100, 18 per cent between 70 and 80, and 7 per cent below 70. The Aycliffe figures for 1949–51 are classified differently, but appear to agree with those for Kingswood.

There is some indication of a rise in IQ, since earlier figures from Kingswood (1950) and for all classified boys (1954) show a mean of 90, and the 1960 figure is 95·4. How far this is a real change, and how far it is due to changes in testing it is difficult to say; but if it is real it is also, of course, too small to make much difference to the general situation. The variation throughout the range of age-groups is not very great. These figures might be modified if Roman Catholic boys were included, but the difference is likely to be small.

It is perhaps necessary to add that while, as is well known, delinquents tend to be on the dull side, when compared with non-delinquents from similar areas it is found that they have much the same IQ distribution. Thus actual IQ is probably not of any great significance in the causation of delinquency (see Woodward, 1955a, 1955b).

Some difficulties were found originally in applying to approved school populations the ordinary intelligence tests, particularly the Terman–Merrill, where some of the words in the questions were unfamiliar or liable to misinterpretation ('conquer' is very like 'conker', a well-known object; and 'Mars' may be a planet or a form of sweet, according to whether one reads *Dan Dare* or not). There were also doubts about the reliabilities and validities of the tests used. An investigation reported by Gittins, however, was reassuring, and demonstrated that Terman–Merrill, Progressive Matrices, and Kohs's Blocks formed an excellent battery for measuring the general intelligence of approved school boys. The study also showed that the boys applied themselves well to the tests, co-operated, and were anxious to do well.

Abilities

There has been a good deal of testing of abilities in approved schools, and it is the usual thing to administer a battery of tests covering reading, arithmetic, and various facets of general intelligence. Much work has been done in trying out tests, particularly at Aycliffe and at Kingswood. The relevant Home Office statistics give reading and arithmetic ages, but not the number of years retarded, although it is clear, from the classification of the schools, that the large majority of the boys are retarded to a greater or lesser degree. For instance, in 1960 in senior schools only 27 per cent had a reading age of 14 or over, and 12 per cent an arithmetic age of 14 or over. If we regard those with a reading age of under 7 as illiterate, about 10 per cent can be so regarded in junior schools and 5 per cent in intermediate and in senior schools. It is almost certain, however, that, in these abilities as in intelligence level, a group of non-delinquent boys of similar ages and neighbourhoods would also show a considerable amount of retardation, though probably not as pronounced.

Gittins found that the average 10-year-old among his boys was graded as 6 years on Burt's Spelling List, the average 11-year-old as 7, the average 12- and 13-year-olds as 9, and the average 14+ as 10 years. Forty-three per cent were retarded three years or more on Burt's Reading Accuracy Test, 65 per cent on Schonell's Silent Reading Test R.4B (Comprehension), and 73 per cent on Hill's Southend Arithmetic Test (Mechanical). The chief factor in these results was the low intelligence of the subjects, and it was estimated that 79 per cent were in fact working not more than two years behind their mental age. Of 146 'intelligent' boys (IQs over 100), seventy-seven were more than two years retarded in attainment, and twenty-five of the remainder were very disturbed and thus unlikely to make the best of their intelligence potential.

On the vocational side, Gittins found that, of 272 cases, 5·5 per cent were rated as suitable for skilled work, 62 per cent for semi-skilled work, and the rest for unskilled work. When a group of 197 boys were asked to choose which occupation they would prefer the most popular choice was farming, followed by joinery; the occupations of clerk, plumber, and gardener were at the bottom. Needless to say, many of these largely urban boys would in fact be unhappy in farming.

Enuresis

There is a certain amount of information from the classifying schools about the number of enuretics. Of the 306 admitted in 1950 to Kingswood, twenty-eight were recorded as 'regular' enuretics and six as 'occasional' (11 per cent altogether). The percentages recorded over more recent years of boys who had been enuretic during their stay at Kingswood are given below:

Year	Percentage
1956	12·6
1957	8·4
1958	10·8
1959	9·9
1960	9·0

At Red Bank in 1956 the enuretic proportion of the intake was 30 per cent, which was rather higher than in the three previous years, the lowest figure being 19·1 per cent. The number of chronic cases had, however, dropped, and was 8 per cent in 1956.

It is difficult to know how far such figures are comparable between schools, and whether the basis of assessment is the same. Some information is, however, available on this point from a study carried out by Stein and Susser (1965). They examined the populations of a classifying school, an approved school, and a day school, and obtained the results presented in *Table 10*. As would be expected, the incidence of enuresis is much heavier in the two approved schools, and an examination of the records of those who were enuretic as against those who were not showed that the former had more often lost their mothers through separation, desertion, or divorce, i.e. through 'a positive act of departure' on the part of the mothers. Their backgrounds were more criminally inclined, and they had some tendency to be more passive than the others. An interesting point is that they seemed to stop wetting when they went into the sick bay. This finding is in contrast with experience reported when children are admitted to hospital, a contrast that the authors explain by pointing out that enuresis is related to the level of anxiety, which would be increased when a normal child went into hospital, but decreased when an already anxious child was admitted to the comparative security and comfort and individualized attention of the sick bay.

TABLE 10 *Prevalence of enuresis among boys*

Age last birthday	Classifying school N	% Enuretic	Approved school N	% Enuretic	Day school N	% Enuretic
9–10	30	20	—	—	106	8
11–12	124	24	85	24	391	6
13–14	277	9	120	7·5	100	1
14–16	285	5	95	6	100	1

Source: Stein and Susser (1965).

Health

Boys arrive with a variety of physical deficiencies and diseases. At Red Bank in 1956, among 423 boys admitted 367 defects were found, including: nineteen infested heads; 122 ear, nose, and throat conditions; and fifty skin complaints. A further 393 defects were noted during their stay in the classifying department. Defective vision was found in ninety-six boys, although only sixteen had spectacles. It is common for minor complaints to have been left untreated for long periods, even to the extent of foreign bodies in ears or noses, easily detected on examination and removed. At Kingswood in 1954, of 522 boys admitted, among other deficiencies three boys were deaf in one ear, and thirteen more had defective hearing. There were forty-two with knock-knees, nineteen with bow legs, twenty-six with flat feet, and twenty-three with some degree of spinal curvature. There was no full inspection by a dentist at this time, but 160 boys were nevertheless found to have dental caries.

Here again we need to approach the figures with caution since we do not know if the standard of health is in fact lower than in comparable non-delinquents.

GIRLS

The information available about girls is much scantier than that about boys, and what follows is taken either from the official statistics or from material kindly made available by the Magdalen Hospital classifying school.

Age

Table 11 shows the age distribution of girls admitted in 1965, and *Table 12* presents the age distribution of those in the schools at 30 June 1965. As with the boys, there has been a distinct tendency towards the higher age-groups although it is much more pronounced with the girls. The over 15s, who in 1938 accounted for 56 per cent of those in the schools, since 1954 have constituted around 75 per cent. Thus there is a strong shift towards the senior school among girls.

TABLE II *New admissions classified by age – girls*
(1965)

Age	Number	Per cent
Under 13	36	4·7
13–14	271	35·5
15	194	25·4
16 and over	263	34·4
Total	764	100·0

D

TABLE 12 *Approved school population by age – girls*
(June 1965)

Age	Number	Per cent
8 and under 13	18	1·6
13 and under 15	240	21·4
15	262	23·3
16 and over	603	53·6
Total	1,123	100·0

Reasons for committal

As might be expected, most of the girls are committed as non-offenders: in fact, the number of non-offenders runs at about one and a half times that of offenders. Where girls are committed for offences, it is almost exclusively for stealing in its numerous legal manifestations. A higher proportion of girls than of boys are straight care or protection cases (section 62 (1)) and this is particularly so in the lower age ranges, although one hears and reads more about the older girls. Similarly, a higher proportion, particularly the older girls, are failed supervision cases (section 66), or are transferred on the breakdown of a fit person order (section 84). On the other hand, there are smaller proportions of beyond control and of truancy cases. In general, some 30–40 per cent of the girl non-offenders are care or protection and some 20–30 per cent failed supervision cases, but the proportions vary from age-group to age-group and from year to year.

Previous careers

There does not appear to be any factual information about the family backgrounds of girls in approved schools, and not very much detail concerning their previous experience in the courts. The Magdalen figures show that from July 1958 to June 1960 only 21 of 632 had previously been in an approved school, whereas 112 had previously been on a fit person order.

Table 13 shows the position for girls placed out in 1959. The number who had previously been in an approved school is very small, and there was no detention centre for girls at this time.

Perhaps the most outstanding characteristic of the girls who come into approved schools is their history of sex experience. We have no means of knowing if this exceeds that of other girls of a similar age and background, but one cannot help thinking that it does, and there are, of course, a number of cases of unusual experience such as incest. The

TABLE 13 *Previous findings of guilt or appearances in court*
(Girls placed out in 1959)

Record prior to admission to approved school	Seniors		Inter- mediates		Juniors		Total	
	No.	%	No.	%	No.	%	No.	%
Offenders with previous proved offence	73	16·1	26	21·0	38	28·4	137	19·3
Offenders without previous proved offence	41	9·1	14	11·3	24	17·9	79	11·1
Non-offenders with previous proved offence	60	13·2	18	14·5	13	9·7	91	12·8
Non-offenders without previous proved offence	279	61·6	66	53·2	59	44·0	404	56·8
Total	453	100	124	100	134	100	711	100

Association of Headmasters, Headmistresses and Matrons of Approved Schools has provided a certain amount of information on this aspect in a monograph entitled *Girls in approved schools* (1954). Of 102 cases admitted to a classifying school (mainly over 14), seventy-five had had sexual intercourse, including one case of incest. In a hundred junior-school cases in the period 1947–53, twenty were said to be sexually experienced (including incest), of whom five were 10 or 11 years old on entry, seven were cases of interference or indecency, and twenty-six were classed as 'malpractice or abnormal interest' (a doubtful category, since many 'malpractices' are probably quite widespread in non-delinquent society). There are also, of course, a small number of girls who are pregnant on entry (twenty or thirty a year), and the Home Office has been considering the possibility of setting up a special school for them.

Intelligence and attainments

The IQ distribution for the girls is much the same as that for the boys, and the mean IQ in 1960 was almost exactly the same: 95·6 as against 95·4. There is also the same indication of a general rise in intelligence level, as shown in the following set of figures from the Magdalen (of girls of 14 and over):

Year	Mean IQ	Year	Mean IQ
1951	89·1	1956	91·8
1952	90·4	1957	94·1
1953	89·5	1958	96·7
1954	91·5	1959	96·7
1955	93·0		

The general picture of backwardness indicated by reading and arithmetic ages seems much the same as for boys, but comparison is difficult because of the restricted age-groups of the girls classified.

Health

Although it is well known that a number of girls need treatment for VD, the only detailed information available seems to be in the monograph referred to above (*Girls in approved schools*, 1954). According to this there was at that time provision for the treatment of 250–300 girls in senior schools, and, though there were only about forty positive cases of VD, other non-venereal conditions arising from sexual experience required a considerable amount of attention. In 1951 there were seventeen cases of pregnancy in girls' schools, and in 1952, fourteen.

Data for 1953, quoted in *Girls in approved schools*, are presented in *Table 14*. In considering these figures, one needs to remember that the rates for these conditions in girls from similar backgrounds who do not go to approved schools are also higher than they are in the population generally.

TABLE 14 *Incidence of venereal disease and pregnancy among girls (1953)*

	Magdalen	Shaw
VENEREAL DISEASE		
Total admissions	331	188
Transfers to treatment schools	44	18
Treated and cured	282	21
Total treated cases	326	39
Gonorrhoea	15	16
Syphilis	3	0
Gonorrhoea and syphilis	1	0
Non-venereal	307	23
Total	326	39

	No. of cases
PREGNANCY	
Pregnant at time of committal	
Placed directly in maternity home	11
Admitted to approved school	6
Total	17
Pregnant during training	
Abscondence	4
Home leave	3
Total	7
Pregnant after training	
(i.e. during period of aftercare)	23

CLASSIFICATION

The concept

The idea of sorting people into groups in order to deal with them more effectively is, of course, an old one. It is obvious that, at the very least, one wants to avoid putting the hardened offender with the unsophisticated youngster, and to separate men and women. Indeed, the judicial process, from charge to sentence, is, and always has been, in a real sense a method of classifying offenders, and the recent proliferation of different types of sentence, particularly for young offenders, has made this aspect more important. In general, the modern juvenile court attempts to assess, by means of its extensive facilities for collecting background information, whether it is best for an offender to stay at home or be sent away; whether he needs punishment or training, or the care of some authority or person substituting for a parent possibly over a long period.

Classification is not, however, a simple idea. In the first place, it is necessary to recognize two distinct functions under this single heading: that of collecting information about the offender, by interviewing him, by observing him, by putting him through psychological tests, and by gathering material about him and his background from relatives, employers, and social workers; and that of deciding where he is to be sent. The first function we shall call *investigation* and the second *allocation*. It should be noted that it does not follow that the same agency carries out both functions – the court in its sentencing function is allocating but not investigating. Nor does it follow that all the information collected by the investigating agency is used in the allocation process, although what is not used may well be invaluable for those who ultimately deal with the offender. These distinctions will become clearer as we look closer at the actual process of classification in the schools.

There is another sense in which classification is not a simple concept. Nowadays we tend to think of it as signifying division into groups of some size, usually in terms of distributing offenders between institutions whose training programmes have different emphases, although they are all within a single system. We think less in terms of classification within institutions, and we do not apply the term at all to the individual assignment of particular cases to particular social workers. We tend to feel that in casework, and also in the type of group work that goes on in institutions, individualization will be the ultimate form and end of classification so that a single person, or a number of people, will shape their dealings with each offender to the pattern of his individual problem.

Where does classification stop and individualization begin? Advocates of the separate system in prisons in the 1830s argued that complete separation by day and night was the perfect form of classification, as opposed to the misguided view of those who merely wanted classification by age and sex groups; it enabled every offender to be dealt with appropriately in complete isolation from his fellows. We no longer believe in isolation as a constructive measure, although we use it as a punishment, or to give the individual an opportunity for cooling off after some mental crisis. We try to see each offender not only as an individual but as an individual in a social setting, but we seek to suit method to problem in each separate case.

Classification, as we now see it, involves the physical separation of offenders into groups in order to make individualization possible, although this may not be at the level of a whole establishment but be carried on as allocation between 'houses'. Where classification ceases to operate is where it is no longer necessary to divide people by physical separation, however much it may remain important to treat them both as individuals and as members of groups.

Development in approved schools

There has always been a certain amount of automatic division into age and sex groups in approved schools, governed by the willingness of schools to take particular types of boys and girls, and, of course, before the industrial and reformatory schools were merged, there were legal distinctions as to who could be sent to each type of school. The system of division into age-groups was well established before classifying schools appeared on the scene, and, in addition, there were a number of schools which provided for a special type of boy. Nautical schools and farm schools, for instance, have existed for a very long time; the short-term schools since the 1930s. Also, there has always been differentiation according to religious persuasion.

Before the Second World War, courts tended to send all types of case to a local school of the appropriate age and sex group, possibly using, in addition, other schools that were known to individual magistrates or the officers of the court, or that were selected, after consultation and inquiry, for cases which seemed to have special needs. A boy might be put on the waiting list of several schools at once if there was a shortage of vacancies, since there was no central or regional pool to refer to.

During the inter-war period there had been much discussion about the setting up of central remand homes where special investigations could be made in respect of selected children, and about the way in which the remand system and these central remand homes could be linked with approved school allocation. The Departmental Committee on Young Offenders of 1927 recommended the establishment of three such centres, but they were kept out of the 1932 Act (the Children and Young Persons Act, 1933, was a consolidating measure) on the grounds of economy, and nothing came of the idea. It is possible that some method of allocation or an advisory service for approved schools might have grown out of this, although the administrative difficulties are obvious.

Whereas the system of allocation to borstals was well developed by 1939 (having started in 1921), there seems to have been no approach towards any similar pattern in approved schools, despite some discussion of the idea, largely because they were jealously determined to preserve their independent operation. Moreover, it is clear from the Home Office reports that the information supplied by the courts to the schools was very limited and unsatisfactory and each school had to undertake its own inquiries. There was great variation in the methods of investigation that they adopted, as also in any psychological and attainment tests that they administered.

The onset of war produced a situation in which vacancies in schools were so scarce that courts were forced to search all over the country in order to find a place, and the lack of any central clearing house for vacancies became all too apparent. In 1942, therefore, the Home Office set up a vacancies pool, and at the same time it took the opportunity, when a new school for boys was opened at Aycliffe in County Durham, to designate it for classifying purposes for the north-east. The premises had been a hostel for women, consisting of a collection of huts; these provided opportunities for a variety of groupings within the school, and rooms were available for classification purposes, which might have proved more difficult in one of the older schools. Aycliffe was a pioneer in its utilization of psychological testing techniques and in persuading the other schools in the area to specialize to some degree, each taking certain types of boy.

A second classifying school for boys, for the north-west area, followed at Red Bank. A special building was put up in the grounds by the boys, and a warden was appointed under the general direction of the headmaster of the school. This pattern was followed for the south-west (Kingswood) and the south-east (Redhill). The system was fully functioning for England and Wales by 1955. Boys in the London area have been dealt with since 1958 by Stamford House, which now operates an interesting combination of remand home and approved school classification – an example, perhaps, of what the central remand home would have been like if it had ever been set up. Stamford House is also reponsible for Roman Catholic boys.[1]

Cumberlow Lodge Remand Home classifies all London girls over 14. For intermediate and senior girls aged 14–17 (non Roman Catholic) two schools were set up, both now closed: the Magdalen, covering the southern half of the country, and the Shaw, which dealt with the northern half. Both started operating the classifying system in 1944.

The division of the boys' training schools for allocation purposes is shown in *Table 15*. There are, in addition, four 'national' schools used by all four classification areas; one short-term school (14½–17 agegroup); two nautical (14½–17); and one for boys of high intelligence (aged 13–15). Each classifying school does some allocation outside its own area as necessary.

TABLE 15 *Training schools within each area of classification – boys*
(1966)

| | | TRAINING SCHOOLS | |
| | | *Intermediate and* | |
Classifying school/centre	*Senior*	*Intermediate/Junior*	*Junior*
Aycliffe			
(north-east)	4	5	6
Red Bank			
(north-west)	3	6	4
Kingswood			
(south-west)	4	4	6
Redhill and Stamford House			
(south-east)	8	6	8

[1] A more detailed description of Stamford House will be found on pp. 178–80. Boys under 12 are dealt with by Redhill or, if Roman Catholic, directly by the Home office vacancies pool.

Table *16* indicates the position for the allocation of girls aged 14 to 17, excluding Roman Catholics.

TABLE 16 *Allocation of girls*
(1966)

| | | TRAINING SCHOOLS | |
Area of allocation	Senior	Intermediate	*Junior* (top range)
Southern (Cumberlow Lodge or Home Office vacancies pool)	9	4	2
Northern (The Moss Remand Home)	7	2	2

Note: One junior school also takes intermediates.

Roman Catholic schools and other schools that accept Catholic children are listed in *Table 17*. These schools will progressively be allocated to classifying areas.

TABLE 17 *Provision for Roman Catholic children*
(1966)

| BOYS | | | GIRLS | |
Category	RC schools	Non-RC schools	Category	RC schools
Junior	6	3	Junior	2
Intermediate/Junior	1	–		
Intermediate	6	1	Intermediate	2
Senior	5	9	Senior	3

In 1964–65 further extensions were about to be made to the system. For a considerable period the existing classifying schools for boys had been in difficulties because their economic working complement of around 500 admissions a year had been considerably exceeded. This was now about to lead to the establishment of a further classifying school for boys in the Midlands. At the same time, negotiations were in progress with the Roman Catholic hierarchy, and it appeared that the inclusion of all Catholic boys would bring all the schools, including the new one, to round about the efficient working complement. Agreement had been reached on this issue, but the publication in 1965 of the White Paper, *The child, the family and the young offender*, prevented any

further action. Recently, however, the situation has altered, and both
these developments are in train (1966).

The procedure

The classifying school is to a considerable extent a secure institution
(locked doors). The reason for this is that it is the first place a boy comes
to. The first few weeks are always weeks of unsettlement, when
absconding rates are high, and the unsettled feeling is increased by the
fact that the boy knows that the school is a temporary port of call and
that he is under observation. The classifying schools are conscious of
these difficulties and try to maintain a relaxed atmosphere so that they
can observe the boys as they really are. This is not quite as difficult as it
sounds.

The intervention of this period of three or four weeks before the boy
goes to a training school has been cited as a criticism of the classification
process, not only in approved schools, but in connexion with reception
centres in child care and allocation centres in the prison and borstal
service. Whether the period in the classifying school increases the degree
of unsettlement in a boy is problematical, since it is no more than an
extension of a long period of instability, which often is rooted in his
experience of life as a whole and may have been intensified by his court
and remand home experience; nevertheless, this consideration must be
weighed against the advantages of early investigation of each child, some
specialization in the schools, and careful allocation. Another point is that,
even with the time spent in the remand home, this preliminary period
is short, and it is followed by a long period in one school which has a
stabilizing effect and gives the individual time to settle.

Classifying schools are generally divided into dormitories: several
small dormitories for each of the two main groups or houses – the juniors
and the seniors. The rest of the accommodation comprises the usual
dining and day rooms and assembly hall, and rooms for the staff. The
staff usually consists of a warden, a housefather for each group, enough
supernumeraries to enable someone to be on duty all the time if required,
and one or more psychologists, teachers, and social workers. The staff
complement needs to be high, in order to carry out the classifying
function and to take care of the necessary security measures. Certified
accommodation is as follows: Aycliffe, 66; Kingswood, 56; Red Bank,
70; Redhill, 70. There are, however, constant pipeline problems, and
actual numbers taken vary considerably.

The classifying procedure is straightforward and obvious enough. The
boy or girl is usually brought to the school by a probation officer or a
child care officer, or sometimes by the police. It is, of course, a difficult

time for the child, and the idea of using a probation or child care officer at this point is to try to maintain the child's morale; the opportunity for contact with the child is also useful to the officers.

Gittins (1952) kept a record of the questions asked by 1,000 boys on admission: 28 per cent asked three questions, 20 per cent two, 24 per cent one, and 28 per cent none. Of the questions, 32 per cent referred to visiting, 26 per cent to letter-writing, 21 per cent to home leave, 13 per cent to vocational training, and only 8 per cent to length of stay under order. The lack of questions on this last point is especially interesting in that, when they were asked, 73 per cent professed that they knew nothing about their period of detention and 10 per cent gave wrong information; thus only 17 per cent were correctly informed.

After a preliminary interview and a bath, each boy is given new clothes, and his own clothes are sent back to his home, or to the remand home if they were provided there. The reason for this is largely that the boy's own clothes would not stand up to the wear and tear of institutional life. The boy is allotted a place in a dormitory and is introduced to the staff member who is responsible for him and who will see that he gets to know the ropes. A medical examination and diphtheria immunization follow soon after.

The boy then goes to the schoolroom, or he may be employed around the school on essential jobs; in the latter case he will also spend some time in the schoolroom. He will be interviewed by the social worker, interviewed and tested by the psychologist, given educational tests in the schoolroom, and generally observed and reported upon by the house staff. A background report will have come with him, and further reports will be obtained where necessary from school or employer, to fill out his previous history. The staff's impressions will be collated, and these, together with the background history and test results, are considered at a staff meeting and made into a dossier of several pages. This records the major events of the boy's life, his present home circumstances, and his test results; it reports his reactions to other boys, to the staff and to authority in general, and to work and leisure; it presents a pen picture of him, and offers a general statement of what his problems appear to be, together with recommendations regarding any specific points in his training (e.g. whether some physical defect or some home problem needs particular attention).

A psychiatric report is not normally included, but a psychiatrist is available for consultation, and where there appear to be unusual features in a boy's make-up, or some form of mental subnormality or mental illness is suspected, a report will be requested. Psychiatrists are, however, in short supply and probably fewer cases are referred to them than should be, and not enough time is given to each. Stamford House has the advantage of having psychiatric aid 'on tap' and it is thus much better off than the other schools in this respect. A further difficulty is that, for the same reason, few psychiatric facilities are available within the schools (although two small special schools for girls, run by the National Association of Mental Health, specifically offer this kind of help), and recommendations for treatment are difficult to fulfil.

Gittins reports that at Aycliffe 7 per cent of the boys were referred to the psychiatrist in the period 1945–52. The criteria adopted for referral were three: where there was suspected mental subnormality; where the problem clearly defied complete or adequate description in the diagnostic terms normally used by the non-medical staff of the classifying school (e.g. where sub-clinical epilepsy was a possibility); and where, apart from the foregoing, a boy seemed unlikely to respond to approved school training and possibly needed some other form of treatment.

A good deal of work remains to be done upon the reliability and validity of assessments made and test results obtained in classifying centres, in the light of what happens later. The views of staff in the training schools are often coloured by their general attitude towards the system of classification which is still new enough to arouse some hostile feelings, but it may be true that in some types of case the classifying school information should be accepted with reserve; and a boy's test performance may change substantially after he has settled in the training school. By and large, however, it would appear that a valid appraisal can be made despite the shortness of the period spent in the classifying school.

Allocation

In many ways the problem of investigation is not as difficult as that of allocation. Investigation is largely a matter of gathering accurate information and putting it together effectively; but allocation involves the consideration of two factors: first, what is available in the way of training schools and, second, how much and which parts of the information collected are pertinent in making the allocation. The two are interdependent because it may well be concluded, after the available data have been examined, that the type of school that would be most suitable for a boy does not exist.

This was, in fact, one of the findings in the analysis carried out by Gittins and reported in *Approved school boys* (1952). He classified 2,100 admissions by age-group (four groups, as suitable for training in a senior, intermediate, junior, or primary approved school); by intelligence (four groups); and according to a general judgement (the four groups listed above, pp. 33–34) of the type of response that could be expected from them. It was noted, first, that a number of these boys were allocated to a particular training school for a specific reason that outweighed any other consideration (e.g. a real desire to go to sea or to work with animals; outstanding ability or special interest in some form of vocational training, or even in a sport that was well provided for in a certain school). In addition, some were unfit for approved school training either on account of physical disability or because they were certifiable. Altogether, 222 boys were accounted for in these ways; most of the special allocations were to nautical training or short-term schools. (Gittins's study relates to the period before 1952; current policy with regard to allocation is to discount special types of school, so that today there would be fewer placements for special reasons.)

The remainder of the boys, who were allocated to their training schools for a variety of reasons, were grouped into sixty-four combinations deriving from the three factors noted above, each with four categories. After further analysis, these groupings were condensed to give a number of categories representing the types of school required that could be considered viable. The following categories were suggested:

Senior schools for reasonably normal boys.
A senior school for boys requiring longer training and some psychological advice for the more apathetic types.
A very small school for senior and intermediate boys of the more intelligent type who need definite psychological treatment.
A small school for senior and intermediate boys who are borderline defectives.
Schools for more intelligent intermediate boys.
Intermediate schools for boys of low intelligence.
A junior school for intelligent boys.
A junior school for less intelligent boys.
A junior school for dull and backward boys.
A junior and primary school for boys of very low intelligence or graded as psychopathic.
A primary school for brighter boys.
A primary school for duller boys.

Unfortunately, apart from the observation that 'in some respects it [the plan] is not unlike the present provision in the north-east', there is no indication of how far these schools existed at the time, although it seems very unlikely that there was anything approximating the more specialized types of school.

As a further indication of the types of school required, as soon as an allocation had been made at the classifying meeting, it was assessed according to the suitability of the school available; from this it appeared that, of 406 cases, 6·6 per cent were placed unsuitably.

The nature of the allocation process has until recently run something like this. There is first of all a rough division into age-groups, taking into account actual maturity and sophistication; second, those who, for one reason or another, are clearly destined for particular schools are eliminated. These reasons may include those already stated; but sometimes there is a very clear indication merely because of very high or very low intelligence, where this is uncomplicated by other problems, or because particular difficulties need physical or psychiatric treatment. The next stage of sorting out according to more subtle characteristics depends very heavily upon a close acquaintance with the available schools (and it is at this point that attempts to push the work of the classifying schools back a stage into the remand home have tended to break down), since it is obvious that experience and judgement play a large part in the decision.

Unfortunately, a statistical assessment of the suitability of a placement, based on the results of the training experience, is difficult to get (the standards by which such an assessment should be made are open to question), but it is a pity that no concerted attempt is made to link the allocation process with the experience of the boy in his training school. It is only recently and reluctantly that schools have begun to accept the idea that some boys need to be transferred or re-allocated, it being a point of honour in a system that does not regard itself as a system to consume one's own smoke.

There is the added problem that a number of these boys ought to be kept for a time at least in closed conditions – anathema to most approved school staff – and it is only recently that closed blocks have been attached to the classifying schools. In other systems, such as borstal, where the security risk is an integral element of allocation and of the training system, a closed block for 'cooling off' and re-allocation is provided for boys removed from their institutions.

It will be seen that the information collected as a result of investigation has been used in allocation in varying degrees according to the type of problem encountered. One fact may be overriding, or the whole dossier may be inadequate, but in most cases the nature of the limitations means that comparatively little of it is used at the allocation stage. The limiting factor is usually the number and type of schools available. By the time the schools in a region have been split up into age-groups, and the special characteristics of some of them taken into account, the chances are that there is not much actual choice. This is inevitable in view of the wide variety of problems that are encountered and the administrative necessity of limiting the number of schools. The difficulty can be met either by having a larger number of very small establishments – a system that, in Sweden, has resulted in some lack of heterogeneity in each – or by regarding allocation as one stage in the sorting-out process, to be carried further by sub-allocation to 'houses' in the schools – which is virtually the present system.

We have little or no knowledge of the best combinations of types of boys so far as training is concerned, and our efforts are only too often in the negative direction of excluding those who cannot be fitted in. Recently, the weaknesses of the system have been underlined by a new approach to classification. This stemmed initially from reviews undertaken in several areas as a result of falling success rates, and it appeared from these that headmasters felt strongly that the work of the schools was being negated by lack of attention to the home while the boy was away.

Detailed examination of the numbers and location of schools showed that, in fact, most boys could be accommodated reasonably near home. The major source of approved school boys is, of course, the large towns, and the schools also tend to be grouped round these towns. It is necessary to except from this new pattern those boys who need specialized treatment, and they will go to special schools which might be anywhere in the classifying area. They include boys in need of intensive psychiatric treatment; very dull boys in the intermediate and senior ranges; boys of high intelligence who need appropriate schooling; and persistent absconders and very disruptive boys, who will be dealt with in the closed blocks attached to classifying schools. All others go to schools near their homes, and it appears possible to have two or three schools in both the intermediate and the senior range in each locality.

This is, of course, a major change in the system which will have far-reaching consequences. It has seemed appropriate to defer discussion of them until rather more has been said about the working of the system, and further comment will be found in Chapter 9.

4

Training and aftercare

The aims and means of approved school training can be expressed very briefly and generally in the following way. The major aim is so to alter the behaviour of a boy or girl that delinquency is no longer considered a desirable course, and to reintegrate him or her into family and community to live the life of the non-offending citizen. The means are formal and informal education in their widest sense, combined with close personal contact. To say this, however, is to say little, for these are no more than broad statements of intention. The actual process of training is considered in detail in Chapters 9 and 10. At this point I want to describe the methods employed, and to indicate some of the problems encountered in the institutional situation.

OBJECTIVES OF TRAINING AND THE INSTITUTIONAL SITUATION

The object of putting a child into an approved school is to achieve some change in his attitudes towards life, and to try to ensure that he imbibes, at least to some extent, new standards by which to live. The average boy in an approved school has not merely committed an offence; this is the symptom rather than the disease. He is at odds with himself, with his family, and with society at large. The reasons for this, even in the case of younger boys, are often, but by no means always, deeply embedded in that immense collection of emotionally charged experiences which goes under the name of family life. Often enough the boy has been exposed to shocks which it would be difficult for anyone to contend with: deprivation of affection, loss of parents, misunderstanding, neglect, insecurity. He is not strong enough to withstand such pressures, as some others who experience them may be; and he offends in anger, in rebellion, in misery, or for the pleasure of outlawry, according to his own personality. The balance of causation for this state of affairs ranges from heavy weighting on the side of the parents to equally heavy weighting on the side of the child, for parents with the best will in the world and some skill in the art of parenthood may be defeated by the unusual temperament of their children. The resulting problem, always different, though depressingly the same, may be soluble by the boy

54

himself with very little or no help other than removal from the immediate pressures of his environment; it may be soluble by the means at the disposal of the school; it may need special professional attention; or it may not be soluble at all within the ambit of our present knowledge and abilities.

Thus if the aim is to effect an alteration in the way in which a boy lives, it is in each case a different alteration that is to be achieved, and one that requires, very often, not merely some change in the boy himself, but also change in his circumstances; in the setting in which what he thinks and does and feels are only a part of what other people who live with him and around him think and do and feel. The nature of the adjustment is such that it covers his whole field of living. The consequence of this is that we need to know a great deal about him, his family, and his background, so that he stands out as a person in a solid and real environment. A second consequence is that we need to be in a position to use this knowledge to help him and his family to effect whatever changes are necessary, which may mean convincing all of them in the first place that some changes are essential; or even that offending matters – and not offending matters even more.

In all institutional treatment the first thing we do is to create great problems for ourselves by transferring the individual from one community to another. We do not necessarily do this because it is the best solution, a deliberate action taken after conscious study of the situation. In most cases we do it because other measures have been tried and failed; and, in a state of mixed desperation, exasperation, and righteous rebuke, we pick up Tommy Smith of Hoxton and make him into Tommy Smith of Blank School. But Tommy Smith of Blank School, although he is very much like Tommy Smith of Hoxton, is not quite the same lad, for he needs to find some way of adjusting to all the social and organizational pressures of the school. If he cannot find a way, even by retreating into himself, he is better off somewhere else, for no one can flourish in an environment which is insupportable for him, even if it may not be so for others.

Thus the first thing we want to know is how Tommy Smith fits into the school community. This sounds easy but it is not so. There are in all institutions, and particularly in correctional institutions for children, two communities with different cultures and, especially in correctional institutions, with different standards and ways of living. For some boys, going to an approved school is a relief, but pride and the need to keep the goodwill of one's fellows make it difficult to say so. Boys do not choose to go to a school: they are sent there; if they abscond they are brought back. No matter how admirable the staff may be, it is almost

E

inevitable, in these conditions, that the scale of values in the inmate community will tend to be anti-authoritarian; and the boy who can foster such expressed attitudes, without bringing his hearers and admirers into open conflict with the staff, is likely to lead the others. Like the appeal to pride in the regiment, the appeal to pride in one's peers, entailing resistance to those who threaten to undermine their cherished defences, is very strong.

This division between the staff and the 'peer community' (a convenient term to use in preference to 'inmates' or 'boys and girls') is one that it is often difficult for staff to accept. Nor is it easy to accept the idea that it takes skill and experience, preferably based on appropriate training, to bridge the gap. Indeed there are several factors, all tending to maintain the division, to be surmounted at the same time: the differences between adults and children (and 'children' here includes adolescents); the wide differences in ways of living, affected as they are by social class; the walls put up by a child to preserve himself from the indifference, or even the dislike, of those of whom he has had most experience; and the conflicting elements in the prevailing aims and attitudes of peer group and staff. There are numerous ways of overcoming the handicaps with which the adult starts out to do something for the child, but they all depend initially on an awareness of the real problems of institutional training.

They depend also, however, upon the advantages of institutional training. These are the obverse of the disadvantages, since removal of the child from his home reduces the impact of home problems, and provides a new environment which can be manipulated, to some extent at least, in order to provide security, understanding, and sometimes affection, and against which the boy can test not so much his physical or mental abilities, although these cannot be neglected, but his social and emotional strengths. If he can put up with the strains of institutional life, not least the strains of creating and maintaining new relationships with his peers and with the staff, then he is beginning to build the mechanisms that will allow him to bear the strains of life outside, even those that led him into conflict with the law.

These objectives will be familiar to those who have experienced, or who have thought about, any kind of boarding-school education. Moral fibre is the theme of many a prize-giving speech. Boys who get to approved schools in some ways need moral fibre much more than those who attend public schools; their moral strength is much more likely to be put to the test every day. But how to achieve it? Are cold baths and compulsory sports the answer? Or is the problem too complex for such simple mass solutions?

It does not take much thought to see that mass exercise, or any attempt at a solution that involves the indiscriminate application of the same process to numbers of boys, is no more than laying about with a blunt instrument in the hope that some of the blows will land on those to whom they will do some good. It is obviously much better to suit the solution to the problem, the training to the boy. In order to do this one needs to know the boy intimately; to cross the barriers referred to above. But also it is necessary to utilize consciously and deliberately the web of community living to serve the purposes of each particular case. Yet this is difficult because school life must have structure and routine, rules that govern everybody and entail sanctions if broken. And individual treatment has repercussions on the whole society. A boy who does not work when everyone else has to work is likely to be punished because of the possible reactions of his peers, however much it may appear necessary to the staff to let him roam.

The pressures towards conformity to routine are always great. They exist in the staff because they facilitate easy handling. They exist in the peer group because it is suspicious of favouritism and afraid of betrayal. To achieve sufficient flexibility to allow, to a reasonable degree, the modification of routine in accordance with individual needs, while maintaining the bony structure of community rules upon which discipline rests, is one of the major tasks of the headmaster of any school.

In sum, therefore, there are two problems. The first is to get close enough to the boy to find out what he wants of life and what he could get from the school; the second is to arrange the stream of institutional living so that there is the maximum possibility of giving him substantially what he wants as an individual without damage to the interests of other individuals, or to the permanent structure of the community. These are the primary objectives which should always be kept in view.

Nothing at all has yet been said about educational attainments, good work habits, training for industry, sportsmanship, active leisure pursuits, fitness, cleanliness, tidiness, table manners, politeness, or all the hundred and one other things that a school is supposed to inculcate in a boy. These are all means. And as means they will fail if there is no real readiness on the part of the boy to take advantage of them – a positive attitude that he is likely to have only if he believes, in spite of what is said by his more aggressive dormitory fellows, that the staff are on his side. You cannot teach a deaf man by shouting loudly in his ear, and you cannot teach a boy whose concern is primarily with his own internal problems by emptying buckets of advanced educational technique and good advice over his head.

In saying all this I am not unaware of the fact that there are many people who believe that what these boys really need is a 'good clip round the ear'. That is to oversimplify the issue. But this is not the place to engage upon another weary trudge around the ever-repeated arguments about corporal punishment. All that need be said here is that a violent method of punishment will be effective only if it is used in love and anger, where the love tempers the anger and wipes out the hostility and resentment engendered by the violence. It may be that such a relationship between boy and adult can be reached in an approved school, or in other institutions. Certainly this is put forward as a justification for the use of the cane in the schools as a disciplinary measure, though how far the precondition exists is a matter for conjecture. For the central problem is exemplified in every renewal of the public argument about corporal punishment; the issue generates so much emotional heat and so little rational light that it is obviously extremely dangerous to place this method of punishment in the hands of people in authority in the expectation that it will be used in the judicial and discerning manner in which it should be used.

MEANS AND METHODS

Formal education

We must now consider the means of training in approved schools. The most obvious of these is formal education, which occupies the major part of the working day in junior schools, and is used extensively in intermediate schools, and to a lesser extent in senior schools. In the junior schools the teaching programme and the other activities of the school are largely carried out by the same people, so that there is an easy transition from schoolroom activities to less formal education. In schools for higher age-groups, craft instruction and a variety of practical work play a large part, so that there tends to be a school within a school, run by the principal teacher and his assistants, who carry out formal classroom teaching. In such a situation the teaching often takes on a more remedial character, aimed at giving boys, who for various reasons have passed through the educational system at the back and the bottom of the class, the opportunity to attain a simple standard of literacy and the ability to manipulate numbers.

In a number of the girls' schools, which are usually quite small, the girls go out to school. This is less often true of the boys' schools, although some boys attend courses in outside educational establishments.

Formal education is perhaps a poor description of the teaching process since approved schools have more opportunity than many others to teach the basic subjects in an informal way: the classes tend to be small, comprising twelve to fifteen children, and the whole of the child's time is supervised by the school. It is difficult to assess how far these advantages are used creatively. Educationists tend to argue that the teaching methods practised in approved schools are apt to be antiquated, because the teachers are not in close touch with the mainstream of the educational system from which the newer developments would filter through. To what extent this criticism is valid it is difficult to say. It is true that all residential institutions run the risk of losing touch in this way, but refresher courses in teaching techniques are available, and a fair number of approved school teachers have some special school experience. There is no scheme for the interchange of teachers between approved schools and schools for the educationally subnormal, which have much in common, but there is some movement both ways.

Craft instruction and practical work

The equivalent of formal education for some of the intermediates and for the seniors is craft instruction. This is undertaken, again in small groups, by instructors who are essentially craftsmen but who have a bent towards using their skill in this particular way. Here again there is some doubt how far the methods of instruction are up to date. There are a number of 'refresher courses' for instructors – the quotation marks are used because there is, in fact, no basic instructor's training to refresh, although there is, of course, a basic craft training – and these are sometimes held in Institutes of Education and include lectures on method. They are, however, very brief, of about two weeks' duration, and it is unlikely that the majority of instructors will have attended such a course.

The next major activity is work, which, strictly speaking, is only for those over school age. Institutions for adolescents commonly offer a range of work facilities as well as training departments. The work is largely domestic (interpreted widely to include maintenance), building (including the building of additional school blocks, of staff houses, and even classifying schools), and agricultural. A limited amount of work is undertaken in outside industry.

The range of craft training and of work activity is very wide, and no purpose would be served by attempting to detail it. Staple activities are carpentry, farming and horticulture, cookery, painting and decorating, and a variety of building trades. But facilities exist for many other types of work in addition. Two boys' schools are entirely concerned with training for the merchant navy, and a number are mainly concerned with farming; in recent years, however, there has been a move away from one-industry schools, and an attempt to provide some variety everywhere.

Other activities

Similarly, there is little point in trying to enumerate the leisure-time and sporting activities of the schools, which again cover almost everything there is. Teams from approved schools must by now have won trophies in every ordinary sport, game, or cultural pursuit (e.g. music, drama), from gymnastics to tiddleywinks. Approved school boys and girls often win Duke of Edinburgh Awards, and they go on outward-bound type courses whenever places can be found for them. They belong to scouts, guides, cadets, local youth clubs, and other similar associations, and they are usually well known, and well liked, in connexion with local community activities of all kinds.

Religion plays a varying part in the school life according to the principles upon which the particular school is run; the specifically Christian foundations tend, naturally enough, to lay more emphasis on this aspect. Attendance at a Sunday service is generally compulsory; at other services attendance is voluntary. Approved schools usually patronize the churches in their locality, but there is always a chapel in the school, and, of course, clergy of various denominations are available. If there is little discussion of religion here, it is not because it is thought unimportant by the schools, but because, like the other activities referred to above, it is an integral part of their organization.

Mark systems

Most schools have mark systems. These usually determine the amount of pocket money a boy receives, although a minimum sum is laid down by the Home Office. The mark systems are sometimes extremely complex, marks being awarded for almost everything that the individual does, and for joint activities such as the tidiness of the dormitory. Although headmasters maintain that even the dullest boys understand how marks are awarded, it is difficult to believe this. It seems more likely that the boys look upon marks rather as most people look upon income tax – that is, marks represent the assessment of experts and one accepts them, unless they seem blatantly unfair, as one accepts any natural catastrophe.

A few schools have established grades through which a boy passes according to conduct and effort, and his progress will affect his discharge date; such systems are comparatively rare. A considerable number have instituted some form of house system, and this practice is increasing rapidly. Many of these schools, however, do not have housemasters designated as such, and the houses function largely as competitive units. A competitive spirit is, in fact, heavily relied upon by many headmasters who believe in maintaining a brisk atmosphere and in giving the boys goals to strive for – marks or attainments in educational subjects or in sports – throughout the day.

Punishment

Punishment is a means of training, and one of the most difficult to use effectively. Reference has already been made above to the dangers inherent in the belief that punishment in the sense of penal deprivation is what is needed, rather than attempts to re-educate. In any institution which is dealing with material as explosive as approved school boys can be, especially the older ones, it is necessary to enforce some sanctions. The imposition of sanctions is not necessarily a mark of failure unless they are used as a last resort; but punishment is always a dangerously easy substitute for the careful handling of the situation that has given rise to the offence, and its incidence is indicative of the way in which the school in general is run. If there is great emphasis upon adherence to routine, then it inevitably follows that there will be many minor punishments for infringements of the regulations; loss of marks, leading to loss of special privileges, is a typical method of punishment.

The extent to which punishment is used also bears on two related points: how far the type of boy taken can be successfully trained within the range of the school's resources, and how skilled the staff are in handling their charges. An incident nipped in the bud before it has time to develop into a major infringement of the rules; sympathetic handling of an act of defiance; the link between a boy and a staff member which brings the boy to talk when he feels himself on the verge of absconding: these are the elements of discipline, and punishment is employed often enough because they are lacking.

In the application of punishment, both the public good and the individual good have to be taken into account. Justice seen to be done can be a sound basis for trust. Yet it is a mistake to deal with the offence that represents the protest of a boy who is in agony of spirit, or a welcome sign of life in a withdrawn or passive boy, in the same way as one would deal with the offence of a potential antisocial leader, even though the actual offences might appear equally grave. Thus the headmaster is faced with the same situation as the magistrate: he has to weigh criminal and crime against each other, and in his case the task is made all the more difficult because his decision operates within a tightly knit community.

Punishment in approved schools is strictly governed by the 1933 Rules:

'*Rule 34* When punishment is necessary for the maintenance of discipline, one of the following methods shall be adopted:

(i) Forfeiture of rewards or privileges (including pocket money) or temporary loss of recreation.

(ii) Alteration of meals for a period not exceeding three days: provided that any such alteration shall be within the limits of a special dietary scale approved by the Chief Inspector.

(iii) Separation from other boys: provided that this punishment shall only be used in exceptional cases and subject to the following conditions:

    (a) No boys under the age of twelve shall be kept in separation.

    (b) The room used for the purpose shall be light and airy and kept lighted after dark.

    (c) Some form of occupation shall be given.

    (d) Means of communication with a member of the staff shall be provided.

    (e) If the separation is to be continued for more than twenty-four hours the written consent of one of the Managers shall be obtained and the circumstances shall be reported immediately to the Chief Inspector.

(iv) Corporal punishment. Every effort shall be made to enforce discipline without resort to corporal punishment. Where it is found necessary its application shall be in strict accordance with Rule 35 or 36 as the case may be.

Rule 35 Corporal punishment in boys' schools shall be subject to the following conditions:

(a) It shall be inflicted only with a cane or tawse of a type approved by the Secretary of State.

(b) If applied on the hands, the cane shall be used and the number of strokes shall not exceed three on each hand, but no boy over 15 shall be so punished.

(c) If applied on the posterior with a cane or tawse, it shall be applied over the boy's ordinary cloth trousers and the number of strokes shall not exceed six for boys under 15 or eight for boys of 15 and over: provided that in exceptional cases, with the special approval of one of the Managers, twelve strokes may be administered to boys of 15 and over.

(d) No boy with any physical or mental disability shall be so punished without the sanction of the Medical Officer.

(e) No corporal punishment shall be inflicted except by the Headmaster (or during his absence by the officer appointed under Rule 21 to exercise the duties of the Headmaster) or by an officer of the school in his presence and under his direction.

(f) It shall not be inflicted in the presence of other boys.

(g) Notwithstanding the provisions of paragraphs (e) and (f) of this Rule, for minor offences committed in the schoolroom by boys under 15, the principal teacher may be authorized by the Managers to administer with the cane not more than two strokes on each hand. Where the principal teacher is so authorized by the Managers to administer corporal punishment, he shall keep a book to be known as the Schoolroom Punishment Book and he shall at once enter therein any corporal punishment inflicted by him under this paragraph.

Rule 36 Corporal punishment in girls' schools shall be subject to the following conditions:

(a) It shall be inflicted only on the hands with a cane of a type approved by the Secretary of State and shall not exceed three strokes on each hand, but only girls under 15 shall be so punished.

(b) No girl with any physical or mental disability shall be so punished without the sanction of the Medical Officer.

(c) It shall only be inflicted by the Headmistress (or during her absence by the officer appointed under Rule 21 to exercise the duties of Headmistress) or by an officer of the school in her presence and under her direction.

(d) It shall not be inflicted in the presence of other girls.

(e) Notwithstanding the provisions of paragraphs (c) and (d) of this Rule, for minor offences committed in the schoolroom by girls under 15, the principal teacher may be authorized by the Managers to administer with the cane not more than two strokes on each hand. Where the principal teacher is so authorized by the Managers to administer corporal punishment, she shall keep a book to be known as the Schoolroom Punishment Book and she shall at once enter therein any corporal punishment inflicted by her under this paragraph.

Rule 37 The Headmaster shall be responsible for the immediate recording of all corporal and other serious punishment in the Punishment Book which he is required to keep under Rule 18, except corporal punishment inflicted by the principal teacher under Rule 35 (g) or

36 (e) as the case may be, and he shall enter therein such details as may be required by the Chief Inspector.

The Headmaster shall examine the Schoolroom Punishment Book, if any, at least once a week and shall sign it.

The Punishment Book (and the Schoolroom Punishment Book, if any) shall be examined at each meeting of the Managers and shall be signed by the Chairman. They shall also be shown to the Medical Officer at least once a quarter.

Rule 38 Except as provided by these Rules no member of the staff shall inflict any kind of corporal punishment. The term "corporal punishment" includes striking, cuffing, shaking or any other form of physical violence. Any person who commits a breach of this rule shall render himself liable to instant dismissal.

Rule 39 No boy shall be allowed to administer any form of punishment to any other boy.'

It seems likely that a revised list would not include 'alterations of meals' (i.e. the withdrawal of puddings or 'seconds'), a form of punishment which is in any case rarely used. It would also probably cut the maximum number of strokes with the cane. It might include, however, the imposition of 'fatigues', which is quite common and does not appear as an official punishment. It is a matter of some dispute also whether 'separation', or 'segregation' as it is sometimes called, should be considered as a punishment since it is often used to give an extremely disruptive boy or girl an opportunity to quieten down rather than in any disciplinary sense. The line between the use of the measure as a punishment and its use in other circumstances is, however, rather finely drawn. In senior girls' schools hysterical behaviour and violent incidents are not infrequent; in addition, the schools receive boys and girls who would more properly be considered as mental hospital cases, but they are not accepted for treatment because of the failure of the hospital services to face up to the problem of dealing with difficult adolescents. If such a child has to be 'separated', the important point is whether the other boys or girls regard what has been done as a punishment or as an unfortunate necessity; they might take the latter view more readily if 'separation' was not designated as a punishment in the Rules.

There is no published record of punishments given in approved schools, as there is of punishments in prisons (although it might be thought more important that this kind of information, which bears on the safeguarding of individual justice, should be available in respect of the schools, since minors are less able than adults to protect themselves against abuse by members of staff. Moreover, both the Franklin Committee, which reviewed punishments in prisons, borstal institutions, approved schools, and remand homes (Home Office, 1951) and the Durand report on disturbances at the Carlton approved school (Home Office, 1959) mentioned instances of unauthorized punishments in approved schools).

The Franklin Committee (1951) did provide some data on the incidence of punishment in approved schools during the last six months of 1949. The numbers punished over the period were expressed as percentages of the school populations as at 3 December 1949, plus an allowance for turnover during the six months of 25 per cent of that population for senior and intermediate schools and of $16\frac{2}{3}$ per cent for junior schools. In the sample of schools studied the rates of punishment varied considerably, as the following figures for corporal punishment show:

Category of school	No. of schools	% of population punished
Senior boys	6	11–34
Intermediate boys	6	0–15
Junior boys	6	2–52
Senior girls	6	9–71
Intermediate girls	6	16–88
Junior girls	6	2–17

It is difficult to ascertain to what extent these schools may be considered representative. The returns showed more canings in senior than in intermediate boys' schools, which the committee put down partly to a tougher type of boy and partly (and very questionably) to their contention that the cane used in senior schools did not hurt as much; but there were enormous variations in the rates in junior boys' schools, and the high-punishment schools could hardly be explained in terms of having tougher children to deal with. Among the senior girls' schools also, widely differing rates were shown; at this level, where the most difficult girls are found, the schools are usually small and the method of punishment they most frequently use is separation in a special room. Some of the intermediate girls' schools had high punishment rates; in this group, loss of recreation and the allocation of additional tasks are the main forms recorded. The incidence of punishment is notably lower among the junior girls' schools; caning is more frequently reported at this level. One cannot help suspecting that what is recorded as serious punishment among the girls' schools varies considerably from school to school; whereas, among the boys' schools, corporal punishment seems to be the only method consistently recorded. It must also be concluded, in general, that the Franklin Committee were remarkably unpenetrating in their acceptance of such dubious information.

The subject of punishment has been dealt with at some length; it is an issue that is immediately raised whenever there are criticisms that the schools are too lenient. From the analyses made by the Franklin Committee it would appear that the main offence for which these recorded punishments were given, and corporal punishment in particular, was that of absconding, an offence which it is particularly important to restrain others from committing, and which tends to bring the school into disrepute in the neighbourhood.

A question of a different kind arises from the regulations concerning punishments in approved schools: namely, how far self-government should be allowed to go. The Rules provide that no boy should administer punishment to any other boy, and this can be interpreted as meaning that self-government should not be practised to the extent that a house or school council is allowed to evaluate offences and award punishments. The Franklin Committee considered this type of development very undesirable and doubted whether there were many boys in approved schools fit to exercise self-government in this way, but one could also, and more constructively, take the view that it would be a considerable triumph upon the part of the staff of a school if a system of this kind could be made to work effectively. Fortunately, there is some ambiguity on this point in the Rules, and there is still room for enlightened experiment.

THE PROBLEM OF ABSCONDING

Absconding is one of the schools' most worrying problems, often having an adverse effect on the relationship between a school and its local community, yet little is known about the subject and little research has been attempted. There are no published figures, but it is estimated that about one-fifth of the population of boys abscond, rather more in senior schools, rather less in junior; and about one-third of the girls, showing similar trends with age. The proportion of boys has been constant over the last three years, and that of girls has been declining towards the same level.

Chernuchin (1957) carried out a small study of seventy boys, thirty-five from each of two schools. The age range was 13 to 18 years, with an average of 15·5. He used a variety of personality tests devised by Haggerty, Olson, and Wickman, and found that absconders had more difficulty in sustaining attention, were less easily fatigued, were more virile, behaved less well, were more confident in personal relationships, more critical of authority, more assertive over others, more moody, impatient, suspicious, and impulsive. In general, they showed a greater degree of maladjustment. Chernuchin suggests that the absconder is not recognized as he would like to be by other lads and the absconding is an attempt to gain status, to which the punishment he receives may also contribute. Chernuchin devised a new test called the pictograph, which, he claims, is predictive of absconding.

In a more recent investigation, Gunasekara (1963) studied nineteen absconders and twenty-five non-absconders, selected at random from approved schools in England and Wales. He divided the absconders into two groups of eight persistent absconders (those who had absconded five times or more, or where there was an interval of six months or more between the first and last abscondings) and eleven casual absconders. The three groups of persistent absconders, casual absconders, and non-absconders were then compared in relation to eighteen characteristics. The casual absconders were shown to be akin to the non-absconders, but the persistent absconders were all rootless boys and confirmed truants; in general they had poorer backgrounds than the other groups, and were characterized as being 'affectionless', solitary and withdrawn, indifferent, suspicious, highly impulsive and immature, persistent thieves, and unable to make good social relationships; they had a limited span of attention and low frustration tolerance, were escapist on Rorschach test, had known early separation from the mother, and had been in care before their committal to approved school. They had not run away from home as often as the non-absconders, however.

Only one other study of absconders is known to me, and it was carried out in the Illinois State Training School for Boys (Levine, 1962). The subjects of the investigation were seventy-four boys who absconded over a sixteen-month period in 1958–59. Apart from the usual finding that the absconding rate was high in the first month of detention, there were some other interesting results. The absconders were almost exclusively white, although 45 per cent of the population were coloured; half of them were recalls; and they were, more often than the numbers in the institution warranted, boys from outside Chicago. In a survey of 412 boys, who were asked why abscondings occurred, homesickness and anxieties about the home were mentioned in 65 per cent of the replies. Attempts to test the validity of this reason by applying a scale purporting to measure anxiety were unsuccessful, probably owing to the inadequacy of the scale. Another interesting finding was that boys convicted of offences against the person showed an absconding rate one-third as high as the rate for the whole sample.

It is well known that a good deal of absconding takes place soon after the boy comes into the school and before he settles down, and absconding rates would be more revealing if they were calculated over the period up to, say, one month after admission, and then for the rest of the time spent in school. There are also, in practice, some difficulties in deciding on what population figure the rate should be calculated since this is, strictly speaking, the number of boy-days in the year, or, as the prisons put it, the daily average population. This figure does not, however, exist in approved schools, although an approximation could be made.

Furthermore, it is difficult to know what an absconding rate means when one has it, since we have only vague ideas about the reasons for absconding. In general, however, it is felt that the proportion of absconders is indicative both of the type of child in the school and of the school's morale. A small, strongly anti-authority group can induce a good deal of absconding by making life difficult for other boys in the school, even if the members of the group do not actually abscond themselves. Similarly, any sign of unsettlement, such as frequent staff changes, is likely to lead to a general unease which will put up the absconding rate. The reasons for absconding are often obscure, but this does not justify the lack of attention that has been given to the problem.

It would not be a fair measure of a school to look at the absconding rate alone, but it has some relevance in an assessment of what is happening; the same is true of groups of schools, or of all the schools. A general assessment of achievement is complex since it may be that an increase in the intensity of treatment, and thus in its eventual success, will heighten the risk of emotional reactions which may express themselves in running away. Nevertheless, the trend in the absconding rate is a statistic that it is useful to have, and, indeed, that each school does have, though the rates are not published.

Absconding is quite clearly regarded as a serious offence by the schools, as it is by all correctional institutions. The reason for this is partly practical – one cannot reform a boy who is not there – but mainly because of the immensely unsettling effect absconding has on the school itself. In any system whereby people are forced to reside in a particular place and to be subjected to a particular régime, however much it may be for their own good, regaining freedom is inevitably much in their minds. This fact is essentially recognized in the idea of the indeterminate sentence, i.e. the earning of early release, and is utilized deliberately as a spur to effort. Unauthorized freedom is a rejection of the régime, and a reminder to other boys that they are being forced to stay where they are. For those who like being where they are, or are prepared to put up with it, this does not matter; for those who do not like it, it may well increase their unsettlement.

As far as the individual is concerned, absconding is an incident in his career at the school, and the wise staff member will see it in this light. In this setting it is very important to know why it happened. An impulsive 'scarper' in the early days may mean very little; if absconding is the result of persuasion, of planning, or of fear of others, it may demonstrate salient facts about the boy. Certainly in studies of borstal boys, the failure rate is consistently higher among those who abscond compared with those who do not, so that absconding may be an indication of trouble to come. It is interesting, however, that absconding does not seem to be significantly associated with those factors which govern the general failure rate.[1]

There have been several attempts to provide special facilities for absconders in the form of closed blocks and of extra psychiatric help. One boys' school has had a closed block for some time; arrangements have been made to deal with absconders in the training school associated with one of the classifying schools; and a girls' school was at one time set aside especially for absconders from other girls' schools. Official opinion is firmly in favour of closed blocks at classifying schools, but the usual organizational difficulties combined with serious doubts on the part of a number of headmasters have made progress slow. We shall discuss later the problem of transfers and the difficulties it entails in a system which is only half-conscious that it is an organized whole.

ROUTINE

We have now discussed, somewhat cursorily, the objectives of training and some of the means of attaining them. Perhaps, however, a more realistic idea of the day-to-day life in a school can be obtained from a brief description of a normal day. The account that follows is not drawn from any one school and the routine obviously varies according to age and the season of the year. This description refers to boys, but the routine in girls' schools is not substantially different, unless, of course, the girls go out to school.

a.m.

6.30–8.0   Boys called by bell and by staff getting them up. Staff note enuretics, and anyone not feeling well. Boys wash and dress under supervision. An unobtrusive count is taken to see that they are all there. Boys make beds, fold blankets, carry out assigned domestic jobs. Inspection for marks when these are done.

[1] See Mannheim and Wilkins (1955, p. 117); also Wilkins, unpublished approved school study, quoted by Chernuchin (1957).

8.0	Breakfast.
	Most schools are fairly zealous about table manners, and the staff present (usually one or two, according to size of school) are expected to see that the boys eat without too much disturbance to others and that they take a proper range of food, i.e. that they eat the greens too. Meals are noisy, but orderly.
8.30	Teeth-cleaning under supervision. Matron does surgery. If boys are old enough, usually over 15, they may be allowed to smoke.
8.45	Morning assembly. All staff on duty. Another count is sometimes carried out.
9.0	Boys go to work or school. They usually go by themselves, but may be collected if they need to be taken some distance as a party.
10.30–10.45	Morning break: milk for younger children; a special drink for the older ones, if practicable; smoking permitted.
p.m.	
12.0–12.30	Return from work or school and wash for lunch.
12.30	Lunch.
1.15	Lunch interval: smoking allowed, games can be played, but boys are not usually allowed in their dormitories.
2.0	Work or school. There is another check here to ensure that they all arrive.
4.0–5.0	Return from work or school, time according to age. Wash and general clean-up, and change if necessary, for tea.
5.0–5.30	Tea.
6.0	Activities.
onwards	This is when staffing problems usually become most acute. Any spread of activities which results in the boys' being in different places means also the extension and thinning of staff coverage, since most activities have to be supervised. It is usual for boys to be expected to undertake some activity; the boy who wants to sit and do nothing is anathema to most school staff. There is also the problem that the staff themselves must have some time off in the evenings. The general rule is that boys go to some defined place and stay there and do not wander about without specific permission from a member of staff.

8.0–9.0
according
to age

Supper: a hot drink and a snack taken informally.

9.0–10.0
according
to age

Teeth-cleaning, undressing, folding and putting away of
clothes, all under supervision; and bed. Lights out at the
latest for the older boys about 10 p.m.

Saturday is usually treated as a half-day, with sport or free time in the
afternoon. Sunday morning is largely taken up with churchgoing, and
there is free or organized activity in the afternoon.

The way in which all these activities are carried out depends not only
on the headmaster but on the individual staff members concerned. There
are schools (too many of them) where cleanliness and tidiness are something of a fetish, and one is conducted round large featureless dormitories
without any visible sign of habitation, not even a photograph of mum.
There are others where smaller dormitories look lived in and even
reasonably untidy. Too few schools are as yet organized in small enough
units to be homely, and this is only partly the fault of the buildings. As
to observance of routine, the tone is usually set by the headmaster, but
some staff members, obviously, are stricter than others.

What should be noted about a routine system of this kind is not so
much that it facilitates more or less continuous supervision, which may,
in fact, be very much abated as a boy passes through the school, but
that it does not provide opportunity for close individual contact between
staff and boys. Boys are always in groups, and always, at least in theory,
doing something. The headmaster sees each boy when he comes in,
and he will call him up for a talk occasionally or speak to him when
some special problem arises, but there is no easy way for a staff member
to have a heart-to-heart talk with a boy. Many schools are not organized
so that a particular member of staff is responsible for a specific group
of boys; rather, the out-of-school or out-of-work duties of the staff
rotate. Staff members who are interested in a particular hobby, sport,
or activity may find that by this means they can establish close contact
with small groups of boys – but here again it tends to be groups, not
individuals, that are involved.

This problem is one of some difficulty. It has been stressed above that
constructive training needs to be built upon close personal relationships,
but a conflict arises between the need to organize a routine and provide
a range of interesting activities and the need to create opportunities for
close contacts between staff and individual boys. There is also the further
problem, not always fully recognized, that a boy has to be able to explain

F

to his mates why he has had a talk with a member of staff if he is not to be accused of crawling. Few occasions arise for a staff member and a boy to be alone together in the pursuit of some activity; in girls' schools there is less difficulty in this respect since it is often possible, in the course of domestic work, for a member of staff to talk quietly with a girl while they are jointly engaged on a task. Providing for close contact between staff and boy is not as easy in practice as it sounds.

Moreover, few schools are organized round the need to develop and maintain close personal relationships. Work, leisure, activities in general, are not normally weighed and planned with a view to creating maximum opportunities for staff to maintain prolonged and close contacts with individual boys. There are a number of reasons for this: there is the traditional attitude, dating from a time when little attention was paid to the needs of the individual; there is the overlarge size of many schools and the shortage of staff; furthermore, a headmaster may consider that only one or two members of his staff can handle this type of relationship effectively. It demands both time and skill to deal with the complex emotional problems of a number of boys.

Indeed, it is often difficult to avoid the general impression that approved school staff are obsessed with means to the exclusion of ends; that they are content to fill the boy's day with constructive activities in the hope that these will, in some mysterious way, strike a spark in him; and that they insist on good personal and work habits in the belief that these will take root, if rubbed in hard enough. How many headmasters evaluate the week's activities to establish how much each contributes to opportunities for close relationships between staff members and individual boys, or for free communication in groups or between individuals, or for direct discussion of personal problems? This lack of emphasis on individual relationships is often enough reflected in the types of records kept, which are unlikely to offer a detailed running report on each boy in the form of case notes (although regular progress reports must be maintained) and which frequently, moreover, are accessible to only a few selected staff members.

There is, of course, nothing wrong with hearty and constructive activity, but the fundamental problem with every type of institutional training is how to widen its range sufficiently to be of use not only to the boy who will train himself and who will benefit from such activity but to the boy who needs the most careful individual attention in order to get anything at all out of his period in residence. The inevitable logic of this is that the school must be organized to deal effectively not with the easier type of boy but with the majority of more difficult boys; therefore each boy must have the opportunity of experiencing close individual care and constructive group pressures, although they will not all need these in the same proportions, as the skilled staff member will recognize. To achieve a balance between group and individual training is by no means easy, and it cannot be done unless the organization envisages, and encourages, the development of personal relationships, and allocates time for constructive staff discussions. There are various ways of providing for individual care, but it is quite clear that a school in which the personal element is submerged by a welter of duty rotas and brisk healthy activities is not fulfilling its function.

AFTERCARE

'Aftercare starts when the boy comes in.' This is an oft-repeated and often unhelpful phrase, embodying an idea that it is extremely difficult to carry out in practice. Ideally, by the time a boy leaves an approved school he should know well, and be well known to, the person who will be responsible for supervising him after his discharge. In fact, for practical reasons this is seldom feasible. If a school takes local boys only, it may be possible (though not easy, since it takes up a great deal of staff time) for a member of the staff to continue to visit a boy after he leaves. If, however, as has been the practice until recently, the boy has been allocated to a school some distance from his home because it was considered most appropriate to his needs, then someone else will have to carry out the aftercare duties and that someone will be best situated in the boy's home area. In either case, even when there is a strong desire to do so, it is very difficult to provide opportunities for a boy and his aftercare supervisor to get to know one another well while the boy is still at school. It is common practice to try to assign a supervisor at an early date, and the boy may be told to see him, if he is in the school area, well before he is due for discharge. This is, however, a fleeting contact; moreover, schools do not always report adequately, or indeed at all, to the supervisor in respect of the boy's progress. When the supervisor is based in the boy's home area and this is some way away, it is rare for him to be able to visit the school, and if he does so the visit tends to be brief.

Thus, in practice, it is often impossible for a school to maintain contact by using its own staff, or even a social worker attached to the school, and it is equally impossible for the aftercare agent to make any real contact before the boy leaves the school and comes directly under his wing.

Legal provisions
Under the 1961 Act (section 14 and Second Schedule) the managers are

empowered, and may be required by direction of the Home Secretary, to release a child under supervision, at any time during his period of detention in an approved school, in order to live with his parents or any suitable person who is willing to receive or take charge of him; but they must obtain approval from the Home Secretary if they wish to release him in the first six months. To this end they must, under the relevant Rules and circulars, review the progress of each child and all the circumstances of the case towards the end of the first six months in the school and thereafter as often as may be necessary and at least quarterly, and must put the child out under supervision if this is desirable. (Before this Act, strictly speaking, a child was on licence until the period of detention terminated, and under supervision subsequently.)

When the child leaves, the managers also have a duty to provide him adequately with clothes, and, if necessary, with means for travelling and subsistence, and to inform his parent or guardian and the local authority responsible for his maintenance. They must make satisfactory arrangements for aftercare and appoint a suitable person to carry it out. They must see that the child is advised, assisted, and befriended (famous words from the Probation of Offenders Act, 1907), and give him any kind of material assistance or get him a job as necessary. They must find a hostel or suitable lodgings if the home is unsatisfactory or non-existent.

The period of supervision lasts two years from the date of release: the managers remain legally responsible for the boy during this period, and are throughout the whole period of the order *in loco parentis* except that, where the boy is, with their consent, living with the parents, the parents exercise their usual rights over him, although they must do so in such a way as to help the managers to continue to exercise their control. At any time a boy may be required to return to the school and may be kept there for the remainder of the detention period or up to six months, whichever is the longer, but not beyond the age of 21. After the age of 19, a boy can be recalled only with the consent of the Home Office. If the child runs away during the aftercare period he becomes an absconder and may be dealt with as an absconder, i.e. apprehended without warrant and returned to the school, or brought before a court.

Thus the managers remain responsible for the boy throughout. This means that the aftercare agent reports to them; in practice, to the headmaster. There are standard forms to be completed on the appointment of an agent, and before the boy's release, and standard report forms are provided for the agent's use. A Home Office memorandum on aftercare, issued in 1955, lays it down that the agent should send in a report in the first month of the aftercare period, then at quarterly intervals during the first year, at four-month intervals in the second year, and subsequently at six-month intervals. Schools are less good at giving the agent progress reports while the child is in the school, but it is becoming increasingly the practice, under Home Office pressure, to send the agent regular progress reports at quarterly or similar intervals, and these often serve as the progress reports in the school's running record. The agent is usually also asked to make a home surroundings report before a child has home leave, and the child is told to see the agent while on leave.

Choice of aftercare agent

Various possibilities are open to the school in deciding who should carry out supervision. For the boys, but not for the girls, there has been a system of welfare officers, fifty-one in all. They covered the main centres of population and were nominally based on specific schools, although their areas were not related to the catchment areas of these schools. Welfare officers were brought in for supervisory purposes as a wartime expedient consequent upon the breakdown of the system that had obtained before the Second World War, whereby each school had a local catchment area. The shortage of school places during the war period led to the creation by the Home Office of a vacancies pool, which allocated boys according to the places available, giving as much consideration as was possible in the circumstances to the suitability of the school for the particular child. It was inevitable that boys were often sent far from home and the school was thus unable to supervise them on release. The welfare officer system was the result. It has, however, always operated under handicaps. The areas covered by the welfare officers were originally very wide, entailing a great deal of travelling. Although they have been restricted to a certain extent, a considerable amount of travelling was unavoidable. Caseloads were always high, with the result that there was a tendency to concentrate on emergency situations to the exclusion of less critical cases which might, nevertheless, need intensive work. The majority of the welfare officers were not trained as social workers. No information is available on their previous experience, which is thought to be widely varied, but they were obviously chosen as being suitable for the job. This service has been run down and ceased to operate in 1966.

The probation service plays a large part in the aftercare of approved school leavers. Before 1952 this was done on a voluntary basis, but since that date, by an amendment of the Probation Rules, probation officers have had a duty to accept these cases if asked to do so by the school managers. Managers and headmasters are divided about the wisdom of employing probation officers in this capacity, the main objection being that they are unavoidably associated with the courts.

(An equally valid objection can be made to the idea of the school as the aftercare agent – the boy may not want anything more to do with the school.) It may be, indeed, that a probation officer finds himself aftercare supervisor of a boy who has been in his care at an earlier date while on probation. Probation officers claim that such an experience does not affect their attitudes in the aftercare situation and that any disadvantage deriving from their association with the courts is offset by the knowledge and skill they bring to the handling of this type of boy. Opinion seems to be moving in favour of the probation officer and the proportion of boys allocated to them is rising.

Children's departments are also used widely, especially by girls' schools, and a number of the larger children's departments employ officers who deal with reports to courts and with aftercare. In general, child care personnel are not as experienced as probation officers in respect of the special problems of offenders, but they are less closely associated with the courts and have more resources to draw on in dealing with children who are homeless or who cannot go back to their families. Furthermore, under section 6 (4) of the Children Act, 1948, a local authority may, with the consent of the managers, receive into care any approved school leaver under the age of 18, where the managers think that this is desirable because the child has no home or his home is unsatisfactory. This provision is used proportionately more often for girls than for boys. It produces a somewhat ticklish situation since the managers remain responsible for the child but must rely upon the children's department to do the actual work, and schools are often reluctant to put their children so completely into the hands of another department. They like to feel that they themselves can deal with any problems that arise. Children's departments have no duty to take on an approved school case if requested to do so, although they have a specific power to do so under the Children and Young Persons (Amendment) Act, 1952, and the Ingleby Committee has recommended that this should be converted into a duty, which would put them in the same position as the probation service.

The other main aftercare agent is an officer of the school concerned. A few schools have social workers whom they employ both for maintaining contact with the family while the boy is in the school and for carrying out aftercare; but it is uneconomic to use them as aftercare agents except where the school takes the majority of its cases from a near-by urban area (as in London), or where it specializes in cases of such a type that it has many leavers who can be satisfactorily boarded out in the neighbourhood, e.g. working on local farms. Housemasters are sometimes selected for the supervisory tasks, or a particular member of the staff may be designated the aftercare agent. In either case the principle of continuity may be undermined, for though it is often useful that the agent should be a staff member who knows the child to some extent, and in some cases is highly effective (provided, of course, that the boy is not unwilling to be closely reminded about his stay in an approved school, which is not necessarily the case), the most suitable person for the job is the staff member with whom the boy has formed some real, emotionally charged association during his time at the school. To give effect to this last recommendation would mean making arrangements that allowed all members of staff to be away from school every now and again – a formidable problem.

Tables 18 and *19* present the proportions of boys and girls placed out with the principal aftercare agents in 1954, 1961, and 1965. For 1961 the figures are broken down by type of school; for 1954 and 1965 only the total percentages are given, for comparative purposes. The tables show that the probation service is being increasingly used, especially for girls. Children's departments are also being more often employed; they tend to be used rather more for the younger age-groups.

It has sometimes been argued that the aftercare system for approved schools is untidy and that all the work should be done by one type of agent, as indeed it is in the case of borstals and young prisoners, where the probation service is used almost exclusively. It should be remembered that approved school children cover a very wide age range, and it is no more than sensible to have some choice of aftercare agent. The schools have insufficient contact with the people doing the job to be able to make a real choice, but the bulk of the children tend to be drawn from the main centres of population and the schools do get to know what they can expect from probation departments and children's departments in these areas; the result is that they choose whoever appears to show most interest and do the job best. The problem of contact with the actual agent remains a difficult one, however, since there is constant movement of staff in the services concerned, they are usually overworked, and only too often it is necessary to rely upon general knowledge of the kind of service provided rather than upon knowledge of individuals.

The Home Office Advisory Council on the Treatment of Offenders has issued a report on *The organization of aftercare* (Home Office, 1963a), in which consideration has been given to problems of aftercare in approved schools. The report refers to an analysis of the work of twenty-seven of the forty-nine welfare officers in post in 1962, which showed that, on average, each officer was dealing with boys from twenty-five schools. The caseloads varied considerably but averaged about eighty actually released and a similar number still in schools.

TABLE 18 Use of aftercare agencies – boys (1954, 1961, 1965)

Aftercare agency	Classifying	Placed out by school, 1961								Total 1961		Percentages placed out	
		Senior		Inter-mediate		Jun. sec.		Jun. primary				1965	1954
	No.	No.	%	No.	%	No.	%	No.	%	No.	%	%	%
Approved school welfare officer	—	748	56	714	52	465	56	18	36	1,945	54	15	62
Probation officer	—	366	27	392	28	161	19	18	36	937	26	43	15
Local authority children's department (section 6 (4))	—	40	3	21	2	32	4	7	14	100	3 }		
Local authority, others (almost exclusively children's department)	—	96	7	159	11	120	14	7	14	382	10 }	38	19
School officer other than welfare officer	—	71	5	67	5	46	5	—	—	184	5	3	3
Other	—	20	2	26	2	13	2	—	—	59	2	1	1
Total	—	1,341	100	1,379	100	837	100	50	100	3,607	100	100	100

TABLE 19 Use of aftercare agencies – girls (1954, 1961, 1965)

Aftercare agency	Classifying No.	Placed out by school, 1961							Total 1961		Percentages placed out	
		Senior		Inter-mediate		Junior					1965	1954
		No.	%	No.	%	No.	%			No.	%	%	%
Approved school welfare officer	—	15	3	2	1	—				17	2	—	—
Probation officer	—	321	68	92	56	83	50			496	62	65	30
Local authority children's department (section 6 (4))	—	18	4	2	1	7	4			27	3	25	50
Local authority, others (almost exclusively children's department)	—	63	13	43	26	52	32			158	20		
School officer other than welfare officer	—	26	5	21	13	17	10			64	8	8	12
Other	2	29	6	4	3	6	4			41	5	1	8
Total	2	472	100	164	100	165	100			803	100	100	100

The Ingleby Committee had already recommended that the welfare officer service should be run down, and the Home Office report supported its general theme of turning aftercare over to an extended probation service. The Committee was, in general, against a small separate aftercare service in the larger centres of population – which would be the only way of having a viable separate service – on the grounds of lack of promotion opportunities, lack of comprehensive coverage, and the need to unify services for delinquents at various levels. Its recommendations have received general approval from the Home Office and, despite opposition from approved school organizations, are being carried out.

There has been criticism of the low standards of work of the welfare officers. If such adverse comments are justified, it is entirely the responsibility of the Home Office, which has failed until recently to make any decision about the future of the service, and has allowed the officers' caseloads to become much too heavy instead of placing a reasonable limitation on them – which it would have been perfectly easy to do. The unfortunate welfare officers have thus been placed in an invidious position.

The aftercare report recommends that the school managers should continue to exercise responsibility for aftercare and that, although the new probation and aftercare service and children's departments should take most of the cases, the managers should retain the power to use others if necessary. The report also recommends that in the larger centres of population some officers should specialize in aftercare work.

It is difficult to evaluate the findings of this report without treating the whole subject of aftercare at rather greater length than would be merited in the present context. Briefly, the major problem is the amount of time likely to be spent on the job. Aftercare, if it is to be carried out adequately, is extremely time-consuming. The boys released from approved schools are likely to be more difficult and more experienced in delinquency than ordinary probationers, and their homes tend to be in a more advanced state of breakdown. Furthermore, any real attempt to maintain continuity between school and home involves the aftercare agent in numerous visits to schools, entailing a great deal of travelling. There is grave doubt whether aftercare will receive sufficient attention in a service whose primary responsibility is to the courts, and must remain there. No amount of rearranging probation committees to turn them into probation and aftercare committees can obviate the dangers of adding what must almost inevitably be a second string to an already highly overworked service. Other problems arise in trying to avoid mixing boys on probation and boys on aftercare, and in dealing with a range of aftercare extending from 15-year-old boys and girls to old lags leaving preventive detention prisons. (Will probation officers' waiting-rooms consists of individual sound-proof cubicles? Or will the officers have to depend almost entirely on visiting?) Aftercare has an expertise of its own which needs to be developed, and this is unlikely to happen under the arrangements now suggested.

Changes in the grouping of schools to bring their pupils nearer the main centres of population will serve to throw back the problems of aftercare to the schools themselves. These trends are discussed elsewhere (cf. pp. 181–3 below).

The report tends to envisage a long-term solution when there will be adequate numbers of well-trained probation officers to carry out after-care. The immediate situation is, however, a balancing of inefficiencies. Is the overworked, understaffed probation service likely to be able to cope any better than the overworked, understaffed schools regrouped to facilitate home-visiting? The school personnel have the advantage that their knowledge of the boy and their relationships with him are based on the experience of having lived with him; and where the boy's period at the school has been of significance to him, it may well be valuable for him to continue to see someone he has got to know there, provided that any really difficult cases are referred to trained workers outside if the school personnel have not the necessary skill. In other cases, no doubt, the boy is only too glad to have done with the school, and a new face, or the familiar face of his previous probation officer, is to be welcomed.

In this connexion, the safeguard lies in the recommendation that the managers (i.e. the headmaster) should retain the power to choose the aftercare agent. This provision introduces a flexibility that is in keeping with the great variety of boys and home situations concerned – a flexi-bility that is lacking in other parts of the aftercare organization. It also places the schools in the position of being able to defeat an intended administrative change to hand over their aftercare to probation officers. The loss of the welfare officers is bound to raise the problem of what to do with individual boys, and it remains to be seen in what proportions they will be shared out among the schools' own staffs, the children's departments, and the probation service.

The Ingleby Committee considered the question of establishing and maintaining contact between the school staff and the home, emphasizing the role of housemasters and housemistresses in this respect, and welcoming the appointment of school social workers (at the end of 1962, thirteen had been appointed to boys' schools, including six at classifying schools, and nine to girls' schools). It is, of course, illogical to have a system of school social workers as well as an aftercare service, and the former is necessary only because the latter does not work very well. While it is obviously advisable for the schools to maintain as many links as possible with the homes as the system is at present organized, it is uneconomic and inefficient to operate from the schools if a better alternative is available, except where the homes are within easy reach.

EVALUATION OF TRAINING

Lack of systematic data

It is only recently that a reasonably reliable system of collecting statistical information about approved schools has been devised on the basis of a centralized punched-card system. Most of the earlier attempts to assess the results of approved school training must be regarded with suspicion, since they are based upon what managers have been able to learn about the subsequent careers of the children from a somewhat inadequate aftercare service. Notification of actual reconvictions seems to have gradually improved; nevertheless, as late as its 1938 report the Home Office could say: 'An obvious criticism is the question how far the school authorities know if a girl or boy has been before the courts. There is one satisfactory reply to this: it is almost the universal practice of boys and girls from Home Office schools who come before the courts to ask that the school be notified.' This statement, if true, might well have been gratifying to the Home Office, but it is much less helpful to the statistician.

Most of the information available on outcome relates to the position three years after the initial discharge from the school; failure means reconviction only. There is not much point in going back too far, but it is interesting to note that in the 1925 report, which gives figures for those discharged in 1921, the success rates are 90 and 92 per cent respectively for boys and girls in reformatory schools, and 93 and 99 per cent for those in industrial schools. The 1928 report does not present the figures in a comparable form. In the 1938 report the data are elaborated to take into account those who have died, those who have been certified insane, and those who have been lost sight of, but it does not keep separate those who were recalled without offence. From 1938 onwards, as stated in the 1951 report, the number recalled without further offence is specified, but, together with those who have died or have been certified, it is deducted from the numbers placed out; those lost sight of (who had previously been deducted before the success rate was calculated) were put in separately. From 1946, those lost sight of are included again with the deductions. Thus the figures over the years are not exactly comparable, though the differences in the methods of calculation do not affect the results in any significant way.

More recent figures refine the procedure by indicating the numbers who were and who were not reconvicted before they were recalled, certified, or lost sight of, or before they died. Examination of the later figures suggests that the earlier figures for recalls must have included some who were originally placed out at a prior date. The later figures omit those recalled without a finding of guilt.

Measurement of success

Reconviction is a very inadequate determinant of success or failure in this context. In the first place, it is a crude measure of failure in that it takes little account of the total aftercare situation of the boy or girl and gives no indication of the seriousness of the offence that led to reconviction; moreover, approved schools are concerned not only with offenders but with non-offenders – care or protection and beyond control cases. The numbers of non-offenders in boys' schools are too small to distort the overall figures, but they predominate in girls' schools; in any case, a success rate based on reconvictions has little relevance for girls.

It is debatable whether a recall who has not committed an offence should be regarded as a failure. It can be argued that the whole period from entry to the school to the end of aftercare should be treated as one process; or, again, that success and failure are in any case being assessed from the date of discharge, therefore any recall must be counted a failure. Strictly speaking, if supervision is part of the process, then assessment of outcome should cover a follow-up period after supervision ends. It would have been difficult to do this because the period of supervision varied in length up to the 1961 Act. The most reasonable procedure seems to be to base assessment of success and failure on the initial major period in the school, including all recalls. However, recalls are not included in the more recent data and the difficulty remains that a substantial number of them relate to earlier years.

There is, perhaps, some justification for deducting, before success rates are estimated, the mentally disordered, those who have died, and those who have been lost sight of, if there is no record of how many of them were reconvicted before they came into these categories; but the argument about those recalled to the school is more complex. A recall has already had a period on aftercare and therefore he is in a special position as regards measurement of outcome from various points in the process. Three separate success rates are thus required: that measured from the end of the initial major period in the school; that measured

TABLE 20 Success rates three years after initial discharge from school – boys

Year	Placed out No.	Readmitted or recalled No.	Readmissions and recalls as % of total placed out %	Satisfactory as shown in official reports %	Without finding of guilt after deducting nos. certified or dead and counting readmissions and recalls as failures %
1928–30[a]	1,290	—	—	79	—
1931–33[a]	1,348	—	—	77	—
1938	3,321	296	8.9	75	69
1939	3,346	229	6.9	73	68
1940	4,919	537	10.9	71	63
1941	4,232	464	11.0	69	61
1942	4,623	629	13.7	68	58
1943	4,670	577	12.4	66	57
1944	4,110	487	11.8	63	56
1945	4,698	482	10.3	67	60
1946	4,309	312	7.2	65	61
1947	4,228	261	6.2	66	62
1948	3,681	221	6.0	66	62
1949	3,628	219	6.0	63	60
1950	3,914	235	6.0	63	61
1951	3,737	244	6.5	64	60
1952	3,657	168	4.6	65 (65)[b]	62
1953	3,750	349	9.3	62 (64)[b]	58
1954	3,649	320	8.8	61 (63)[b]	57
1955	3,337	325	9.7	56 (58)[b]	53
1956	2,778	284	10.1	51 (53)[b]	51

[a] Annual averages; readmissions and recalls not shown separately.
[b] Percentages in parenthesis are calculated upon the same basis as those for previous years.

TABLE 21 Success rates three years after initial discharge from school

Year	Placed out	Readmitted or recalled	Readmissions and recalls as % of total placed out	Satisfactory as shown in official reports	Without finding of guilt after deducting nos. certified or dead and counting readmissions and recalls as failures	Without finding of guilt counting those lost sight of as failures
	No.	No.	%	%	%	%
1928–30[a]	228	—	—	81	—	81
1931–33[a]	181	—	—	81	—	82
1938	671	147[b]	22·0	83	65	c
1939	739	203[b]	27·5	84	63	c
1940	777	152[b]	19·6	82	66	c
1941	752	128[b]	17·0	85	70	c
1942	869	147[b]	16·9	82	68	c
1943	764	75	9·8	79	72	68
1944	934	123	13·2	80	70	68
1945	1,060	116	10·9	83	74	72
1946	1,132	86	7·6	84	78	75
1947	1,074	60	5·6	85	81	76
1948	692	39	5·6	80	77	72
1949	714	36	5·0	83	80	75
1950	656	40	6·1	80	77	70
1951	670	51	7·6	82	77	73
1952	651	40	6·1	82 (82)[d]	77	74
1953	764	106	14·0	83 (82)[d]	71	68
1954	805	137	16·8	85 (87)[d]	73	67
1955	767	110	14·4	88 (89)[d]	77	71
1956	685	96	14·0	84 (85)[d]	74	68

[a] Annual averages; readmissions and recalls not shown separately.
[b] Includes a small number of certified and died.   [c] Number lost sight of not given.
[d] Percentages in parenthesis are calculated upon the same basis as those for previous years.

from the end of a recall; and that measured from the end of the super-vision period. The present measure of success is therefore a hybrid one, combining the first two and ignoring the third.

In *Tables 20* and *21* I have attempted to rectify the figures by showing the numbers recalled and including an additional column counting all the recalls as failures; i.e. measuring success from the end of the initial period in the school only. Among the girls *(Table 21)* the numbers lost sight of are considerable and an extra column lists them as failures. I need hardly add that these are rough and ready techniques and that probably only the more recent figures can be considered reliable. Since 1 January 1963 the Home Office has altered the basic list of offences counted as reconvictions by omitting some minor ones, and figures for later years are not strictly comparable with those given here.

The Home Office figures for later years allow of analysis in rather more detail, as in *Table 22*. The figures for girls are probably more meaningful at the lower end of the age range. It is interesting to note that success rates are higher for senior and intermediate than for junior boys (the variability in respect of junior primary boys is probably due to small numbers).

TABLE 22 *Success rates three years after initial discharge from school (Boys and girls – 1954–60)*

| | Three years after discharge | | | | | | |
	1954	1955	1956	1957	1958	1959	1960
BOYS	%	%	%	%	%	%	%
Senior	64	62	54	52	44	46	47
Intermediate	66	61	52	52	45	46	42
Junior (secondary)	53	46	46	46	39	38	39
Junior (primary)	47	37	46	32	38	31	39
All boys	61	57	51	50	43	43	43
GIRLS							
Senior	84	90	88	86	86	83	86
Intermediate	84	86	82	83	89	83	84
Junior	89	85	73	82	85	78	81
All girls	85	88	84	85	86	82	85

Factors influencing success and failure

The recent figures also provide some indication of the seriousness of the failures that are occasioned by a subsequent offence, since they specify the award of the court (presumably the heaviest penalty is given, if there were several). If absolute and conditional discharges and fines are excluded on the grounds that they suggest minor offences, then the success rate for boys placed out in 1959 would be 61 per cent rather than 43 per cent; moreover, the extent to which the two rates differ has been increasing recently (for 1955 placings the difference was only 9·5 per cent). The success rate for girls, on the other hand, would be little affected by this manipulation.

In *Table 23* the success rates for boys and girls placed out over a five-year period are broken down according to their records prior to admission to approved school. In considering these measures, it should be remembered that, among the girls, there are very few reconvictions at all; and that, of the reconvicted boys, the great majority have committed an offence prior to their admission to approved school. Among boys placed out in 1959, for instance, of 1,707 with subsequent findings of guilt, 1,511 were in this category.

What these statistics do not provide, however, is any information on the *number* of previous offences committed that could be related to subsequent behaviour. An investigation by Dr P. D. Scott (1964) throws some light on this aspect in the course of answering the question, 'When approved school boys commit further offences after release, are these offences serious or not?' Scott studied 149 boys released consecutively from an intermediate school; date of release was early enough to allow at least a three-year follow-up in each case. There were 100 failures (67 per cent), as judged by the criterion of a further finding of guilt within three years from release. The mean age on release was 15 years, with a range from 14 to 16. Of the 100 failures, thirty-four committed more than two offences and nine more than three. The average length of previous delinquent record (that is, from first charge to approved school committal) was 2·23 years, yet the average number of charges in this period was greater than in the three-year follow-up period (3·13 per boy as against 2·1). The decline may be partly explained by the general falling-off of crime in these age-groups; but time spent in institutions is also a relevant factor. Some 30 per cent were 'out of circulation' in various institutions before their committal to approved school, compared with 64 per cent afterwards; however, the periods in institutions at the earlier stage were markedly longer.

With regard to the quality of the offences, 27 per cent of all the offences committed in the follow-up period were minor traffic offences or taking and driving away. Nevertheless, only five boys would have been classed as successes but for offences of this nature. In general, the offences committed were not very serious, and the great majority would come out as trivial on the Sellin–Wolfgang scale (Sellin and Wolfgang,

G

TABLE 23 *Success rates by previous record (boys and girls placed out 1956–60)*

Record prior to admission to approved school	Year placed out									
	1956		1957		1958		1959		1960	
	Boys	Girls	Boys	Girls	Boys	Girls	Boys	Girls	Boys	Girls
	%	%	%	%	%	%	%	%	%	%
Offenders with previous proved offence	50	75	49	80	43	83	42	60	43	82
Offenders without previous proved offence	57	81	53	80	47	84	53	75	48	84
Non-offenders with previous proved offence	54	87	57	88	45	82	52	83	46	78
Non-offenders without previous proved offence	56	88	60	86	46	89	63	87	55	87
Included above										
Those previously in approved school	44	70	44	71	29	88	31	77	33	83
Those previously in detention	42	—	41	—	50	—	68	—	37	—

1964). This scale may, of course, reflect the greater seriousness of crime in the United States, and may not be applicable in every respect in Britain. It was found that the post-release offences of these 100 boys were no more serious than the offences committed by 100 boys of the same age who went through a remand home but were not sent to a correctional establishment.

A comparison of the successes and failures in the total sample of 149 boys showed the expected greater disturbance in work records and family situation among the failures. Moreover, the failures seemed to come from larger and more delinquent families and were more often middle or only children (but there are no significance tests).

In general, the evidence of the study suggested that subsequent reconviction was a good indication of serious personality disorders and seriously disturbed family backgrounds – a somewhat unexpected, but useful, result.

It is hard to say whether the results given above should be considered good or bad. Obviously, success rates for boys have declined rapidly in recent years, and the service is not doing anything like as well as it used to, but to what extent the lower rate reflects an intake of more difficult types of boys is unknown. Direct comparison with the success rates of other services is impracticable, since selection by the courts gives them different intakes. Some comparative material was included by the

TABLE 24 *Indices showing results of sentences compared with expectation for first and recidivist offenders (100 = expected rate of reconviction within five years)*

| | Indices of reconviction among offenders under 17 years of age | |
Sentence	First offenders	Offenders with previous offences
Discharge	89	100
Fine	75	83
Probation	118	101
Approved school	138	102
Borstal training	—	101
Detention centre	—	106
Attendance centre	—	119
Imprisonment	—	—
Corrective training	—	—

Source: The sentence of the court (Home Office, 1964).

Home Office Research Unit in Part VI of *The sentence of the court* (Home Office, 1964). It examines the reconviction rates among 4,239 cases convicted, and variously sentenced, in the Metropolitan Police District in March and April 1957 and followed up for five years. Expected rates of reconviction were calculated for first offenders and for offenders with previous offences, and the actual rates were expressed as indices in relation to these expected rates. *Table 5* of the Home Office publication is partially reproduced in *Table 24*.

On this basis, it is seen that approved schools deal much less efficiently with first offenders than the other methods cited; for offenders with previous offences, however, the results are similar for all methods except fines, which appears to be more successful. It should be remembered that these expected rates are crude measures based upon limited data.

5

Staff

It is axiomatic that any method of training offenders is as good as the people who operate it. This statement is especially pertinent where the method of training is residential, since, though attempts may be made to avoid it, the institution takes on some of the aspects of a separate and self-contained community with its own laws, its own standards of right and wrong, its own view of which ends and aims are desirable and which are not. The dangers of institutions are often stressed but there is also a positive side. It is the intention of those who are concerned for the welfare of the delinquent or difficult child, and who decide to remove him from his home, that he should be placed in an atmosphere which will exert on him, in every possible respect, those pressures that are necessary to alter his attitudes and feelings in such a way that he no longer offends. An approved school is no substitute for a normal family, but it provides an experience in community living and offers opportunities for the formation of warm relationships that can have lasting impressions. And it is the staff who both control the operation of authority and offer compensating relationships to offset those that have already failed the boys and girls who come under their care.

Of the nature of the task of maintaining and working in this type of community, and of the difficulties encountered, more will be said in later chapters, but it is evident that it is not an easy job and that the staff concerned must be carefully selected and carefully trained. There need to be reasonable rewards, promotion prospects, and conditions of work. A sense of vocation is admirable, but only a minority are motivated solely in this way; thus, as far as the majority of approved school staff are concerned, their interest and dedication must be underwritten by those material rewards that make life worth living – after all, there are many good causes that call for a lifetime's devotion, and it is not surprising that most people choose those that offer them a reasonable return and a minimum of personal inconvenience.

STRUCTURE

The actual structure of the staff in any particular school depends, of course, upon the size and type of school. The general pattern consists of a headmaster in charge, a deputy headmaster, and a number of assistant teachers (with their counterparts in girls' schools). Many schools have housemasters and housemistresses and/or housefathers and house-mothers. Where appropriate, there are instructors in various types of craft or in agriculture, and there may be a farm bailiff and farm staff. The domestic side is the responsibility of the matron, who is often the headmaster's wife; in girls' schools this is not a separate post; there may be some assistance in looking after the linen, and there are the usual cooks and cleaners. All schools have medical officers, usually part time, and a number of educational psychologists, psychiatrists, and nurses are employed. Social workers and welfare workers are included on the staff of some schools. Together with the usual clerks and boilermen, etc., a complex establishment is made up, the positions being graded on various national and local pay scales. *Tables 25-28* (pp. 93-5) show staff and vacancies in each of the main grades at the only dates for which it was possible to obtain these figures.

Headmasters and headmistresses

The headmaster (or headmistress) is obviously the very kernel and core of the school, around whom everything is built. From him stem the prevailing tone and methods of working, and, if he stays at one school for a long time he can, through his influence in the appointment of staff, mould the school closely to his projected image. Under the Rules he is responsible to the managers for the efficient conduct of the school, and, with the approval of the managers, he determines the duties of the staff. If he is to be absent for more than two days he must obtain the authority of the managers.

The headmaster is empowered to impose the punishments laid down in the regulations, including that of the suspension of privileges; he must record all punishments immediately in the punishment book and inspect and sign the schoolroom punishment book at least once a week. Certain safeguards, then, are written into the regulations.

Perhaps the best way to summarize the headmaster's duties is to say that he is in overall control of the school: his control embraces most of the domestic arrangements, the staff, the teaching and training; in addition to exercising control over, he actively participates in, the work of re-educating, retraining, and supervising on discharge the individual boys in his care.

Clearly, the burden upon the headmaster is very great, and traditionally he has been something of an autocrat and arbiter, rather set apart from the rest of the staff, and insistent that nothing should be done without his authority. This situation came about partly because there were few

TABLE 25 Voluntary managements: boys' schools
(Number of full-time authorized posts and staff in post at 30 September 1960)

	Heads[a]	Teachers[a]	Instructors[a]	Housemasters[b]	Housefathers[b]	Housemothers[b]	Matrons[b]	Asst. Matrons[b]	Farm bailiffs[b]	Asst. farm bailiffs[b]	Clerks[b]
NUMBER OF AUTHORIZED POSTS	55	249	182	136	[c]	27	56	55	15	14	[d]
STAFF IN POST											
Qualified teachers	51	232									
Other heads	2										
Instructors:											
Qualified			109								
Substantially but not fully qualified			60								
Housemasters:											
Qualified, Aycliffe	2			13							
Joint Interview Board				85							
Other qualifications				13							
Housefathers and housemothers:											
With CTC certificate					2						
Other					3	18					
Matrons and assistant matrons:											
With nursing qualifications							16	9			
Without nursing qualifications							37	44			
Clerical division											34
General division											73
NUMBER IN POST	55	232	169	111	5	18	53	53	15	14	107
VACANCIES	0	17	13	25	—	9	3	2	0	0	—

[a] Staff within the purview of the Joint Negotiating Committee.
[b] Staff within the purview of the Standing Joint Advisory Committee.
[c] Category not normally recognized in approved schools at this time.
[d] Some schools use the clerical services of headquarters of voluntary organizations.

TABLE 26 *Voluntary managements : girls' schools*

(*Number of full-time authorized posts and staff in post at 30 September 1960*)

	Heads[a]	Teachers[a]	Instructors[a]	House-mistresses[b]	House-mothers[b]	Clerks[b]
NUMBER OF AUTHORIZED POSTS	32	59	114	61	43	[c]
STAFF IN POST						
Qualified teachers	13	53				
Other heads	18					
Instructors:						
Qualified			9			
Substantially but not fully qualified			40			
Unqualified			60			
Housemistresses:						
Qualified	1			1		
Joint Interview Board				33		
Other				14		
Housemothers:						
With CTC certificate					2	
Other					23	
Clerical division						1
General division						13
NUMBER IN POST	32	53	109	48	25	14
VACANCIES	0	6	5	13	18	—

[a] Staff within the purview of the Joint Negotiating Committee.
[b] Staff within the purview of the Standing Joint Advisory Committee.
[c] Some schools use the clerical services of headquarters of voluntary organizations.

TABLE 27 *Local authority managements: boys' schools*
(Numbers of full-time teachers, instructors, and housemasters)

	Teachers	Instructors	Housemasters
AUTHORIZED POSTS	127	64	41
STAFF IN POST			
Qualified	119	34	5
Substantially but not fully qualified		18	
Unqualified	1	11	
Joint Interview Board			27
NUMBER IN POST	120	63	32
VACANCIES	7	1	9

Note: The figures for staff in post are the latest available: for teachers and instructors correct to 10 December 1959; for house staff to 13 May 1960.

TABLE 28 *Local authority managements: girls' schools*
(Numbers of full-time teachers, instructors, and housemistresses)

	Teachers	Instructors	House-mistresses
AUTHORIZED POSTS	4	9	4
STAFF IN POST			
Qualified	4	2	
Substantially but not fully qualified		3	
Unqualified		2	
Joint Interview Board			3
NUMBER IN POST	4	7	3
VACANCIES	0	2	1

Note: The figures for staff in post are the latest available: for teachers and instructors correct to 10 December 1959; for house staff to 13 May 1960.

members of staff whose quality was such that he was able to delegate his duties to them, but, to complete the circle, this in itself was partly the result of an autocratic tradition in dealing with the staff. This type of tradition was not confined to approved schools; it was common in most schools, and particularly in residential schools. In approved schools, as elsewhere, it has been breaking down of recent years, but there are still heads, especially in smaller schools, who keep too much in their own hands. The duties of the headmaster have been defined above in terms of control, but the real control arises spontaneously out of the quality of his staff and of his relationships with them.

Headmasters and headmistresses are nearly all qualified teachers, and they may have other qualifications in addition. Only a few are social workers by training – a reflection of the comparatively recent introduction of staff trained solely in the social sciences. There is virtually no direct entry into the grade, appointments going to experienced approved school staff, and no special additional qualifications are required. The Central Training Council for Child Care does, however, run refresher courses for headmasters and headmistresses.

Deputy headmasters and headmistresses

As the term 'deputy' implies, these are the senior staff members who substitute for the headmaster when he is absent, and generally assist him. The grade was instituted as a consequence of a recommendation of the Reynolds Report (Home Office, 1946). The deputy headmaster has the powers of the headmaster, under the regulations, when he is acting for him. Nearly all schools have deputies; and most schools also have a senior assistant (third in charge).

Here, again, appointment is by promotion, not necessarily from within the school, and most of those holding these posts are teacher-trained.

Teachers

Most of the staff are teachers or instructors. The teachers are nearly all qualified according to Department of Education standards, but usually they have had no additional training. A similar situation is found in special schools run by local education authorities (for the maladjusted, the educationally subnormal, the physically handicapped); for teachers in special schools, however, a number of special post qualification courses are available, whereas, despite the recommendations of the Reynolds Report, there is no further qualification specifically designed for approved school teachers. They usually come to the work from teaching in ordinary schools, sometimes via special schools, and they learn on the job under the guidance of the headmaster and deputy.

The duties of teachers are twofold: schoolroom teaching, and general supervision outside the schoolroom. The amount of schoolroom work depends, of course, on the age range. For those under 15, and thus in all junior schools, there is full-time education. Of those in intermediate schools some will have full-time education and some will have what amounts to part-time education, the arrangements varying considerably. In senior schools educational activities tend to be part time and are rather more directed to the remedying of major defects, particularly illiteracy. The amount of time devoted to supervision is also determined by the type of school, and supervision ranges from overlooking the changing of boots to creating and maintaining a close relationship with a boy and helping him with his emotional problems. These activities are described for salary purposes as 'extraneous duties': there could hardly be a more inappropriate name for them.

Instructors

Instructors are the counterpart of teachers for craft and industrial training, and the number per school depends upon the age-group of the children. The schools vary enormously in the types of craft or industrial training they provide. Some have farms and concentrate largely on agricultural pursuits; some are engaged entirely in other types of work. Among instructors, therefore, a wide variety of crafts and skills are represented.

Instructors are classified for pay purposes as qualified, substantially qualified, and unqualified, the classification following that of the Department of Education, which prescribes the kinds of qualification that are acceptable. The qualified man has some technical qualification, such as a Higher National or City and Guilds Certificate; the substantially qualified has a lesser qualification plus experience.

Instructors may be recruited from industry or from other types of school. No further qualification and no special training are required for work in an approved school.

Housemasters and housemistresses

This is a comparatively new grade in approved schools, dating only, as a general grade, from the Reynolds Report. Borstal institutions have been built round the idea of houses since very early on and the system was well established by the 1920s. Following Mettray, Redhill approved school was based upon the house system, but the pattern did not become general. Thus, though most schools are divided into houses for competitive purposes – for games, and for marks for tidiness, industry, and good conduct – these are not yet run as separate administrative divisions as borstal houses tend to be. Of recent years there has been a move away from emphasizing the competitive aspects of the house system in borstals, coinciding with the emergence of smaller institutions, and the trend has been to regard the housemaster rather as a social worker who is primarily responsible for doing what can be done with a specific group of boys – a function which, in approved schools, had remained with the headmaster.

As *Tables 25* and *27* show, there were 175 authorized posts of house-master in boys' schools in 1960.[1] The existence of the grade is generally accepted, but many heads are not very sure how to use housemasters, whose duties range from those of a roving supernumerary, mainly concerned with routine jobs such as dealing with boys' correspondence, through those of an aftercare officer, to those of a staff member responsible for a specific group of boys. The difficulty has been to fit the housemaster into an organization based largely on the school rather than on the therapeutic institution. It is easy to acknowledge that a school needs a social worker for contact with parents or for aftercare; it is less easy to accept the fundamental reorganization involved in realigning teaching and social work functions in the school itself. To place a housemaster in charge of a group of boys is to change both the role of the headmaster and the roles of the other teachers on the staff; it is difficult to effect such changes, even if their objectives are well understood.

The generally accepted qualification for a housemaster is a social science diploma. Special courses are available, as detailed below (p. 104.) The need for staff at this level is so great, however, that any individual with relevant qualifications or experience, or a graduate expressing an interest in the work, would be eligible for appointment.

Housemothers and housefathers

Another comparatively recent grade is that of housemother (house-father), and its introduction reflects a spilling over of the developments in child care work. In the latter sphere the small-group principle rapidly became pre-eminent: large homes were replaced by family group homes for a maximum of eight children, with houseparents in charge, and any communal homes that remained were operated as far as possible on the group method. A similar principle is being adopted in residential schools, and is beginning to establish itself in approved schools. Problems, however, arise. To what extent is the housemother to be regarded as the domestic head of a group of children, without any real responsibility for their training, and to what extent is she to be regarded as the friend and colleague of the trained social worker? The fact that, in the period 1955–59, there was a higher turnover among housemothers – 36 per cent per year – than for any other grade of approved school staff would seem to indicate that some of the problems have not yet been solved.

[1] By 1966, there were over 300 housemasters in post.

Matrons and assistant matrons

The role of matron in boys' schools is more clear cut: she is in overall charge of the domestic side. In girls' schools, where there is a general emphasis on domestic training, a separate post of matron is not necessary. In boys' schools the matron is often the headmaster's wife, an arrangement that is obviously advantageous from the financial standpoint. Whether she remains primarily the domestic manager or is able to participate in more positive training depends upon her own personality and that of her husband. There are advantages in having a couple in charge, where they may be seen and may act in a substitute parental role; there are also disadvantages when boys identify the matron with the main source of authority, as must inevitably happen in these circumstances. The key point here is whether the school is organized in such a way that it is possible to establish and maintain a close relationship between a small group of children and substitute parents, which bears some resemblance to the family situation. Distance lends no enchantment to an institutional child's view of authority; he has seen too much of 'them' already.

Assistant matrons usually attend to the more routine side of the matron's work in a large establishment. This job also has a large turnover, 31 per cent per year in 1955–59, which suggests a lack of satisfaction in the work.

Method of appointment

In general, staff are appointed by a committee of managers with the headmaster in attendance; auxiliary and domestic staff are appointed directly by the headmaster. How far the headmaster's views are accepted with regard to staff appointments depends upon his relationship with the managers, but obviously he is the man most concerned and most managers defer to his wishes. The managers also appoint the headmaster, but under the Rules they must obtain the prior approval of the Home Office and in practice the regional inspectorate is usually fully consulted. Vacancies for headmasters and deputies must be advertised; in effect, vacancies of all grades tend to be advertised.

Since committees of management vary widely in experience and ability, it is not surprising that many different standards are exercised in the making of staff appointments. The system of selection is akin to that in operation for ordinary and special schools, but it is quite unlike the centralized selection and appointments system of the Prison Department. The probation service has an elaborate central selection procedure, but probation committees are not restricted to its products and often appoint directly; such appointments must be confirmed by the Home Office after one year, however, if a grant is to be paid.

STAFF ASSOCIATIONS AND NEGOTIATING MACHINERY

A word about staff associations is appropriate here. For senior staffs there is the Association of Headmasters, Headmistresses and Matrons of Approved Schools; it seems to have developed, after the First World War, out of the Society of Superintendents, an offshoot of the National Association of Certified Reformatory and Industrial Schools (1881). This Association, having fallen to pieces, quietly dissolved itself in 1927. The Association of Voluntary Managers of Certified Home Office Schools was formed in 1922 (the word 'voluntary' was subsequently dropped and the Association now includes local authority representatives). In 1944 another association was founded to represent the other staff levels, the National Association of Approved School Staffs (NAASS). Membership of this body is open to any member of staff, but it is in fact a counterpart to the Association of Headmasters, Headmistresses and Matrons, and it represents the interests of the remaining staff, including housemasters and welfare officers. There is some overlap of membership between this Association and other unions and professional associations, especially the National Union of Teachers. The latter has an advisory committee on approved schools, upon which the NAASS is represented. A number of other unions also have some members in approved schools, as can be seen in the constitutions of the various negotiating committees. Housemasters have their own association (1949), membership of which overlaps that of the NAASS.

These bodies are represented on the Joint Negotiating Committee for Approved Schools and Remand Homes and on the Standing Joint Advisory Committee for Staffs of Children's Homes, the two main negotiating committees concerned with salaries and conditions of service. The Local Government Manpower Committee recommended new machinery in its first report issued in 1950. The Joint Negotiating Committee was set up in 1953, following a recommendation to this effect by the National Joint Council for Local Authorities' Administrative, Professional, Technical and Clerical Services, a body that deals generally with local authority staff and agrees salary scales for them. The Joint Negotiating Committee, like other Whitley-type committees, is independent of the Home Office. It is concerned with headmasters, deputy headmasters, qualified and unqualified teachers and instructors, and also with superintendents and deputies of remand homes; that is to say, with all those whose salaries are linked to the Burnham scale because they are teachers or instructors. It has twenty-five members, eleven from the management side and fourteen representing staff:

Employers	No.	Staff	No.
Association of Municipal Corporations	3[a]	National Union of Teachers	6
County Councils' Association	3[a]	Association of Headmasters, Headmistresses and Matrons of Approved Schools	3
Association of Managers of Approved Schools	5	National Association of Approved School Staffs	3
		National Association of Remand Home Superintendents and Matrons	2
	11		14

[a] Under review in 1966.

The Standing Joint Advisory Committee of the National Joint Council for Local Authorities' Administrative, Professional, Technical and Clerical Services (the Great Panjandrum himself could hardly think of a more impressive title) was also established in 1953, and deals with the pay and conditions of service of all other administrative and supervisory staff (excluding nurses and grades covered by the Joint Negotiating Committee) in approved schools, remand homes, local authority children's homes, and approved probation homes and hostels. So far as approved schools are concerned, the main grades covered are housemasters, housemistresses, housefathers, housemothers, matrons, and assistant matrons. The Standing Joint Advisory Committee is constituted as shown on page 102.

It will be noted that approved school representatives are decidedly in the minority, on both sides. It is difficult to evaluate the effects of this imbalance. No doubt the other committee members listen with respect when such specialized grades as housemaster are discussed, but they must be much more knowledgeable about the general level of salaries in residential work than they are about salaries in the field of social work.

There is thus a distinct split, in respect of pay and conditions of service, separating teachers and others who come within the Burnham scale from the rest of the staff. It should be noted that this is not a straightforward division between those regarded as teachers and those regarded as social workers; rather, the social workers, i.e. the housemasters and housemistresses, are simply lumped together with the rest

Employers	No.	Staff	No.
National Joint Council (Employers)	7	National Joint Council (Staff)	6
National Association of Homes and Hostels (Employers)	2	National Association of Homes and Hostels (Staff)	2
Association of Managers of Approved Schools	4	Association of Headmasters, Headmistresses and Matrons of Approved Schools	2
		National Association of Approved School Staffs	2
		Association of Hospital and Welfare Administrators	2
		National Association of Remand Home Superintendents and Matrons	2
		Confederation of Health Service Employees	1
		National Union of General and Municipal Workers	1
		National Union of Public Employees	1
		Transport and General Workers' Union	1
	13		20

of the residential staff. It is obvious how this situation came about: it is a direct reflection of the accepted status and the effective negotiating power of teachers as compared with the not yet accepted status and the less effective negotiating power of social workers in general, and of social workers in residential work in particular.

The contrast is, not surprisingly, seen in salary levels also. Actual amounts change from year to year and there is no point in quoting figures. However, a qualified teacher in an approved school receives a salary according to the Burnham scale, plus an 'extraneous duties' allowance. There are additional allowances for certain staff of classifying schools, and for the 'third in charge', the new grade of senior assistant ranking next to the deputy head. Deputy headmasters and headmistresses are on scales related to certified accommodation, as are the heads themselves; they receive assistant teachers' pay, plus allowances calculated according to the numbers in the school. Increments and the extraneous duties allowances are payable in addition. Qualified instructors are paid on the same scales as assistant teachers. These are all staff who come under the Joint Negotiating Committee.

The salaries of those within the purview of the Standing Joint Advisory Committee are lower. Housemasters are of particular concern in this context: their salaries are substantially below those of teachers. A bar part-way along the scale for housemasters is related to acceptance by the Home Office Joint Interview Board, which was set up to try to maintain uniform standards; there is one maximum for those who are qualified in youth work, or hold a residential training certificate for child care, or have been trained and/or approved by the Home Office, and another for those who hold a social science diploma or a senior certificate in the residential care of children awarded by the Universities of Durham or Bristol. There are no extraneous duties or additional allowances. There seem to be no grounds – apart from historical development and the relative strengths of the two negotiating bodies – to justify the differences in scales for qualified staff. By negotiating committee standards in respect of comparable occupations the housemaster's salary is not unreasonable, but it is still anomalous in relation to the pay of his teacher colleagues. Arguments can be put forward, of course, in terms of experience and usefulness, but the problem remains.

When people are doing the same job and receiving different salary scales, friction can result. At present it is doubtful whether the housemaster does, in fact, carry out the same duties as the teacher in most of the schools in which he is employed; moreover, the amount of actual teaching varies considerably in junior, intermediate, and senior schools. Nevertheless, it is likely that, with time, the two posts will gradually move more closely together, especially if the teacher-trained are appointed to housemaster jobs in schools not organized on a house system.

STAFF TRAINING

Very little has been done to implement the recommendations of the Reynolds Committee (Home Office, 1946) that adequate training should be provided for both teachers and housemasters. Responsibility for training approved school staff rests, as it does for children's department staff, with the Central Training Council in Child Care, instituted as a result of the Curtis Committee in 1947. In practice, whether courses are available depends upon demand and upon the ability of the Council to provide in terms of money and staff.

In 1949–50 Sunderland Education Department offered a course for housemasters, but it ran for only one year because further appointments of housemasters were stopped in one of the periodic financial crises.

H

Subsequently, it was decided that a few of the men and women under-taking training in the Council's ordinary fourteen-month courses for residential staff should receive a 'supplementary' period of several months' training. A group of students were given supplementary training in association with the course provided by the Probation Train-ing Board for probation officers; it was found, however, that the arrange-ment did not provide sufficient continuity and the scheme was dropped.

Since 1950 a considerable number of men and women who have qualified by one of the basic courses provided for residential staff have taken up work in approved schools. The number of basic courses available varies from year to year, but has been increasing. The period of training is twelve months, approximately half of it being spent in study at the training centre and half in practical training. If students express an interest in approved school work special arrangements are made for a proportion of their practical training to be carried out in approved schools, and they also receive some supplementary teaching. Women over the age of 18 and men over 21 are eligible for training. No special academic qualifications are required for entry to a course, but candidates are expected to have a good general education and to have had some practical experience in the care of children. Since 1960 this basic course and the senior and refresher courses run by the Central Training Council have been available to those intending to undertake the residential care of handicapped children in special schools, and four additional appointments in the education field have been made to the Council. The courses thus offer training for a very wide field of resi-dential work, but they are not intended primarily to provide house-masters and housemistresses.

A system of training for housemasters and housemistresses has only recently been established. Apart from the abortive effort in 1949–50, there was one other attempt to institute training. This was by John Gittins, headmaster of Aycliffe school, who, through his personal con-tacts with the Institute of Education at the University of Durham, started a course for housemasters, apparently without the backing of the Central Training Council. Since 1957 about six students a year have been taken on to the staff at Aycliffe, where they received a very compre-hensive, careful, and individualized training. This course has now been taken over by the Central Training Council and has emerged as a senior course. There is already one senior course (at Bristol) for experienced staff in residential child care establishments and approved schools.

It was not until 1961 that the Central Training Council inaugurated the first two courses for the staff of approved schools, at Selly Oak, Birmingham, and at the Josephine Butler Memorial House, Liverpool.

In accordance with the Council's policy to mix various types of staff in training, these courses are not specifically for approved school staff only, although most of the trainees go into approved schools. They are primarily intended to train new recruits for the posts of housemaster and housemistress. The period of training is currently one year. Further courses have since been started, and altogether there were twelve in 1965. Not all of those who are trained in this way go into approved schools; but when those trained in the general courses mentioned above are included, output for the schools is seventy to eighty per year.

It is clear that the working party that preceded the establishment of these new courses thought primarily in terms of housemaster training, and there seems to be no likelihood at the moment that courses will be provided to train qualified teachers for approved school work. As a matter of priorities this was the right decision, but the question of special training for teachers will have to be faced sooner or later. Since the Report on the Training and Supply of Teachers of Handicapped Pupils was published in 1954, a number of one-year courses have been set up to train qualified teachers for work in schools for the educationally subnormal, and it is surely equally necessary to train those going into approved schools. There might be some real advantage in instituting a form of training equivalent to that of the Continental 'social pedagogue', not only for teachers in approved schools but for suitable staff in secondary modern schools, since a proportion of these certainly need an approach which is as much social work as teaching. Any system likely to widen the basis of training is desirable, since it would facilitate the valuable interchange of teachers over the whole of the educational field. It is not only better pay that housemasters need; they also need to be accepted and understood by their colleagues.

In addition to these full-time courses, a number of short refresher courses are run for various types of approved school staff, from instructors to headmasters. Some are arranged on a day-a-week basis; others occupy a week or a month. They cover a variety of subjects. Although courses of this type are expanding, it seems unlikely, at the current rate of increase, that many of the existing staff will go through even a short refresher course in the foreseeable future.

6

Control and finance

For the majority of approved schools, there are three main sources of control: the Home Office and its inspectorate, the managers, and the headmaster or headmistress. For local authority schools, which are run by children's departments, two additional points of authority are introduced: the children's officer and the children's committee. Where schools are run by voluntary bodies (i.e. not by *ad hoc* local committees), the secretary and the governing council or committee of the body concerned is involved.

The Home Office has a small administrative staff which is directly responsible for policy concerning the schools (an assistant secretary, two principals, and their train of executive and clerical officers bear the brunt of this side of the work). There is also an Approved Schools Central Advisory Committee, which consists of representatives of the Association of Headmasters, Headmistresses and Matrons of Approved Schools, of the Managers' Association, and of the National Association of Approved School Staffs. The committee meets three or four times a year under the chairmanship of one of the senior officials at the Home Office, and recently it set up two working parties: one on recruitment and training and one on closed and other special facilities. Neither of the reports has been published.

The major work of running the schools devolves, in practice, upon the inspectorate whose members, in the main, deal directly with the headmaster. The headmaster's role has been briefly considered, and there is further discussion in Part II of the relation between the inspectorate, the managers, and the head. This chapter is primarily concerned with the nature of the inspectorate, with the role of the managers, and with the arrangements for financing approved schools.

THE INSPECTORATE

Development and structure

As noted in Chapter 1, the inspectorate grew out of the original legislation on reformatory and industrial schools. It was always handicapped by being too small an establishment: not until 1912 was it increased in size to eight members, one being the chief inspector, and it remained so with little variation up to 1948. By the Children Act of that year all local authorities established children's departments: the amount of work involved and the need for personnel to assist in the reorganization of the whole field of care for deprived children led to a rapid expansion of the inspectorate, and its decentralization into seven regions. At the end of June 1963 there were in all seventy-six inspectors, some forty-six men and thirty women, the majority working in the regions; a chief inspector, two deputies, a senior medical inspector, and other specialized inspectors, including an advisory psychiatrist, were at headquarters in London. Of the headquarters staff, six are concerned with training, one is a specialist in the care of young children, one is a dietician, and four are medical inspectors. Three of these staff are specifically responsible for approved schools: one is for boys' schools, one for girls', and the third is a technical inspector who deals chiefly with farms and gardens; the medical inspectors are also largely concerned with the schools.

The main work is carried out in the regions, each of which has a number of inspectors, according to the amount of work, headed by a superintending inspector (the SI). It is the SI's business to allocate the work, in consultation with the chief inspector, and to keep in touch with schools and children's departments in his area and with the Home Office. There is a meeting of SIs at the Home Office every two months; files are continually passing to and fro, and there is a good deal of daily contact.

Dual responsibility

The inspectorate remains responsible both for child care services and for approved schools, and while the amount of specialization varies from region to region, and in some places inspectors do nothing else but approved school work, in most areas the two are combined. Thus an inspector may have under his wing a number of schools and also several children's departments, and perhaps, in addition, a special subject, e.g. training. The theory behind this structure is that the two fields of work may fertilize each other, but much depends on the actual volume of work. At the beginning of the period of reorganization, inspectors were concerned almost exclusively with child care since a new service had to be set up and guided on its first faltering steps (too much guidance, some people said[1]); consequently, approved schools got rather short shrift. The available money went in the same direction,

[1] See Select Committee on Estimates, 6th Report, Session 1951–52, p. 135.

and the result was comparatively slow development on the approved school side. Subsequently, however, child care departments being well established and less in need of attention from the inspectorate, more energy has been expended on the approved schools, and of recent years the time spent on the schools has probably been greater than that spent on child care.

It follows also from this dual responsibility of the inspectorate that its members are drawn from a variety of backgrounds. Precise data are not available concerning the backgrounds of current inspectors, but some have been in education, some in child care, some in other social work, and only a small minority have had experience of approved school work. This may or may not be a disadvantage, since the best people for the job are those who have the necessary capacities of discernment and judgement. It may be noted, nevertheless, that H.M. Inspectors of Schools are all qualified teachers and that, in the prison and borstal services, governors are promoted to become assistant commissioners, and subsequently directors of various services. The probation inspectorate, which is more closely allied to that of the children's department, though not part of it, is made up of some ex-probation officers and some others with relevant experience.

The inspectorate has quite different responsibilities in its two main fields of work. In the sphere of child care the inspector is dealing with autonomous local authority departments and his function cannot be more than advisory. In the approved school field, however, in addition to advising he has the power to veto, and by this token he participates in the duties of management.

Powers of chief inspector

It is an odd historical quirk that many of the powers of control held by the Home Office are, in fact, powers of the chief inspector and not of the administration. According to the 1933 Rules, the chief inspector has the following powers:

1. The minutes of the managers and any committees appointed by them are open to inspection by or on behalf of the chief inspector.
2. The headmaster cannot leave the school for more than two days without notifying the chief inspector.
3. The managers must tell the chief inspector who is responsible in the headmaster's absence.
4. The dietary scale is subject to the approval of the chief inspector and no substantial alteration can be made in it without his approval.

5. The daily routine (including hours of rising, schoolroom instruction and practical training, domestic work, meals, recreation, and retiring) must be in accordance with a scheme approved by the chief inspector.

6. The schoolroom timetable and syllabus are subject to approval by the chief inspector.

7. The practical training of all boys must be in accordance with a scheme approved by the chief inspector and any substantial deviation from it must be recorded in the Log Book and notification sent forthwith to him.

8. Attendance in the schoolroom at all classes must be recorded on a form approved by the chief inspector.

9. Home leave cannot be granted in excess of thirty-three days without the approval of the chief inspector.

10. Arrangements made for the weekly giving of pocket money must be approved by the chief inspector.

11. 'The discipline of the school shall be maintained by the personal influence of the headmaster and staff and shall be promoted by a system of rewards and privileges which shall be subject to the approval of the chief inspector' (Rule 33 as amended).

12. If separation is continued for more than twenty-four hours this must be reported immediately to the chief inspector.

13. The headmaster is responsible for recording all corporal and serious punishments in the Punishment Book and must enter such details as may be required by the chief inspector.

14. The managers must maintain a licensing register in a form prescribed by the chief inspector.

15. Medical records and dental records must be kept in a form laid down by the chief inspector.

16. Any death, serious illness, or infectious disease or accident must be reported by the headmaster at once to the parent or guardian and to the chief inspector; a report of the proceedings of an inquest must also be sent to the chief inspector.

17. The managers must arrange for keeping all records and returns and for furnishing any information the chief inspector requires.

18. The school must be open at all times for inspection by or on behalf of the chief inspector and facilities must be given for examination of its books and records.

Thus very little of the running of the school can escape the all-pervading authority of the chief inspector as operated through the regional inspectorate. What matters, however, is how this authority is exercised, and only by examining a series of cases in some detail could this be ascertained. In general, it appears that modifications of the daily routine and of the day-to-day administration of a school are usually discussed beforehand with the regional inspectorate, and submission to the chief inspector is mainly formal; formal submissions, however, often need to go to head office for approval. It should be noted that some proposed changes will, in the long run, mean more money; where this is clearly so, head office must be brought in since the regional office has no discretion at all in money matters. It is therefore only minor matters that the regional office has discretion to approve without reference to the centre.

Duties of inspectorate

The varied duties of the inspectorate may perhaps be grouped into three categories:

1. *Informal 'advice'*. This aspect of the inspectors' work goes on all the time. Usually the heads of schools consult directly with the inspectorate in respect of changes they wish to make, activities, or problems. Some of the advice they get is straightforward help derived from the body of knowledge that the inspectors accumulate from their visits to schools. Some of it is in the form of rulings about what head office is and is not likely to accept. Probably this is the most important activity of the inspectors, although their position is anomalous since it is easy for heads to appeal right over them to the Home Office.

2. *Regular visits*. Inspectors are expected to make at least three visits a year to each school in their care, and it is probable that they are now able to do this; it could not be achieved until quite recently since, as noted above, the staff was very small until about 1950 and much concerned with child care immediately afterwards. The three scheduled visits do not preclude visits for special purposes, of course, such as a large development plan, an open day, or when trouble has arisen with staff or boys.

3. *Full inspections*. This system was introduced in 1952 or 1953, and the objective was to inspect the boys' schools at the rate of two per region per year, or twelve altogether; in practice, probably only ten inspections per year are carried out. The project is, therefore, a long-term one, and can have only a general effect, if, indeed, it is continued.

   A full inspection is conducted by a team of inspectors. They descend upon the school and spend a period of time there, going through the whole place with great thoroughness. They then prepare a report in three sections: the aims and intentions of the school; how these are being carried out; and the results so far as ascertained. In this last section, the absconding rate, the official success rate, the punishment rate, and other statistics indicating progress in the educational and vocational spheres are compared with norms worked out for the type and class of school. The recommendations made as a result of the inspection are discussed with the headmaster and managers, but the full report itself is not made available to them. The inspectors thus have the opportunity to write freely, and if necessarily critically, for Home Office consumption only, as well as to talk in some detail with the school personnel. On the whole, the schools are dissatisfied with this procedure and would prefer to see the full report.

There is room for doubt about the value of full inspections of this nature. The rationale behind them is that, preoccupied with the ordinary day-to-day conduct of the school, no one bothers to stop and consider the running of the school as a whole, and its future. A similar procedure is established for ordinary schools. Full inspections tend, nevertheless, to be very time-consuming; moreover, there is a considerable difference between the Department of Education's inspectors and Home Office inspectors in respect of their powers of control over the different types of school. It is clear that there ought to be some review of the progress of each approved school, but it is doubtful whether, under this programme, a school will be appraised once every ten years, and this is too long an interval.

A problem that seems insoluble concerns the relationship between Home Office and Department of Education inspection. This is a long-standing difficulty: it stems from the fact that in so far as approved schools are educational establishments they need to keep abreast of the best educational practice, and the most useful way of achieving this is to have them visited by the ordinary Department of Education inspectors; on the other hand, in so far as they are social work institutions dealing with difficult children, they need the advice of the Home Office inspectors. The issue of dual inspection was argued before almost every commission and committee in the late nineteenth and early twentieth centuries, but, despite various recommendations, nothing successful was done, primarily because both departments were too starved of funds to be able to appoint sufficient inspectors anyway. The position at the time of writing is that the Education inspectors are supposed to visit approved schools also, by arrangement with the Home Office inspectors. It does

not seem possible to ascertain how many inspections of approved schools
are made by Education inspectors, but one gets the impression they are
comparatively few. The educationists feel that the child welfare experts
have insufficient knowledge of, and are not interested in, modern educational methods, whereas the child welfare experts think that the
educationists do not know enough about and do not care enough about
dealing with difficult and delinquent children. Both, of course, are
right, and it is to be hoped that, eventually, higher staffing ratios in
both inspectorates will give each time to find out more about the other.

THE MANAGERS

Types of management

'"Managers" in relation to an approved school established or taken
over by a local authority or by a joint committee representing two or
more local authorities means the local authority or the joint committee
as the case may be, and in relation to any other approved school means
the persons for the time being having the management or control
thereof.'

Thus the definition given in the 1933 Rules, charmingly phrased, and
utterly circular. For more useful information we must look further.
There are two major types of management, voluntary and local authority.
Of these, the voluntary agencies are by far the older, and some of them
are managing schools that have been in operation for over a hundred
years. Most of the original boards of managers were local *ad hoc* committees brought together specially for the purpose, but a number of
schools are run by voluntary bodies of various kinds. (Although all the
'juvenile welfare schools' in Sweden have been taken over by the state,
they also have local committees of five members; this system seems to
be the nearest equivalent in another country to the British pattern.) An
analysis of the various types of managing body shows that, of the ninety
boys' schools, forty-four are run by local committees, twenty by voluntary bodies, and twenty-six by local authorities; the corresponding
figures for girls' schools are seventeen, twelve, and four. It is interesting to note that twelve of the boys' junior schools are run by local
authorities and ten by voluntary bodies, out of a total of thirty, whereas
none of the six girls' junior schools is run by a local authority and only
two are managed by voluntary bodies. The voluntary bodies are most
prominent in boys' junior and girls' intermediate and senior schools
(although not in a majority – ten out of twenty-seven, as against thirteen
local committee and four local authority schools).

This preponderance of voluntary action among girls' schools and senior schools in particular is one result of various 'rescue' operations conducted by voluntary bodies. Three schools are administered by the Salvation Army, two by Diocesan organizations of the Church of England, and five by Roman Catholic 'sisters'. Other organizations running boys' or girls' schools include the Brothers of the Christian Schools (RC), the Southwark Catholic Rescue Society, the London Police Court Mission (now the Rainer Foundation), Dr Barnardo's Homes, the Children's Aid Society, and the National Children's Home. These bodies vary considerably in organization and it is interesting to examine what is in fact a centralized system, with strong direction from the top, and its effects on approved schools.

The National Children's Home is a well-known countrywide organization founded by one of the pioneers in this field, Dr T. B. Stephenson, in 1869. It administers three approved schools, two for junior boys and one for junior girls, in addition to its main work of running six special schools and twenty-eight homes for children of all ages. The National Children's Home is run by an Executive Officers' Committee of five full-time officers, responsible to the General Committee, which is a large and more or less self-appointing body. There are a number of sub-committees, of which the Approved Schools Advisory Council is one. It consists of the general treasurer and the London treasurer, the members of the Executive Officers' Committee, six members appointed by the General Committee, and a local manager of each of the three approved schools; it meets, however, only rarely. Strictly speaking, the officers and the six members of the General Committee form part of the management of all three schools, together with the local managers, but in practice an officer, usually the secretary, goes to a meeting of managers once a quarter, and matters of importance are, unless urgent, reserved for this meeting.

The approved schools of the National Children's Home are self-supporting; the financial arrangements are a little different from those for most of the other schools and the Home is empowered to put its own 'voluntary' cases directly into the schools, though nowadays this rarely happens. Staff are appointed by the central office in consultation with the managers and the Home Office as necessary. The General Secretary of the organization is the 'correspondent' of the managers.

The National Children's Home was a pioneer in the family-group principle and all its homes are run on these lines. Dr Stephenson also founded a sisterhood, which is still an important feature. It is described as 'an Order of women who, with a sense of religious vocation, are trained for the privilege of being housemothers to needy children'. The

Home is Methodist, but the sisterhood is interdenominational and contains members of various religious communities. There are no promises of lifelong service, no vows, and sisters may resign whenever they like. The Home has carried out child care training for a long time, and its course is recognized and financed by the Home Office; thus all the sisters receive training eventually. They are then available for work anywhere, and this supply more or less disposes of the acute staff crisis which has killed a number of approved schools.

Pretty well everything of importance in the Home's approved schools is done through the central office, which has a good deal of expertise at its command and can deal directly, and informally, with the Home Office. Thus things tend to run smoothly and without strain under the control of a full-time administration with adequate resources and wide experience.

Looking at approved schools as a whole one finds, of course, differences in organization according to the type of management. The major distinction is between the local authority subcommittee of the children's committee, which runs the schools for the local authority, and the voluntary committee. The local authority committee is composed of councillors, and, though the newly elected councillor is allowed to say on which committees he would like to serve, the reasons for his choice are unlikely to be related to approved school management, and which committees he is in fact appointed to may be determined entirely by other circumstances. On the other hand, some committees co-opt suitable members from outside (others are strongly opposed to this procedure), and councillors, whatever their interests, may well do a good job when they are allocated to an approved schools committee. Furthermore, they have behind them the children's officer and the resources of his department in addition to the headmaster of the school, although it is also true that the triangle of children's officer, headmaster, and committee can have sharp corners.

Those voluntary boards of managers which are part of larger organizations are also administered by specially appointed committees containing local members, but they tend to be semi-independent of their organization owing to the special relationship in which they stand with the Home Office. It is probable that both these and the *ad hoc* local committees are mainly self-appointing and self-perpetuating. The result may be that excellent local people with much relevant experience are appointed to the committees; again, it may be that local bigwigs or active but not very suitable voluntary workers are selected. One does not want a board to consist entirely of social workers or educationists; people with business acumen and administrative ability are also needed.

Constitution

The 1933 Rules make certain stipulations about the constitution of the boards. Two at least of the managers of a boys' school must be women, and two at least of those of a girls' school must be men (since no maximum number is laid down, however, it is not clear how much in the minority they might be). They must appoint a chairman, a 'correspondent' (secretary), and a treasurer; no member of the staff of the school is eligible for either of these last two offices, although there seems to be no reason why the managers should not appoint any member of the staff to be one of their number and, indeed, to be their chairman, though it is not done. The managers must, so far as is practicable, meet once a month at the school, and a 'sufficient number . . . to ensure adequate supervision' must live within a reasonable distance of it. They must appoint a finance committee, and may appoint other committees, and their minutes and the minutes of the committees are open to inspection by the chief inspector.

Powers and duties

The Rules also cover the powers and duties of the managers. They must 'maintain an efficient standard throughout the school' and for this purpose 'they shall take into consideration any report which may be communicated to them by or on behalf of the Secretary of State' (i.e. the inspectors' reports). Furthermore: 'It shall be the duty of the Managers to ensure that the condition of the school and the training, welfare and education of the boys under their care are satisfactory and for this purpose they shall pay frequent visits to the school.' One manager must visit at least once a month and he must 'satisfy himself regarding the care of the boys and the state of the school, or some part of it, and shall enter his conclusions in the Log Book or other convenient record kept at the school'. The managers choose the name of the school and are responsible for effective control over its expenditure. They are responsible for the appointment, suspension, or dismissal of the staff, but the appointment of the headmaster or his deputy must be approved by the Home Office. They approve expenditure by the headmaster and inspect his log book, daily register, and punishment book. They approve the headmaster's distribution of duties among the staff, and authorize his absence for more than two days. They appoint a deputy when he is absent. They draw up a dietary scale for the boys after consultation with the headmaster and medical officer, subject to the approval of the chief inspector. They act *in loco parentis* so far as the boys are concerned. They determine the intervals at which the boys may receive letters and visits.

On the discipline side, the written consent of one of the managers must be obtained if separation is to last more than twenty-four hours, and the 'special approval' of one of the managers must be obtained where over eight and up to twelve strokes of the cane are to be given to a boy over 15 years of age. The managers can also authorize the principal teacher to administer the cane. They have extensive powers concerning aftercare, which have been referred to elsewhere. They must appoint a medical officer and a dentist. They are also responsible for seeing that all registers and records required by the chief inspector are so kept, and that these, and the school itself, are available for inspection at any time. They must ensure that a copy of the Rules is given to every member of the staff and to the medical officer and dentist on appointment.

If approved schools continue as at present, it is almost certain that steps will be taken to impose an age limit for chairmen of boards of managers, and possibly also for other members, and to restrict the period for which the office of chairman can be held. Such regulations could be included in the new Rules or by issuing Instruments of Management.

Discussion

Perusal of their powers and duties could give an impression of omnipotence on the part of the managers. The reverse is, however, the case. The managers' powers must be read in conjunction with the powers of the chief inspector, and must be related to the effects of the financial arrangements. In fact, the situation of the managers is an extremely difficult one. They are asked to run the school, and if anything goes wrong they are blamed, but inspection and financial control are so close and so ubiquitous that few decisions can be taken without reference to the Home Office either by the managers themselves or, at an earlier stage, by the headmaster. They must visit regularly but it is difficult to know what exactly they are visiting for. They cannot possibly obtain a personal knowledge of the boys; only the staff can hope to do this. They are unlikely to be able to tell whether the school is running well or badly, or even to know which questions to ask. Such insights derive from a wider experience than they usually possess. If they have had experience in cognate fields it is possible that they will be able to apply it, but there is no way of ensuring that this is so. They are expected to decide on discharges, but they must accept the reports of the staff and it is very difficult for them to go against the recommendation of the headmaster. These paradoxes are discussed further in Chapter 11.

Who are the managers? They are presumably much the same people who make up the framework of voluntary committees in other spheres, carrying out a large part of English government. It may be surmised that they include a considerable proportion of retired people and of those whose incomes allow them to give time to this kind of activity. Some boards have teachers or social workers among their members, but this seems to be comparatively rare. The Carlton House board had a distinctly military flavour – very useful in times of crisis, perhaps, but not necessarily so at other times. One gets the impression that the voluntary boards consist, in the main, of people who have been drawn in because of their prestige or status, or because 'it would be nice to have Mrs . . .'. Not that such a system is necessarily bad: there are many people who have much to contribute to the management of the schools. Voluntary committees are liable to be inefficient, although one must hasten to add that local authority committees may well be inefficient for different reasons; behind the latter, however, there is a strong administration used to dealing with problems of this kind.

In the Criminal Justice Act, 1961, the Home Office assumed further powers of control over the managers; these are referred to in Chapter 11 below.

FINANCE

As indicated in the first chapter, one of the major reasons for the succession of government inquiries into the schools that took place between 1884 and 1913 was the problem of finance. As at present, the income of the schools derived mainly from grants from the Treasury, from contributions by local authorities, from voluntary sources (of declining importance as time went on, and now very small), and from parental contributions which always represented only a small part of the total. A complex system grew up, by which the Treasury paid so much per inmate, according to type of school, plus various grants for special purposes; the local authorities paid a flat rate to the reformatory schools, and made up the government grant to an agreed sum for the industrial schools. The costs per inmate varied enormously from school to school (as is still the case, though perhaps with more justification as a result of classification), and what was a sufficient grant for one was insufficient for another. Costs rose steadily, particularly in industrial schools, and the Treasury only reluctantly raised the rates, managing progressively to shift a higher proportion of the cost of industrial schools on to the local authorities, though it paid a higher proportion of the grants to reformatories. The schools and the inspectors wanted to raise standards, which meant more money, and at the same time the schools wanted to preserve their independence. The result was an impasse, with the schools constantly running into financial difficulties, and none of the various committees being able to find an acceptable solution.

The problem was not, in fact, solved until after the First World War, when some unknown diplomatic and financial genius at the Home Office devised a comparatively simple system and persuaded all concerned to accept it. No doubt the experience of the war years and the post-war atmosphere contributed to its positive reception. This scheme, which came into operation on 1 April 1920, and remains substantially unaltered, is a form of pooling based upon expected expenditure. The schools submit estimates, from which is calculated an average cost per child. The Home Office fixes annually a flat rate per child to be paid by the local authority named in the admitting order (usually the authority for the area in which the child resides); this is intended to produce half the cost; the rest is made up by the Treasury. The Home Office maintains an equalization account showing how far the authorities or the Treasury have overpaid their half of the total cost, and an element is introduced into the flat rate for each year in order to bring this discrepancy into balance. This may mean, since the number of children and other expenses may vary considerably from year to year, that either the authorities or the Treasury are overpaying for several years at a time, but the imbalance is gradually corrected. Another factor to be taken into account before the flat rate is determined is the parental contribution, but the courts rarely set these high, and they are difficult and expensive to collect, with the result that they contribute very little to an abatement of the cost. Ten per cent of the parental contribution is retained by the local authority to offset the cost of collection.

The system works as follows. In September–November the schools prepare and return estimates on a form provided by the Home Office. The form for voluntary schools is much more detailed than that for local authority schools. The completed forms are checked and scrutinized by the finance division, in consultation with the inspectors. A number of the items are based on rates laid down by a *pro rata* committee which has already decided what would be a reasonable expenditure per child in terms of food, clothing, household requisites, schoolroom materials, recreation, films, pocket money, and camping (different rates are prescribed for different types of school). The main bones of the estimates, however, concern salaries, superannuation, and insurance, and these are determined by the number and types of staff (nearly all paid on national scales), the establishment being under the close control of the Home Office. On the basis of these estimates and of a forecast of the population, and allowing for the amortization of capital grants spread over a period, the flat rate is decided.

A point that arouses some criticism in the schools is the way in which the actual expenditure works out. Schools are given advances quarterly, but, as in other government services, the principles obtain of no transfer from one subhead to another without authority, and no retention of moneys unspent at the end of the year. The subheads are very detailed: the form contains no fewer than eighteen headings, some of them sub-divided, making fifty headings altogether, and any substantial departure from any of them must be authorized by the Home Office. The principle of spending up one's allocation or losing it is very widely applied in respect of public bodies and presents an apparently insoluble problem, the Treasury claiming that, since it bears the deficits, it ought to get the surpluses, and the recipients arguing that there is no incentive to efficiency. Anyone familiar with the history of regional hospital boards will recognize this perennial issue only too easily.

In general, however, the system as it now operates is acceptable to the schools. It relieves them from the burden of worrying about money and provides a steady and adequate income. Their own resources are usually negligible, and they rely almost entirely upon public authorities, although the Home Office does have some non-exchequer money from which small grants can be furnished. A small variable grant provides for certain contingencies, but such payments are included in the equalization account. By and large, it is likely that, whatever the standards obtaining in the running of the school, the money will be forthcoming without difficulty. *Table 29* gives some details of the actual costs of the schools.

On the capital side things are less easy, reflecting the tight control maintained by the government over capital expenditure in general. No school may undertake any capital project without the approval of the Home Office, whose approval is given in accordance with a capital allocation made by the Treasury to the Home Office. If consent is given, a voluntary school is then free to raise a loan in any way it likes (the activities of local authorities are more circumscribed), the idea being that opportunity is thus provided for the raising of a loan from a bank or an insurance company at a lower rate of interest than that obtainable from the Public Works Loan Board. It is said that loans are usually secured, since the propositions are guaranteed by the Home Office; but if there are difficulties in this respect owing to a credit squeeze, the Treasury will make a capital grant direct. Most of the schools that opened during the war years, for instance, were built on capital grants, repayable over twenty years, the repayments forming part of the annual estimates. Nowadays, few capital grants are issued, but the raising of the money appears to present little difficulty; the real problem is to get the project passed by the Home Office.

I

TABLE 29 Cost of approved schools

Year	Net weekly cost per head			Average number in schools	Total cost	Parental contributions	
						Contributions less collection costs	Average weekly contribution per child
	£	s.	d.		£	£	s. d.
1951–52	6	3	7	9,156	2,956,813	77,730	3 3
1952–53	6	6	2	9,416	3,098,033	88,713	3 7
1953–54	6	16	11	8,930	3,186,697	101,061	4 4
1954–55	7	17	0	7,912	3,238,953	102,430	5 0
1955–56	8	11	5	7,122	3,191,894	103,581	5 7
1956–57	9	2	1	6,810	3,232,157	106,748	6 0
1957–58	9	10	0	7,056	3,495,926	118,150	6 5
1958–59	9	8	1	7,615	3,733,348	128,979	6 6
1959–60	9	19	9	7,912	4,130,714	135,984	6 7
1960–61	11	0	9	7,910	4,552,786	147,831	7 3
1961–62	11	11	6	8,241	4,973,955	154,624	7 8
1962–63	13	4	3	8,605	5,927,635	162,146	7 3
1963–64	15	3	6	8,683	6,889,849	157,350	6 11
1964–65	16	13	5	8,664	7,532,092	161,936	7 2

Notes:

1. Net weekly cost per head: figures exclude parental contributions.
2. Average numbers include Isle of Man, Channel Islands, and non-committed cases.
3. Parental contributions and average weekly contributions: figures relate only to committed cases in England and Wales.
4. Annual instalments of the capital grant, *not* the actual payments each year, are included in the total cost figures.
5. There are slight amendments in past figures from year to year, but they are substantially correct.

This system of approving capital projects may be compared with the control exercised by other departments through the Ministry of Housing and Local Government in giving 'loan sanctions' to local authorities. At the time of writing Treasury policy is moving in favour of approving 'starts' rather than whole projects at a time, a change that increases the number of projects that can be put in train in any one year.

Table 30 shows the capital investment allocations to approved schools since 1950 (including a small proportion for remand homes), and the capital grants actually paid to the schools. The capital grants payments are carried to the equalization account in instalments spread over twenty years, and the local authorities' 50 per cent share is recovered through the medium of the flat-rate payment. The aggregated instalment of capital grant placed in the account for 1962–63 was £76,456.

TABLE 30 *Capital investment allocations*

Year	Capital investment allocation	Capital grant paid
	£000s	£
1950–51	255	140,544
1951–52	275	172,868
1952–53	180	118,084
1953–54	180	95,864
1954–55	220	67,169
1955–56	200	10,555
1956–57	100	28,200
1957–58	156	10,004
1958–59	200	17,907
1959–60	402	3,615
1960–61	750	38,320
1961–62	1,900	282,410
1962–63	3,500	782,272
1963–64	3,800	564,871
1964–65	3,600	459,025
1965–66	3,200	391,387

The very considerable rise in recent years reflects the easing of capital restrictions and the strong pressure to rebuild many of the existing schools upon lines more in accord with current thinking on child care. There is a backlog of neglect to be tackled, as is the case with prisons and mental hospitals. In addition, pressure of numbers has led to extensions to existing schools and to the planning of new ones. If the current rate of rebuilding continues there should be a considerable change in the physical characteristics of the schools in the foreseeable future.

7

The position in other countries

Before embarking upon a criticism of the British system of approved schools, it is wise to take a brief look at what happens in this sphere elsewhere. It is always a dangerous enterprise to compare systems in different countries, since the definitions of many basic terms, such as what is a delinquent, vary considerably. This chapter is based upon information abstracted from the United Nations *Comparative surveys of juvenile delinquency*, and checked and supplemented by reference to the relevant authorities in the countries concerned. Countries that did not respond to the request for information have not been included, and the information that was given is of variable quality. The summaries that follow must therefore be treated with the greatest caution, since the material needs to be seen within the context of the whole judicial and treatment system for minors in the countries concerned. The information presented relates mainly to the years 1962–63.

THE NETHERLANDS

As an example of the complexities of this undertaking, perhaps we might cite the Netherlands. The articles from which this account was drawn have been cross-checked, and reference has been made to two people who know the Netherlands system very well; nevertheless, it is presented with some trepidation.

The Netherlands is divided into nineteen districts, each served by a district court, at which at least one of the judges deals almost exclusively with child offenders (up to 18 years old). Each district also has a child protection board, set up and maintained by the Ministry of Justice. Anyone has a right to bring to the notice of this agency a child who is in physical or moral danger, or being neglected. The board investigates the case and makes a recommendation to the court, but it is the court that makes the decision, except in emergencies when the public prosecutor, whose action must be confirmed by the court, places the child in the care of the board, which can then send him to a school or family.

Under civil law, since 1901 it has been possible (a) to deprive of parental authority parents who grossly neglect or exploit their children, and (b) to release from parental authority parents who are unfit, or incapable of educating their children.[1] The latter can be done only with the consent of the parents. In 1921 supervision (akin to our probation) was introduced in addition. Under criminal law, a child can be 'placed at the disposal of the government' or sent to a correctional school. The latter is for a definite period of a maximum of three months up to age 14, and of six months between 14 and 18. The minimum period is one month. There is one correctional school for boys, and one for girls, both run by the State; they appear to be similar to our detention centres. The above measures are often not applied, however, since they are given in the form of a suspended sentence.

A child may be sent to an approved institution, which may be a home, a school, or a hostel, under any of these measures, including supervision (except, of course, when he is sentenced to a correctional school). If the child is 'placed at the disposal of the government' he may be sent to a State institution, of which there are three for boys and two for girls, but he is more often sent, at least initially, to an approved voluntary institution.

The Dutch system of social services relies more heavily than most upon voluntary activities, and there are 144 approved guardianship societies, of various denominational backgrounds, and also including humanist, i.e. non-denominational, societies. These form area associations, and also divide themselves roughly into three main streams: Catholic, Protestant, and non-denominational. They are affiliated at national level to the National Federation for Child Protection. The societies are grant-aided up to 95 per cent of the total cost of the child per day in the institution, but the actual percentage varies according to the type of institution. The children's department of the Ministry of Justice sets the payment per child per day for each institution. The Ministry also exercises financial control to see that the money is properly spent, and has inspectors who, however, are mainly concerned with buildings and staff.

Under the system, then, the child protection board brings the child either before the children's judge, or before a court which consists of three judges, one of whom is the children's judge. The children's judge can order supervision (probation) and, at the end of this, placing in a school, and can also order foster-home placement. Deprivation of parental rights can be ordered only by the courts. After deprivation of parental rights, the child is given into the care of one of the voluntary

---

[1] Judge J. Hudig, *Measures under civil law to protect youth from delinquency and the preventive role of the juvenile court*, European Office of the United Nations, Office of Social Affairs, UN/SOA/SEM/8/WP 8, 1962.

societies, who may place him in a foster home if it thinks fit. The court
may also send him to a State school. He may possibly pass through
an observation centre, of which there are several. He is released (except
from a correctional school) when the voluntary society or institution
thinks fit (but the parent may apply to the court to revoke the order).
The institutions specialize in different ways, covering handicapped and
educationally subnormal children as well as the deprived, the maladjusted, and the delinquent; thus delinquents may well be placed with
non-delinquents. The institutions also vary considerably in size and by
no means all of them are small. About half the staff have some training,
usually in child care.

The distinction between the State educational institutions and the two
correctional schools on the one hand and the voluntary institutions on
the other turns on the fact that the State schools cannot refuse to take
a child, whereas the voluntary institutions can. The State schools
thus tend to get the most difficult children, who do not fit in anywhere
else, and their régimes are said to be adapted accordingly. They are
larger than most voluntary schools. The judge decides whether the child
shall go to a State or voluntary school in the supervision cases, and the
children's department of the Ministry of Justice makes the decision
in respect of those 'placed at the disposal of the government'.
Voluntary agencies only exceptionally ask for a child to be put in a
State school.

The populations by type of institution at the end of 1962 are given
below:

	Boys	Girls	Total
State correctional schools	47	—	47
State educational institutions	146	62	208
State observation centres	54	17	71
Voluntary institutions (all types)	8,368	9,968	18,336

The difficulties of attempting to compare the Netherlands system
with the English system of approved schools are evident from this brief
outline. The problems are equally great in respect of other countries, and
should be borne in mind when the following information, presented in
summary form, is considered.

AUSTRIA

Minimum and maximum ages on committal

The ages of 14–18 are limits only with regard to arrest (youth prison).
There is no minimum age for educational measures, including committal

to a remand home as a result of a judicial decision. The upper age limit is 21. This means that an adolescent may stay in an educational institution up to the age of 21. He can be sent to such an institution up to the age of 20.

Minimum and maximum period of detention

There is no time-limit to length of stay in an educational institution. The period can, as mentioned above, be extended up to age 21.

Average actual period of detention

The average period for which juvenile delinquents are committed to educational institutions (approved schools), under the authority of the Ministry of Justice, is roughly between one and a quarter and two years. There are only two institutions to which judges can make direct committals. Where children under 14 are concerned, or in cases of juveniles who present educational problems of lesser severity, the *Land* Youth Office may, if necessary, suggest 'welfare education'. In such instances the judge will refer the adolescent to welfare education, thereby handing over the educational responsibility to the Youth Office. The latter may then decide on the special measures to be taken: committal to a public home (supported and administered by the provincial (*Land*) authorities) or to a private home, or placement with a foster family. Since the possibilities within the framework of welfare education vary widely it is impossible to state an average period of detention. The judge cannot himself interfere with welfare education; he can, however, order release, even if this is contrary to the decision of the Youth Office.

Period under statutory surveillance after discharge

The period of aftercare (one to three years) applies only to juveniles sentenced by the courts. Aftercare following release from the two educational institutions of the Ministry of Justice usually ends at the age of 20 (because after that age a renewed committal to these institutions is no longer possible).

Number of private schools
Not available.

Estimated number in population of the relevant age-group
Not available.

Administrative organization

The majority of the institutions to which children and juveniles are committed within the framework of welfare education are public. Even if they are not run by the Federal State, they are the responsibility of the provinces, i.e. they are run publicly. Provincial governments also have contracts with private institutions. It is impossible to obtain accurate data, since some of these homes are not exclusively devoted to the work of welfare education.

Training of educators and staff

Special training for educators was started in Austria about 1959–60. So far, various institutions, and occasionally also provincial governments, have attempted to arrange introductory, and sometimes advanced, courses. To date, therefore, the personnel of the educational institutions could not be expected to have any special expert training – apart, of course, from social workers and teachers, who have always had special training. The lack of training will continue to exist for some time to come, despite the opening of a school for educators.

Who decides to which establishment the child is to go?

See under *Average actual period of detention* above (p. 125).

BELGIUM

Minimum and maximum ages on committal

No minimum. Maximum age of criminal responsibility is 16, but young people can be brought before the juvenile court up to 18 in cases of vagrancy, or as beyond control.

Minimum and maximum periods of detention

No minimum. All measures must end at the age of 21, except in cases of serious crime, when they can be extended up to 25.

Average actual period of detention

Twelve to eighteen months.

Period under statutory surveillance after discharge

In principle, up to 21 years of age, except in cases of early discharge.

Number in State schools

At end of 1963:	Boys	Girls	Total
	449	184	633

Number in private schools

At end of 1963:	Boys	Girls	Total
	1,530	1,192	2,722

Estimated number in population of the relevant age-group
At end of 1960: 1,062,416.

Administrative organization

Divided into *Établissements d'Éducation de l'État (EEE)* and private institutions. They are both controlled by the *Office de Protection de l'Enfance (OPE)*, which comes under the Ministry of Justice. *EEE* takes the more difficult cases. There are two establishments for girls (one containing an observation centre); and five for boys, one (Mol-Huttes) being an observation centre and another (Wauthier-Braine) being combined with an observation centre. The largest contains about 180 children (subdivided into smaller groups), and the smallest about forty. There are local voluntary committees for some of these establishments.

State establishments

Staffing: *Éducateurs* (roughly housemasters) and *professeurs* (teachers) must have an academic diploma (*instituteur primaire, humanités complètes,* or equivalent certificate), and be between 21 and 30 years of age on appointment. They are chosen by special examination and can be made *chef de section* or *chef de groupe* after passing another examination. There are also vocational teachers in various branches, appointed on similar conditions.

Directeurs are selected after passing an examination at a high level; they are first-class civil servants.

Training: A training centre was set up in 1962. It provides for educators who have been employed in the State establishments for at least six months a systematic in-service training of 875 hours, spread over approximately three years. For most courses the number of participants does not exceed twelve; thus members have, it is hoped, opportunity to exchange ideas. No fees are charged. The cost of board and lodging is met by the Ministry of Justice.

Other training courses are planned, especially for teachers and administrative staff.

Conferences of magistrates and trained people who are working in the State establishments (superintendents, psychologists, psychiatrists, etc.) take place regularly at the training centre.

Private establishments

There are over 600 of various kinds.

Control: Inspection is by the *OPE*, which lays down certain rules that must be kept. Criteria relating to staff qualifications are also specified.

Finance: The juvenile court judge fixes the daily charge when committing the child; it is paid by the State, but the State can compel the parents to contribute.

Staffing: In the principal private establishments staffing is similar to to that in the State establishments.

Who decides whether the child is to go to a State or a private establishment, and to which establishment he should go?

The juvenile court judge, but he will have reports from the social services and the observation centres upon which to base his decision.

FINLAND

Minimum and maximum ages on committal

State schools: No statutory minimum age; maximum age for committal is 18 years; pupils can be kept in the schools until 21 years.

Municipal and private schools: Minimum age is 9 years; maximum age is 18; pupils can be kept in the schools until 21 years.

(Although there is no statutory minimum age for committal to the State schools, there have been only a very few cases under 9 years and no cases under school age.)

Minimum and maximum periods of detention

No statutory maximum period of detention.

Average actual period of detention

During 1958–61 the average period was 2 years 11 months (boys, 3 years 7 months; girls, 1 year 8 months).

Period under statutory surveillance after discharge

During 1958–61 the average period was 2 years 2 months (boys, 2 years 5 months; girls, 1 year 9 months).

Number of State schools

At end of 1963:	Schools		Places
	For boys	9	496
	For girls	3	149
	Total	12	645

Number of private schools

At end of 1963:

Schools		Places
Municipal, for boys	2	76
Private, for boys	3	205 ⎫
Private, for girls	1	60 ⎭ 265
Total	6	341

Besides the two municipal schools listed above, the city council of Helsinki has three municipal receiving homes; however, since these are used not only as classifying schools for juvenile delinquents but also as remand homes for similar kinds of cases, they have been considered as special children's homes and not as approved schools. All the inmates of approved schools have to be placed under the guardianship of the municipal social committee, but children whose cases are still pending before the child welfare committee (the social committee of Helsinki) can be placed for observation in Helsinki's receiving homes.

Estimated number in population of the relevant age-group

At end of 1962:

Age-group 9–18 years		
Boys	Girls	Total
432,844	415,931	893,775

Administrative organization

At the end of 1963, there were eighteen approved schools in the country. State schools are owned and run by the State (Administration by the Bureau of Child Welfare, Ministry of Social Affairs).

Municipal and private schools are owned by municipalities and private organizations. They are under the supervision of the Bureau of Child

	Type of school			
	State	Municipal	Private	Total
BOYS				
Number of schools	9	2	3	14
Number of places	496	76	205	777
GIRLS				
Number of schools	3	—	1	4
Number of places	149	—	60	209
Total schools	12	2	4	18
Total places	645	76	265	986

Welfare and are eligible for the statutory State grant, which is normally 30–70 per cent of their running expenses. The schools have to submit their budget yearly for approval to the Ministry of Social Affairs. For building and initial expenses, schools can get a State grant of 25–50 per cent of the cost.

The municipalities have to pay a fee for the pupils that they place in the schools. This fee was in 1963 £6 15s. a month in State schools and £8 7s. in municipal and private schools.

The pupils are placed in approved schools by an administrative decision of the local social committee. These committees have to apply for placement in State schools to the Ministry of Social Affairs (Bureau of Child Welfare). The pupils of the municipal and private schools are accepted by the boards of the respective schools. (According to the new amendment to the law mentioned above, all placements in approved schools will be made through the Ministry of Social Affairs. In this way the classifying system for the inmates of State schools will be extended to inmates of all approved schools.)

Staffing of State schools

The posts and the qualifications of the personnel at the State schools are as follows:

1. *Headmaster* (Director):

(a) M.A. with degree in pedagogy or *Heilpädagogik* (in the two biggest schools, the highest degree; in Järvilinna receiving home, in addition, the highest degree in psychology and a good knowledge of psycho-diagnostic methods), or

(b) the qualifications of an assistant headmaster, five years' successful service in approved schools, and the highest degree in pedagogy or the second highest degree in *Heilpädagogik*.

All headmasters have to be familiar with child welfare and school legislation and institutional education.

2. *Assistant headmasters:*

(a) Qualified special school teacher (i.e. elementary school teacher and one-year additional training at the Jyväskyla Pedagogical University), or

(b) three years' successful service as approved school teacher and the second highest degree in pedagogy or in *Heilpädagogik*.

3. *Teacher:* Qualified elementary school teacher, and degree in pedagogy or in *Heilpädagogik*.

4. *Trade teachers:* Technicians in their respective trades.

5. *Educators:* Two years' course in youth work at the School of Social Science.

6. *Social workers:* Training in medical social work or social work at the School of Social Science, with knowledge of casework methods.

7. *Nurse:* Qualified nurse.

8. *Housemothers, housefather* and their *attendants, clerical staff,* and *household personnel,* etc.: Training in their respective fields.

In addition to the personnel mentioned above, the schools have part-time physicians, consultant psychiatrists, etc.

Staffing of municipal and private schools
Similar personnel as State schools, with the same qualifications.

FRANCE

Minimum and maximum ages of committal
No minimum; maximum 18 years.

Maximum period of detention
Up to age 21, between one and three years.

Average period of detention
No data available.

Period under statutory surveillance after discharge
No data available.

Number in State schools
October 1962: State observation centres 540
State approved schools 1,439

Number in private schools
October 1962: Private observation centres 1,999
Private schools 14,801

Estimated number in population of the relevant age-group
1 January 1959: Population between 5 and 19 years old – 10,340,000.

Administrative organization

State institutions are controlled by the *Direction de l'Éducation Surveillée*, which is a part of the Ministry of Justice.

Private institutions are controlled by the *Direction de l'Éducation Surveillée* and the Ministry of Public Health and Population.

State establishments

There are three observation centres, and ten training institutions (seven for boys and three for girls). The boys' establishments take 150–200 children, and the girls' 50–90. They are run by their *directeurs* without guidance or assistance from a local voluntary committee.

Staffing : Staffs are recruited by examination. *Éducateurs* and *instructeurs techniques* are the main grades. There is a training centre.

Private establishments

About 180.

Control : Inspected by the inspectors of *L'Éducation Surveillée* under rules issued by them. Administration inspected by the *Directeurs Départementaux de l'Aide Sociale*.

Finance : The State lays down a rate per child per day.

Staffing : On the same lines as in State establishments.

Who decides whether the child is to go to a State or a private establishment, and to which establishment he should go?

The juvenile judge and the *Direction de l'Éducation Surveillée*.

GERMAN FEDERAL REPUBLIC

In the Federal Republic of Germany an 'approved education order' can be made by:

(a) the juvenile court on account of an offence (section 5, Juvenile Court Act);

(b) the guardianship court on account of neglect or waywardness or threatened neglect or waywardness (section 64, Youth Welfare Act).

In these cases the court entrusts the 'public education' of the boy or girl to the Approved Education Authority, namely, the State Youth Welfare Board (in Bavaria to the Local Youth Welfare Board). The Approved Education Authority has to decide whether the boy or girl should be educated in a home or in a family. The court does not itself commit the boy or girl to a home. Besides 'approved education', which is ordered by a court, there is another form of public education in the Federal Republic, namely 'voluntary educational aid'. This is ordered by the State Youth Welfare Board (in Bavaria by the Local Youth Welfare Board), when those persons who under civil law have the right to bring up the child (parents or guardians) apply for it and the board considers it admissible. This aid follows the same course as approved education. Boys and girls are taken into public education in increasing numbers in this way.

Minimum and maximum ages of committal

There is no minimum age for committal to a home. The maximum age is 19.

Maximum period of detention

A minimum or maximum duration for education in a home is not laid down by law. Release takes place at the latest on coming of age (21 years).

Average actual period of detention

In the Federal area (excluding Berlin) 4,946 minors were released from approved education in 1962, and 9,695 from voluntary educational aid. The average period in approved education was 4·3 years, and in voluntary educational aid 2·7 years. (Periods spent with families are included in these averages.)

Period under statutory surveillance after discharge

The law does not specify duration. The Approved Education Authority is responsible for surveillance until the guardianship court cancels the approved education.

Number in State schools

At end of 1962: In public homes, 3,181 children were in approved education (3,473 at the end of 1961).

Number in private schools

At end of 1962: In voluntary homes, 10,647 children were in approved education (11,041 at the end of 1961).

Estimated number in population of the relevant age-group

At the end of 1960 there were about 16,330,000 juveniles in the Federal Republic, excluding West Berlin. At the end of 1962 there were 25,478 minors in approved education (1·7 per 1,000 under 21), and 26,447 minors in voluntary educational aid (1·7 per 1,000 under 21). (In 1961, the figures were 25,902 and 20,409 respectively.)

Administrative organization

Responsibility lies with the States or the Federal Republic; in each State, with the Ministry for Social Affairs or a Special Minister for Youth Affairs.

There are sixty-four State homes for approved education and voluntary educational aid, including special schools for the maladjusted. (Homes run by lesser local authorities not included.)

The main voluntary welfare organizations have 614 homes. There are observation homes among both the special schools for the maladjusted and the approved education homes, although the latter often have only an observation wing. Unfortunately, no figures are available.

State homes

The administration of the State or local authority homes lies in most cases with the director. Committees are not usual. The State Youth Welfare Board supervises all State, local authority, and voluntary homes. The director has to keep the State Youth Welfare Board informed of certain facts about staff, equipment, etc. Officers of the State Youth Welfare Board visit each home regularly. There is a move to establish a uniform training but this is not yet accomplished. In some homes there are specialist advisers (e.g. psychologist, psychiatrist).

Voluntary homes

Administration, supervision, staff, and training are the same as for the State homes.

Voluntary homes are financed by their parent bodies. State or local authorities often give grants. The Approved Education Authority pays in addition a specified fee for every boy or girl sent to a home.

Who decides whether the child is to go to a State or a private establishment, and to which establishment he should go?

The Approved Education Authority decides whether the boy or girl for whom approved education has been ordered shall be educated in a family or a home, and in which family or home, State or voluntary.

If a period in an observation centre or observation ward precedes committal to a home, a report about the child concerned is taken into account.

GREECE

Minimum and maximum ages on committal

For approved schools: minimum age 8 years; maximum 18.
For borstals (adolescents): minimum age 13 years; maximum 17.
For borstals (post-adolescents): minimum age 18 years; maximum 21.

Minimum and maximum periods of detention

In approved schools (homes for re-education): no maximum period but never over 21. The period of detention depends on the behaviour of the child and the possibilities of social rehabilitation.

In borstals (correctional homes): maximum and minimum lengths are fixed by the sentence of the juvenile court. The minimum can never be below six months and the maximum never exceeds twenty years, according to the penal law.

Average actual period of detention

In approved schools: two years.
In borstals: one to five years.

Period under statutory surveillance after discharge

For children released from approved schools: one year.
For children released from borstals: it depends on the conditions of the release.

Number in State schools

At end of 1963: Approved schools 550 approx.
  Borstals 400 approx.

Administrative organization

There are no private institutions. The State institutions are homes for re-education (approved schools) and correctional homes (borstals). They are financed directly by the State.

Approved schools

(a) for boys, for school education (8–14 years of age)
(b) for boys, for vocational education (15–21 years of age)
(c) for girls, with two sections (1) 8–14 years of age
  (2) 15–21 years of age

Borstals

(a) farm for boys, adolescents (13–18 years)

K

(b) open institution for boys, adolescents (13–18 years)

(c) farm for boys, post-adolescents (18–21 years)

(d) institution for adolescents and post-adolescents

(e) special section in women's prison, for girls, adolescents and post-adolescents

(Because of the very small number of girls needing borstal treatment – maximum ten – there is no special borstal, but girls are detained in a section of the women's prison)

State institutions do not take the physically handicapped, the mentally disturbed, or the feeble-minded. There is no observation centre; no specialization besides age. The Ministry of Justice is in charge of these institutions.

There are no advisory or executive committees. There is a board of trustees, consisting of voluntary workers, who give moral and material help to children released from approved schools.

There are also Children's Aid Societies, working under the Ministry of Justice. They, too, help children released from approved schools and borstals.

Staffing

The director of a borstal must have a law qualification; in approved schools the director can also be a pedagogue (graduate from a school for teachers).

Housemasters and housemothers are trained in a special course for two months immediately after their appointment.

Teachers are qualified according to Ministry of Education requirements, as are all teachers in public schools. Instructors in vocational education are qualified as technical instructors according to the general regulations for vocational education.

Who decides to which establishment a child is to go?

So far as approved schools are concerned, the Ministry of Justice decides, taking into account the recommendations of the juvenile judge; in cases of delinquency, the court decides on the institution.

In so far as borstals are concerned, it is the prosecutor who specifies the institution. But the Ministry of Justice can always transfer children from one institution to another.

JAPAN

The usual procedures for judging juvenile delinquents are carried out in the forty-nine family courts, but there are some cases that the family court judge considers as criminal offences, and these are referred to the public prosecutor to be judged in criminal courts. Juveniles are defined in Japanese law as all those under 20. Juveniles under 16 years of age cannot be sent to the public prosecutor (Juvenile Law, Article 20).

There are three educative measures for those juvenile delinquents who are ordered to be sent for re-education by public facilities. They are:

1. Homes for the training and education of juvenile delinquents, and protective institutions, both under the child welfare law.
2. Reform and training schools.
3. Probationary supervision by the probation-parole supervision office, under the jurisdiction of the Ministry of Justice.

Juvenile delinquents who are punished for crime and are sentenced to a penalty must be placed in a juvenile prison.

Under the jurisdiction of the Ministry of Justice, juvenile detention and classification homes are provided for juvenile delinquents who have been before the family courts and need to be assessed as to their character and personality. In the juvenile detention and classification home, special medical-psychological studies of the delinquents are carried out. The maximum period for juvenile delinquents in these homes is, in principle, two weeks, but if a longer period is needed they can be held for an additional period of two weeks (Juvenile Law, Article 17, item 2). The average period in 1960 was 21·7 days. Further details are given below.

Ages of delinquents in juvenile detention and classification homes
(Japan 1963)

Age		Males		Females	
		No.	%	No.	%
Below	13	255	0·8	34	1·1
	14	1,996	6·4	406	12·9
	15	3,048	9·7	597	19·0
	16	4,776	15·2	633	20·2
	17	5,275	16·8	479	15·3
	18	7,217	23·0	495	15·8
	19	8,767	28·0	492	15·7
Over	20	15	0·05	4	0·1
Total		31,349	100·0	3,140	100·0

Number of juveniles judged in family courts (Japan 1952–63)

Year	Total	Sent for prosecution in the criminal court	Put on probation	Sent to juvenile education and training homes	Sent to reform and training schools	Dismissed or given no sentence	Others
1952	167,000	5,318	22,220	294	10,645	126,483	2,040
1956	349,967	15,358	16,841	249	7,826	269,224	40,469
1958	521,841	39,174	20,669	306	8,733	397,375	55,584
1959	621,624	48,634	23,265	315	9,275	421,067	119,068
1960	828,348	79,049	24,433	255	8,999	574,580	150,032
1961	841,567	130,056	23,131	341	8,713	643,250	36,076
1962	896,816	139,843	21,904	427	16,309	642,780	75,553
1963	977,927	126,247	22,761	358	7,642	733,433	87,486

Period of placement by the court with families (Japan 1959–63)

Year	Total	Months								Over 1 year
		Under 1	2	3	4	5	6	9	1 year	
1959	9,231	368	692	1,147	1,406	998	1,211	1,819	863	727
1960	8,626	323	607	1,004	1,318	938	1,208	1,753	770	705
1961	8,934	306	542	935	1,306	996	1,327	1,845	825	852
1962	14,597	1,646	1,077	2,028	2,248	1,340	1,634	2,483	1,142	999
1963	22,638	6,545	1,481	2,634	3,107	2,416	1,726	2,720	1,083	926

In exceptional cases custody in a prison is possible and these offenders are sent by the public prosecutor's office. The period of custody must be no more than ten days before prosecution, and two months after prosecution, but this may be extended one more month (Code of Criminal Procedure, Article 60, item 2, and Article 208, item 1). The average detention period for custody is not recorded in the statistics. From the point of view of the protection of juveniles, prosecutors are, except in special cases, forbidden to ask the judges to keep juveniles in custody (Juvenile Law, Article 43).

The only non-residential educative measure is the probationary supervision of the probation-parole supervision office, which is prescribed in the Juvenile Law, Article 24. But family courts may use observation as a kind of intermediary measure (Juvenile Law, Article 25). This is a form of temporary placement with families, under supervision (see data opposite).

Homes for juvenile training and education, protective institutions, and reform and training schools are provided as facilities for the treatment of juvenile delinquents.

Homes for juvenile training and education (government, two; public, fifty-three; private, two) are organized on the cottage system and try to provide a family background. The government homes for juvenile training and education accommodate those juvenile delinquents whose misdeeds are considered to be serious and those who need to have medical, psychological, sociological, or educational treatment according to modern scientific techniques. As at 31 December 1962 the number of staff in the homes was 1,296 and the number of children 6,156.

Reform and training schools are all financed by government funds. As at the end of 1962, there were fifty-eight main reform and training schools, and three branch schools; the number of juveniles accommodated was 9,297. These reform and training schools are divided into four types: elementary, secondary, advanced, and medical, in accordance with differences in age, differences in delinquent tendencies, and varieties of maladjustment. There are three types of institution: open, semi-open, and closed. Those who are committed must stay for at least one year. In the fiscal year 1963 the number of staff working in these institutions was 2,695. Those who are discharged from reform and training schools are usually placed under the supervision of probation officers (Offenders Rehabilitation Law, Article 33, item 1).

For the training of staff for work in juvenile prisons, reform and training schools, and juvenile detention and classification homes, there is the Central Training Institute for Correctional Personnel, together with local training institutes for correctional personnel (in eight main cities throughout the country).

In the Central Training Institute for Correctional Personnel there are two courses, namely, the regular course and the postgraduate course. The former is divided into two. The first division trains the chief gaolers or the vice-chief gaolers who work in detention houses, prisons, and juvenile prisons. The second division trains the teaching staff and the officers who work in the reform and training schools, the juvenile detention and classification homes, and the women's guidance homes. The postgraduate course offers a variety of higher training, especially professional academic skills to the staff of the training institutes for correctional personnel, according to the work and to their different positions.

The training period in the regular course is one year, but it may be shortened so long as the total of the class time is not less than 800 hours. That of the postgraduate course is prescribed as within three months; it depends on the kind of training, but usually it is one or two months.

The local training institutes for correctional personnel offer three different kinds of course, namely the elementary course, the regular course, and the special course. The regular course has two divisions. The elementary course trains newly employed officers and teaching staffs. The first division of the regular course trains the chief officers, and the officers who are working in the penal detention institutions, the prisons, and the juvenile prisons. The second division trains staff for the reform and training schools, the juvenile detention and classification homes, the women's guidance homes, and the teaching staffs of the juvenile prisons. The special course, which is divided into the regular division and the postgraduate division, gives the staff of the training institutes for correctional personnel special training according to type of work and to their position.

The training period of the elementary course is, in principle, four months, but it may be shortened so long as the total of the class time does not fall under 360 hours. That of the regular course is six months, but it also may be reduced so long as the total class time is not less than 400 hours. That of the special courses can be two months, but usually it is around one month.

POLAND

Minimum and maximum ages on committal

In Poland there are two types of establishment for children who have come into collision with the penal law: *educational establishments* (for children in need of special educational guardianship), under the Ministry of Education; and *houses of correction*, under the Ministry of Justice.

Juvenile courts send to these establishments about 10·5 per cent of the total number of accused children (educational establishments, 4·7 per cent; houses of correction, 5·8 per cent).

Minimum and maximum periods of detention

Both types of establishment take children between 13 and 17 years of age. At an educational establishment, a ward's age cannot exceed the 18th birthday, and at a house of correction the 21st birthday.

(In addition, educational establishments take children (from 10 years of age) referred by education committees, or by parents who face serious difficulties in bringing up their children. These children form 29 per cent of the total number of wards in educational establishments.)

Average actual period of detention

About two years. Release requires the approval of the juvenile court.

Period under statutory surveillance after discharge

The court may decide to appoint a court curator to supervise further guardianship over the child when released from the establishment. Final discharge is at the discretion of the court.

Number in State establishments and schools

At 31 December 1962: In educational establishments, 4,432 children.
In houses of correction, 3,274 wards.
All these children attend classes in schools on the premises.

All educational and correctional establishments are run and paid for by public bodies. Educational establishments are paid for by local councils, and maintained as independent budgetary units. However, parents partly cover the costs of maintenance.

Educational establishments

In the school year 1961–62 the total number of educational establishments was fifty, providing 4,866 places. These establishments included:

34 for boys	3,624 places
10 for girls	757 places
3 for morally neglected, underdeveloped boys	170 places

Educational establishments, subject to the Ministry of Education, are supervised by inspectors of the relevant school districts and by inspectors for special schools at the Department of General Education at the Ministry of Education.

Matters concerning organization, administration, and economic problems are settled by statute and regulations.

The staff employed at educational establishments, in addition to the qualifications required in ordinary schools, should be graduates of the State Institute of Special Pedagogics, or pass a qualifying examination covering the programme of this Institute.

Houses of correction

In the school year 1961–62 the total number of houses of correction was twenty-four. Staff require similar qualifications to those mentioned above.

PORTUGAL

Minimum and maximum ages on committal

Juvenile courts may send minors between 9 and 16 years of age to institutes for re-education.

However, in certain cases, criminal offences committed by minors of 16 to 18 years of age are also judged by juvenile courts.

Minimum and maximum periods of detention

Detention is discontinued as soon as the minor attains 21 years of age, if the court has not already released him because he is considered socially readjusted. The directors of institutions must review the minor's situation at the close of every three-year period of detention as from the court's latest decision. Moreover, the minor's situation may be re-examined at any moment on receipt of a proposal from the directors of the institution.

Average actual period of detention

The average period of detention is now about four years for boys and four and a half years for girls.

Period under statutory surveillance after discharge

After leaving an institution, minors are kept under supervision for three years.

Number in State schools

At end of 1963:	Boys	Girls	Total
	997	331	1,328

Private schools

There are no private institutions of this type. All re-education institutions in existence belong to the State, though the administration of four of them has been entrusted by agreement to religious orders specializing in educational problems.

Estimated number in the population of the relevant age-group

There are approximately 1,940,000 in the population between 9 and 21 years of age. (According to the census of 1960, there were 1,845,678 in the population in this age-group: 892,043 boys and 953,635 girls.)

Administrative organization

The institutions are run by the Ministry of Justice, General Directorate of Tutelary Services for Minors.

There are at present (1963) ten re-education institutes – six for boys and four for girls. All the institutions are intended for boys and girls between 9 and 21 years old. They are divided into sections or pavilions, where the minors are separated according to age. As a rule, minors are classified into three sections depending on their intellectual and physical development. School capacity varies greatly.

Institutions for boys	Accommodation for	No. of inmates 1963	Institutions for girls	Accommodation for	No. of inmates 1963
Caxias	270	230	Benefica	100	57
S. Fiel	270	246	S. Bernardino	84	38
Guarda	80	56	Corpus Christi[a]	150	118
V. Fernando	250	211	S. Jose de Viseu[a]	150	118
Izeda[a]	120	107			
V. do Conde[a]	150	147			
Total	1,140	997	Total	484	331

[a] Institutions managed by religious orders.

There are three observation centres, in the cities of Lisbon, Oporto, and Coimbra. No minor can be admitted to a re-education institution without having previously passed through an observation centre.

The institutions are controlled only by their director, and by the General Directorate of Tutelary Services for Minors through the inspection services.

Staffing

In addition to the director – who has to hold a university degree – the doctor, and the administrative personnel, re-education institutions have education and supervisory personnel. Educators have to be qualified primary school teachers.

The personnel of these institutions have to take the special courses provided for them by the School of Practical and Criminal Sciences. In addition, they have to undergo a training of two years before being finally appointed.

Who decides to which institution the child is to go?

The Ministry decides upon the institution to which the minor should be sent. The taking of this decision is based on the report of the observation centre, on the study of the trial, and on the magistrates' verdict.

SWEDEN

Minimum and maximum ages of committal

Not below 10, and only in special circumstances under 13. Maximum age 21. Committal is normally by being placed 'in public care' by a child welfare council.

Maximum period of detention

One to one and a half years.

Period under statutory surveillance after discharge

One to two years.

Number in State schools

At end of 1962:	Boys	Girls	Total
	659	265	924

Number under surveillance of the schools

At end of 1962:	Boys	Girls	Total
	328	280	608

Estimated number in population of the relevant age-group

At end of 1961: 1,100,000.

Administrative organization

Since July 1950 all approved schools have belonged to the State and are called 'youth welfare schools'. They are controlled by the schools section of the State Social Welfare Board. There are twenty-five schools, of which nine are for girls. There are two main types: for those of school age; and for those above it. The boys' schools range in size from twenty to eighty places, and the girls' from fourteen to seventy. They are divided into groups of seven to fifteen, usually in open cottages, but in ten boys' and four girls' schools there are one or two closed houses, each for a maximum of eight persons. There are two schools for the mentally subnormal, one for boys and one for girls, and two schools for those with exceptionally high intelligence.

Each school is governed by a local board of five. These managers are responsible for running the school, including the methods of treatment and supervision of those discharged.

The ideas of conditional release, trial release, or subsequent care are not included in the new child care law. Instead, it refers to care within and care outside the school. In this way, care outside the school has been equated in significance with care in the school. There are no other rules as to when the one or the other of these forms of care is to be used than that care outside school should be resorted to 'as soon as possible'.

The board and headmaster of the school are responsible for the care, both within and outside the school.

Before a pupil can be released for care outside the school, the board must have arranged for him housing, employment or further training, clothing, and a supervisor.

The following arrangements exist for care outside the school:

(a) Supervised family care: that is, families in the neighbourhood of the schools take in the pupils and are paid for it. This placement may be combined with continued treatment and schooling or vocational training at the schools or elsewhere. The youth welfare school, through its social worker, gives support, help, and advice to the families.

(b) Courses of training in various kinds of school.

(c) Employment and supervised boarding-out.

(d) Boarding homes with mixed clientele are run by married couples. The husband has an ordinary job and the wife, with the help of a maid, takes care of a house or a large apartment, accepts boarders, up to ten persons, half consisting of ordinary homeless youths and the other half of pupils placed for care outside the school.

These homes are under the supervision of the State Social Welfare Board.

(e) Hostels with eight to ten places for short stay.

(f) Camps for road and forest work.

(g) 'Operation Wilderness': groups of four or five boys live under primitive conditions, together with a housefather, who is also the work leader, and a housemother, who is also the cook. They undertake to cut a plot of forest, clean off a nature reservation, build a fence for reindeer, repair the border markings between Sweden and Norway, or the like.

The Social Welfare Board has special consultants who are responsible, each in his own district, for the various arrangements for care outside the schools and for the recruitment and leading of supervisors.

Finance is directly by the State.

Staffing

The *headmaster* and *assistant headmaster* usually hold a university degree or diploma from a school of social work, or a teacher's certificate plus advanced studies in psychology, mental hygiene, sociology, etc.

Teachers and *teachers in vocational training* have the same qualifications as are required for teachers in the ordinary educational system.

The *head matron* usually has a training in home economics and is specialized in the care of boarding schools or similar large establishments.

Wardens have so far had no special training outside the in-service training courses run by the State Social Welfare Board. In 1961 a special course was started in one of the approved schools: ten young persons are recruited each year for training for a period of six months. The training consists of theoretical studies and practical work in institutions. In September 1962 the State started a special basic course for wardens in various kinds of institution.

Who decides to which establishment the child is to go?

The Social Welfare Board decides which establishment the child goes to on the basis of reports made to it by the local child welfare council.

SWITZERLAND

Switzerland consists of twenty-five small States (cantons or half-cantons). It is only the basic principles of law that are the same for all. There is a Swiss code of common law and a Swiss penal code, but there are twenty-five different codes of civil and criminal procedure. The administration, too, is divided between the twenty-five cantons.

Minimum and maximum ages on committal

The Swiss penal code discriminates between children and adolescents. The minimum age for committal is 6 (in 1964 it was about to be raised to 7). Slightly different measures are applied in the cases of children (6–14 years) and of adolescents (14–18 years). The maximum age for application of the juvenile criminal law is 18.

It has been planned to establish another category: young adults from 18 to 25 years of age, who could benefit from special measures of re-education.

Children are never imprisoned even during the preliminary investigations. If necessary, they are placed in institutions or in foster homes. Children (6–14 years) are not imprisoned but they may be given detention at school.

Maximum period of detention

According to the Swiss penal code, the legal authority – which may be either a court of justice, a guardianship, or an administrative authority – says that:

(a) If the child or the adolescent is in need of care, he is then placed in foster care in a reliable family, or in an institution, or he may remain in his own family, but under supervision.

(b) If the child or the adolescent needs special care (if he is mentally or physically handicapped), then treatment should be prescribed.

(c) If the child or the adolescent is neither in moral danger, nor depraved, nor in danger of becoming depraved, then he can be punished; adolescents can be imprisoned for a period ranging from one day to one year.

In Swiss law, one measure can be replaced by another: for adolescents, the sentence can be suspended or they can be conditionally discharged. A fine can be imposed on its own, or in addition to detention.

There is no fixed maximum duration of stay; if the adolescent is placed in an approved school (*maison de rééducation*) he can be released conditionally after one year of placement. At the age of 22, he must be discharged.

Average actual period of detention

It is not easy to give an average period of detention, for ideas differ from one canton to another; in most cases the sentence is suspended, with a supervision period of six months to three years as a rule.

Number in State and private schools
It is very difficult to estimate figures, because the majority of both private and State schools receive juvenile delinquents as well as other adolescents who have not committed offences, but whose behaviour makes their placement necessary. Moreover, there are no statistics concerning the number of pupils in the institutions.

Administrative organization
In Switzerland institutions may be classified as follows:

  Residential schools (*maisons d'éducation*)
  Approved schools (*maisons de rééducation*)
  Observation centres and probation hostels (*foyers de semi-liberté*)

At present, a great problem is the creation of a home for very difficult children.

Detention usually takes place in an approved school (*maison de rééducation*). However, it is rarely used because, even in cases of revocation of suspended sentence, detention is changed into a placement in a residential or in an approved school.

It is noteworthy that institutional placements are very often carried out in the institutions of other cantons. The balance is maintained, because some cantons are specialized in one kind of institution: some have probation hostels; others have approved schools.

Finance: The State institutions are supported by the cantons. Each canton fixes a *per diem* allowance. Nearly all the private institutions receive State grants.

Training: Institutional staff have social work training, but many are trained in the establishment itself or have qualified in schools abroad.

Who decides whether a child is to go to a State or a private establishment, and to which establishment he should go?
Sometimes the judge, and sometimes the administration.

UNITED STATES
Any attempt to summarize what is happening in the United States immediately comes up against the problem that, apart from a few schools for federal offenders, the treatment of offenders is a State responsibility. As with many other matters, provision varies enormously. At one end are well-staffed and ably run institutions, and at the other conditions are such as would cause a public scandal in most European countries.

All that can be done here is to present the best general picture available. It has been taken largely from the *Comparative survey of juvenile delinquency, Part 1, North America*, prepared by Professor Paul W. Tappan (United Nations, revised edition, 1958). This has been supplemented by information from the Children's Bureau of the Federal Department of Health, Education and Welfare, which collects and publishes *Statistics on public institutions for delinquent children*.[1] Each of the reports has a special supplement: 1956, on administrative and intake policies; 1958, on employees; 1962, on the administrative transfer of children from juvenile institutions to penal institutions. The Bureau has also published *Institutions serving delinquent children – guides and goals*,[2] which is intended to set standards. Information is also available in texts on the subject of juvenile delinquency,[3] and in Deutsch's exposé *Our rejected children* (1950).

There is, of course, a considerable variety of legislation relating to juvenile courts and their powers of commitment. The term 'delinquent' tends to be interpreted widely and often includes what would in England be considered as care, protection, or control. The procedure is often much more informal, and approximates more to the Scandinavian inquiry into what can be done than to the English insistence on proving an offence, or at least the existence of a state of affairs defined fairly closely by statute. There is also a strong tendency to deal with cases unofficially in one way or another, and this may to some extent involve placements in institutions, though these would usually be private. Most United States juvenile courts have jurisdiction to 18 years of age, though there may be power to remit to a criminal court, or concurrent criminal jurisdiction, which may be either exclusive or selective. The commitment is usually indeterminate with an age limit of 21.

The information available is almost entirely restricted to training schools publicly provided. In 1962 there were 230 public institutions for juvenile delinquents in the United States (including Puerto Rico and the Virgin Islands). This total includes 140 State training schools (one a federal school), forty-three local training schools (run by local authorities below State level), and forty-seven forestry camps (one a federal camp). There are also something in the region of 130–140 private institutions receiving delinquents.

[1] There are three reports, all in the Children's Bureau Statistical Series: No. 48, 1956; No. 59, 1958; and No. 70, 1962.

[2] Children's Bureau Publication No. 340, 1957.

[3] Particularly P. W. Tappan, *Juvenile delinquency* (1949); and N. K. Teeters and J. O. Reinemann, *Challenge of delinquency* (1950).

'Provision is made under the laws of a number of State jurisdictions and of the federal government for the use of private institutions for the treatment of delinquents. In the more progressive jurisdictions the attempt is made to determine whether the particular private institution's treatment programme and facilities best meet the needs of the particular child. Some private institutions, however, limit their intake on such criteria as the seriousness of the child's offence, his personality disturbances, his prior offence record, and his religion. Characteristically, these institutions establish upper and lower age limits and are for either males or females. In many cases the private institution restricts the proportion of court cases that it will take and refuses court referrals on this basis. Some courts determine the appropriateness of using private institutions on the basis of the gravity of the delinquent's offence or his prior record: in general, the tendency is to commit him to a State institution when his behaviour is deemed quite serious. Federal information indicates that every effort is made to avoid placing in institutions children who are under the age of 14. Children with outstanding scholastic abilities may be placed in private schools. On the other hand, youths in the 17-year age-group who have extensive histories of delinquency, who are aggressive and assaultative, and who have lengthy histories of running away from training schools or other institutions, may be placed in reformatories which house the 18 to 24-year group.

Private training schools are operated both by sectarian groups and by independent non-sectarian organizations. There is probably a somewhat greater preponderance of sectarian institutions. In some jurisdictions the law requires that such institutions must be licensed by the State before they may be used by the courts or public welfare agencies. Generally they are subject either to State inspection and licensing or to inspection by the judges of the juvenile court. The regularity of such inspections varies. Sometimes they are made once or more a year. Sometimes, though authorized, the inspections are very rare and quite superficial. For the most part they constitute a rather poor source of evaluation of the institution's programme. Those facilities used by the federal courts are visited regularly by the United States probation officer during the period a child is in residence, and where it appears that the programme is not adequate to the needs of the child, he may recommend a change in placement. The costs of care of children placed in private institutions as federal juvenile offenders is borne by the government of the United States. In some State jurisdictions the State pays the entire cost on a *per capita* basis; elsewhere costs may be shared by the State, private welfare agencies, and/or the funds of the institution itself. In a number of jurisdictions the parents must share in the cost when they are able, and in some their ability to pay determines whether the child can be committed to a private facility' (*Comparative survey*, pp. 63–4).

The tendency is thus for the private institutions to cream off the 'better' cases, and for the public training schools to take the rest. A greater proportion of boys than of girls are in public schools. A census by age and sex as at 1 April 1960 gave the results shown below.

Juveniles in training schools in the United States
(1 April 1960)

	Under 15			15–19		
	Male	*Female*	*Total*	*Male*	*Female*	*Total*
	%	%	%	%	%	%
Public schools	82	77	81	90	72	85
Private schools	18	23	19	10	28	15
Total	100	100	100	100	100	100
	(9,556)	(3,129)	(12,685)	(22,847)	(8,469)	(31,316)

Source: U.S. Census, *Inmates of institutions* (1960, Table 11).

The amount of public training school provision varies considerably from State to State, as do the provision and use of private schools. Of the 226 institutions making returns in 1962, 56 per cent had accommodation for fewer than 150 children, this being the standard recommended by the Children's Bureau; 42 per cent of the boys' and 39 per cent of the girls' institutions had accommodation for a greater number. No fewer than fourteen boys' schools had more than 400 places. It is probable that size goes with neglect of this service by the State; certainly the figures show that the median number of those recommitted (mainly for failure on aftercare) rose with the number in the schools. There is heavy overcrowding (measured as an occupancy rate of more than 100 per cent of the number designed to be accommodated) and the percentage of institutions experiencing this has risen from 27·8 in 1956 to 44·7 in 1962. Overcrowding is at its worst in the largest institutions. Almost half of the institutions with a capacity of 200–300 children and almost two-thirds of those with a capacity of 300 or over had occupancy rates of more than 100 per cent.

On 30 June 1962, 38,725 children were in the 230 institutions, of whom 30,288 (79 per cent) were boys and 8,437 (21 per cent) girls.

L

These figures represent an 8 per cent increase over 1958, the number in the relevant age-groups having increased by only 6 per cent. No information about age-groups is available. Fifty-two per cent were admitted as a result of court commitment, 12 per cent were returned as failures on aftercare, and 36 per cent were transfers from elsewhere. Transfers happen mainly in the North Central and Pacific regions, where they result from attempts to provide better treatment – these are the areas with better school systems. The length of stay was quite short: 9·2 months for boys and 10·8 months for girls. As one would expect, it was shortest in the forestry camps. It is not possible to analyse length of stay by age.

Nor is it possible to say what proportion receives some form of supervision after discharge, because of the difficulty of separating out transfers, but it is in the region of 60–70 per cent. Of these, some 80 per cent are supervised by the institution or its parent agency. The decision to release is generally made by the school, but provision concerning periods of supervision and its quality vary considerably.

'As to type of accommodation in special government institutions, both congregate and cottage systems are employed in the United States. Cottage structure is preferred and this constitutes the main trend of development. Many of the so-called cottages in institutions using this system, however, are excessively large, particularly in government institutions. Often each unit houses thirty-five, fifty, seventy-five or even 100 children, rather than the ten to twenty that are considered desirable. As a result, many of the special advantages inherent in the cottage plan are lost through lack of the close relationship of the children to the cottage parents or counsellors and the inability to provide individualized attention. The individual cottages tend to approximate congregate institutions in effect. When there are several such cottages, however, the system does permit some measure of classification of the population for treatment purposes. By and large, such classification into the various cottages is mainly according to the age and size of the inmates rather than specifically in relation to educational or clinical treatment requirements. For the most part the congregate institutions emphasize security features more than is characteristic of cottage facilities. There has also been an increasing development of open (minimum-security) facilities of a camp type with more temporary types of frame structure. The federal juvenile institutions are of a cottage type' (*Comparative survey*, p. 69).

About 16,900 full-time employees were working in the schools in 1962, an increase of some 20 per cent since 1958, and 865 part-time workers. Of these, some 60 per cent were treatment and educational personnel. Shortages of staff are general but about a half of the institutions reported no vacancies and presumably could not obtain increases in establishment. Turnover is apparently high: about one-fifth of all staff left their jobs in 1962, and two-thirds of these were treatment and educational personnel. On 30 June 1962 about one-quarter of all employees had been in their jobs less than one year. These rates have changed little between 1958 and 1962.

The Children's Bureau calculates the ratio of children to full-time employees. This ratio, for treatment and educational employees only, was 3·8 in 1962 as against 4·3 in 1958, but lack of breakdown or comparative material makes this, as well as the turnover figures, difficult to evaluate.

In 1958 a number of questions were asked of 3,870 male and 2,480 female full-time treatment and educational staff. The most interesting part of the findings is that which relates to previous experience: 87·5 per cent had had less than one year's previous experience in an institution for delinquent children before taking their present post, but, once in post, only 18 per cent had been there for less than a year and over a third had been there for more than five years; 40 per cent had no education beyond high school, and 21 per cent had not even completed high school. These figures are, however, heavily weighted by the fact that 2,853 of those questioned were houseparents or others employed in cottages (although college graduation is considered a desirable qualification for such posts). Of the academic teachers, all but 6 per cent had a college degree or diploma, and, though only 22 per cent of the 519 social workers had a full training, 18 per cent had done some postgraduate social work training. Only 8 per cent had no degree or diploma at all; 34 per cent had a degree or diploma at undergraduate level. Methods of recruitment, pay, security of tenure, conditions of service, and superannuation provisions vary from State to State, and a minority of staff do not appear to be well served in these respects.

Most of the public institutions are directly administered by States though the actual authority varies. Some are under Departments of Welfare, Education, or Corrections, and in other States there are independent boards of commissioners or a Youth Authority. In most States there are no special provisions for study and classification before placement in a school, and classification takes place only within the institution; a few states, however, have Youth Authority schemes. In California there are a number of small forestry camps; and New York State, following New Jersey, is developing short-term institutions on the Highfields pattern.

GENERAL DISCUSSION

It will be seen from the above accounts that one of the major problems is how to deal with the more difficult children. In countries that rely to a considerable extent upon a voluntary system, the tendency is for the voluntary schools to get the 'better' cases, difficult though these may be, and for the most difficult to gravitate into State institutions, which are often too large, badly understaffed, and altogether unsuitable, not only for this type of child, but for most types of child. This system is seen at its worst in some of the American States, where there is a fairly wide range of voluntary provision, often well staffed, alongside very large reformatory and industrial schools, badly neglected by the public authorities. There are always, of course, some children who will be beyond the resources of any school, and it may well be true that they must be dealt with in a public system in closed blocks; but such provision must be a consequence of careful classification and of deliberate policy, and constant attempts should be made to discover some more constructive method of training. The English system has not really tackled this problem, let alone solved it, but it does avoid the pitfall of letting the voluntary bodies take the cream by giving all schools an equal, if somewhat uneasy, status.

Most countries have arrangements of some kind for certifying, controlling, or inspecting the private institutions to which the court sends juveniles. These vary enormously, and it is impossible to say without detailed study in each country (and in each State of federal countries) how effective such arrangements are. They seem, however, to be very well organized in France, Belgium, and Finland. It is also usual for the State to pay for its cases, and/or to subsidize the institutions concerned, although, again, the actual financial arrangements vary immensely.

Practice also varies as to which department of the State has the responsibility for these institutions, State or private. There is some tendency for the younger children to come under Education and the older under Justice, as in Norway and Poland, but in many of the United States there are special bodies set up to control these institutions, alone or in conjunction with other forms of treatment as, for example, the Youth Authority. In France there is a department called *L'Éducation Surveillée*, and in Belgium an *Office de Protection de l'Enfance*, but both are under the Ministry of Justice. In Norway the main responsibility falls on the Ministry of Church Affairs and Education, in Denmark and Finland the Ministry of Social Affairs is responsible. Thus in some States the schools are associated with child protection, as in effect they are in England through the dual role of the inspectors; in some they are associated with the special school system, as in Norway; and in some they come under the Ministry of Justice or its equivalent, as in Italy and many parts of the British Commonwealth.

These arrangements often reflect the type and powers of the committing body, but it by no means follows that a court with wide powers, covering not only delinquents but other children needing protection, will be matched with a State agency covering the same range. The Scandinavian Child Welfare Councils, which are administrative agencies, strictly speaking, have very wide powers, but the controlling bodies for schools differ in the various countries. Juvenile courts in some of the United States have powers very similar to these Councils, but there is an immense variety of bodies controlling institutions. Obviously, to consider the history of the relevant social services in each country is more useful than to attempt a logical classification.

The English approved schools take, of course, both delinquent and non-delinquent children, but they are all sent by the court. In many other countries those coming through the courts are successfully mixed with those coming from other agencies, but there is usually an element of selection and the more difficult children remain together, often in State institutions.

So far as classification goes the English system is one of the most advanced. The classifying school system, even though it does not cover everyone, is probably more comprehensive than the system in Belgium, which applies only to government institutions. Similarly, the schools themselves are well diversified, possibly as well as anywhere else, including the Scandinavian countries.

It is not possible to add very much about the institutions themselves. In size they range from 600–700 places to 30–40. In the United States some 40 per cent of State schools have a capacity of over 200, and some are very large; in most countries 200 seems to be the top limit. In Sweden and Denmark most of the schools are quite small. Where the numbers are large, however, there is very often a cottage system or some form of house system. In Belgium, for instance, which pioneered this type of organization, the schools take about 200, but are split into units of twenty-five. On size, the English institutions come out quite well, but they generally lack any adequate system of organization in smaller units – this is just coming.

English institutions tend to be lacking in house staff as compared even with United States State institutions. They also have rather less specialized personnel than the better institutions in the more progressive states, i.e. psychiatrists, psychologists, and trained social workers. There are even a few trained group workers in American institutions, and some in Holland also. Apart from this, however, the standard in England is reasonably high. It is common for institutions to be largely staffed by people who have a teaching qualification, and England is no exception in this respect; nor in its use of a considerable number of untrained or partially trained other staff.

The reason for this is partly shortage of staff, which exists in most countries, but there is also a world-wide lack of training facilities. Even the limited facilities provided in England are rather better than pretty well everywhere else (excepting France, Belgium, and Japan), and most countries rely on in-service training (probably, in most places, amounting to very little) and such short courses as can be arranged locally. Training of staff is quite clearly the most important element universally lacking.

The system in England, then, is by no means bad if seen in an international setting. It is divorced from special education and child protection agencies to a greater extent than in some countries; but not more so than in others. This aspect is examined in the next chapter. The classification system is more effective than most others. Size of institution and staffing are reasonable, though differentiation within institutions is not well developed. And training is at least starting, which is more than can be said for many places. All in all one might say that, if we do not have any occasion to cite the English system as a shining example, it is distinctly in the 'good average' class, and that in itself is quite an achievement in a heavily populated community with a fairly high crime rate.

PART TWO

Mainly Argumentative

8

Education and social work

No attempt will be made in this part of the book to discuss all the problems of correctional schools. The problems selected have been chosen, in fact, largely because they appear to be somewhat neglected at present. Because of its close link with local authority children's departments through the inspectorate, the approved school system is moving nearer to the child care system. We look first of all, therefore, for comparative purposes, at similar schools in the education system, and later consider how far local authorities should be involved at all.

Approved schools obviously resemble certain kinds of special school, particularly those for the educationally subnormal and the maladjusted. Indeed, Unesco's *Statistics on special education* (1960) includes 'correctional schools' among its definitions. The data in that volume are based upon questionnaires and national publications; the questionnaires used (issued in 1953 and 1955) and the published material specifically refer to children who 'have no fixed home', 'are in correctional institutions', or 'are delinquent children'. The information given for England and Wales (for the year 1958) does not cover approved schools, but many other countries included data about similar schools in their returns.

The fact that approved schools were not included in the United Kingdom returns is due, to some extent, to our methods of dealing with delinquent children. In so far as we insist upon a judicial process based upon criminal proceedings, we tend to emphasize the distinction between those who appear before the courts and are the subject of compulsory orders and those who are not brought before the courts. The distinction is, of course, blurred in its effects by the existence of a wide range of treatment methods applicable not only to those found guilty of an offence but also to care, protection, or control cases. Nevertheless, the court order remains an essential ingredient. In many countries the age of criminal responsibility is near or above the upper age limit of our juvenile courts (the seventeenth birthday), and the methods of dealing with children, though backed by authority, tend to depend much less on formal judicial processes. Thus the authority concerned is likely to think less in terms of forms of treatment related specifically to the judicial process (e.g. probation, approved schools) and more in terms of what we would call child care provisions (e.g. foster homes, small children's homes) or educational provisions (e.g. schools or hostels for the maladjusted or the mentally subnormal).

SPECIAL SCHOOLS WITHIN THE EDUCATIONAL SYSTEM

So that we may now consider English approved schools in relation to schools for the educationally subnormal and for the maladjusted, let us look briefly at the development and nature of these special schools.

Schools for the educationally subnormal

Schools for the educationally subnormal (termed ESN schools) are a comparatively recent innovation. Homes of various kinds, taking dull and mentally defective children, have been in existence for a long time, and many such children could be found in poor-law institutions in the nineteenth century. The first day school for the category of children we would think of as ESN was opened in Leicester in 1892, and the second in London a few months later. In 1899, the Elementary Education (Defective and Epileptic Children) Act gave local education authorities power to provide for these children between the ages of 7 and 16, and the power became a duty in 1914. Provision was, however, only slowly built up. The 1944 Education Act introduced the present system of special schools, and the first post-war report in 1947 showed the number of special school places as 12,000 in 135 schools, as against some 38,000 ascertained as ESN.

Restrictions on capital expenditure meant slow development, limited almost completely to the conversion of country mansions, but it soon became apparent that there was an enormous reservoir of cases that would have been ascertained as ESN if there had been any point in doing so. In the Ministry of Education Pamphlet No. 5 on *Special educational treatment* (issued in 1946, reprinted in 1951) it was estimated that 10 per cent of all registered pupils, amounting to some 500,000, required some form of special educational treatment because they were ESN, though not all of this would need to be provided in special schools. Most of the children concerned, it was suggested, could be dealt with in special classes. The pamphlet accepted the recommendation of the Wood Committee on mental deficiency (Ministry of Health, 1929) that 1·2 per cent (about 60,000) would need education in special schools, of whom 0·2 per cent (about 10,000) would need to go to boarding schools.

As the number of ESN places available increased, the waiting list increased with them. In 1956, the Ministry of Education asked local education authorities to estimate the numbers requiring ESN places in special schools, as distinct from those ascertained and waiting for places; the total returned was 27,000, or more than double the number ascertained. It was split roughly into 19,000 day places and 8,000 boarding places. It is likely that a similar inquiry today would find a great many in the pipeline. The waiting list has been about 12,000 since 1949, and only in 1962 went down to 10,400, at which figure it remained in 1963. Of these, 5,100 had been waiting more than one year.

In January 1964 there were nearly 41,400 pupils in ESN schools. The number in boarding schools was 9,200; in day schools, 33,200. The waiting lists were 6,500 for boarding schools and 3,800 for day schools. Together with those being educated elsewhere, the total number ascertained was 51,800. The total number on the registers of grant-aided and independent schools was 7·7 million; 1·2 per cent of this gives 92,500, and 0·2 per cent (boarding) is 15,500. If the Wood Committee was anywhere near right (and it based its estimates on limited evidence), we still have a long way to go.

It should be remembered, however, that the demand for places in ESN schools is closely related to the availability of, and the standard of, special teaching in ordinary schools. It by no means follows that a child with an IQ of below 70 should automatically be sent to an ESN school. Even very backward children may prosper exceedingly in a special class in an ordinary primary or secondary modern school. As Dr M. F. Cleugh (1957) points out, there is a difference between 'special' education and 'suitable' education, and it is sometimes possible to provide in the ordinary school methods of teaching that are appropriate to a wide range of pupils at the lower end of the intelligence range. Indeed, primary and secondary modern schools vary greatly in the balance of provisions needed for various levels of intelligence, and some schools may well have to approach teaching in a way that is far removed from book learning.

What is more pertinent in the present context is the reasons why children go to ESN schools. 'Everyone knows,' says Dr Cleugh, 'that in practice behaviour is often the chief factor which determines a head-teacher's decision to refer a child for statutory examination but the question we are concerned with here is whether this emphasis on behaviour is justifiable', and she goes on to distinguish between '(1) those in whom the low intelligence is primary and who are "naughty" because the ordinary school does not and never can meet their needs, and (2) those who are troublesome and fail in school as a result'. She thinks that, in the selection of children for ESN schools, preference should be given to those who are really too unintelligent to cope in any ordinary school, rather than to those whose intelligence is limited in its application by emotional problems.

There is little doubt that the actual population of the schools is a mixture of those of distinctly low intelligence and those whose intelligence is not all that low, but who are prevented by their own difficulties from making the best of what they have. Furthermore, there are within the category of those of low intelligence many with personal and family problems, who need special treatment, and this is probably more so in the boarding than in the day schools. Whether the ESN school takes a particular child often depends as much upon the form in which his difficulties are expressed as upon the level of his intelligence, but the emphasis is upon teaching, not social work, so that the more obviously difficult child tends to be excluded.

Provision for the maladjusted

Some of these obviously difficult children will go to special schools for the maladjusted. As has been indicated, attempts to provide schools for the mentally defective came up against the problem of those whose intelligence was not in fact low though they were educationally backward. The development of the school psychological service, stemming largely from the appointment of Sir Cyril Burt as psychologist to the London County Council in 1913; the work of Dame Evelyn Fox; the founding of the Central Association for Mental Welfare, also in 1913; the opening of the Tavistock Clinic by Dr Crichton Miller in 1920; the beginnings of the child guidance service in 1927 – all contributed towards an increased interest in difficult children.

In the late 1920s a few independent boarding schools began to cater specially for this type of child, and in 1932 Leicester became the first local education authority to open a day school, consequent upon the development of its own child guidance service. From 1929 onwards it had been established, as a result of a case put forward on behalf of a child under treatment at the Tavistock Clinic, that local education authorities could pay for the boarding-out of maladjusted pupils either in schools or in foster homes, and this led to a gradual increase in the numbers of children so placed.

The Education Act, 1944, and the regulations made under it established the maladjusted as one of the categories requiring special educational treatment. This gave the Ministry the opportunity to approve for this purpose both the old-established special schools and boarding homes and also a number of more recent ones which had grown out of evacuation problems during the war in the form of hostels for difficult children.

The situation regarding schools for the maladjusted is thus somewhat complex. There are special schools maintained by the local education authorities, and there are special schools not maintained by the authorities but recognized as such by the Department of Education; also, children can be sent by the authorities concerned to a number of independent schools which, to a greater or lesser degree, cater for the maladjusted but are not, strictly speaking, special schools.[1] In addition, several places are available in what may be described as homes or hostels: in some, where the child is of school age, he goes to school outside the home; others, which take children who are so disturbed that schooling in any accepted sense is not applicable, might be more accurately described as hospitals.

The Ministry of Education's pamphlet mentioned above gave 1 per cent as the proportion of children in maintained schools needing special educational treatment under the heading of maladjusted. According to the Underwood Committee (Ministry of Education, 1955b) this is intended to mean that 1 per cent would need treatment in any one year (about 75,000 at the moment). Dr Blacker estimated, also in 1946, that 1 to 2 per cent of all children need guidance each year. The Underwood Committee obtained information from a number of local authorities in 1952–53. Their estimates of the proportion of children in the school population who required treatment as maladjusted ranged from 5·4 to 11·8 per cent. Taking an average of 8 per cent it seems likely that Dr Blacker's upper figure is nearer the mark, and that some 150,000 children a year should be coming forward for treatment, and 600,000 should be under treatment at any one time.

These figures are open to question, however, since they rest on a very narrow factual basis and since the assessment of maladjustment is made *in vacuo* without the need to suggest actual treatment, and without knowledge of natural remission rates or of what proportion of cases could be dealt with by non-psychiatric social workers or by teachers. It is wiser, therefore, to be content with the statement that extensive developments could well be envisaged in this field. The Underwood Committee recommended a massive expansion in child guidance staff, a doubling of the number of teachers, and a considerable increase in house staff in the schools over the next decade; it seems doubtful, in

---

[1] Action has now been taken to bring the independent schools under the special school umbrella for all categories of the handicapped. As from 1 January 1965, local education authorities may send children only to schools that are inspected and approved (Circular 4/61).

view of all the other calls for more personnel in other services, that this will be achieved.

The waiting lists for schools for the maladjusted have always been lower than for ESN schools, amounting only to 1,100 in January 1964, of whom 1,000 were waiting for boarding-school places. The figures have been steady in recent years. This is probably attributable to the unequal and restricted development of school psychological services, to the wide range of problems to be met, requiring, correspondingly, many different types of school, and to the general view that treatment away from home should be avoided if possible. There were, in January 1964, fifteen day schools, accommodating 541 pupils; and forty-six boarding schools, accommodating 1,634 pupils. There were also 681 pupils boarded in homes and 1,909 attending independent schools (sent by local authorities). Altogether, there were 4,500 pupils in schools for the maladjusted, of whom 3,800 were in boarding schools.[1]

Against these figures relating to the provision of services for ESN and maladjusted children, the problems of approved schools seem much less acute. The supply of approved school places must meet the demand, and generally does so; until recently, indeed, it was in excess, with the result that a number of schools – including some of the more ancient and unsuitable – were closed. Latterly, some children have had to wait in remand homes before they could get into classifying schools, and schools have been filling what ought to be a 10 per cent margin for eventualities. Even if it were desirable to provide 1,000 more places – which would mean a very considerable expansion, and is probably an overestimate of the need – it would still be much less of a problem than that presented by the shortage of provision described in the other fields. By any reasonable standards of comparison it must be accepted that approved schools are well ahead in terms of number of places to number of clients, even if this favourable situation is largely the result of more adequate provision of other methods of dealing with delinquents.

FACTORS INFLUENCING CHOICE OF TREATMENT PROCEDURE

We must now think about the needs of the children involved. As far as IQ levels are concerned, it is evident from the figures given in Chapter 3 that there is considerable overlap between approved and ESN schools; this point is underlined when one considers the wide

---

[1] Assuming that the independent schools are boarding schools.

range of IQs found in ESN schools alone, some taking children with IQs in the 80s and 90s if they are deemed suitable for other reasons. It is equally obvious that a broad range of temperaments must be represented in both approved schools and ESN schools, and in schools for the maladjusted also. It is extremely difficult to estimate the extent of the overlap. In so far as low intelligence is the predominant feature and the major problem is to provide the right type of education, not to deal with behaviour disturbance, then clearly the ESN school is the right environment; but backwardness may itself be the source of behaviour disturbance (though this by no means follows), and behaviour problems stemming from this or other sources are inextricably mixed up with the nature and effects of intellectual lack. Perhaps it is more sensible to think in terms of the degree and kind of behaviour problem than in terms of its genesis.

So far as society is concerned, the main consideration is not so much whether there are rows and unhappiness in the family, or whether a child is difficult to manage, as whether the resulting stress can be contained within the family's defences in depth, or is of such a nature that it affects others adversely and needs the attention of the community's resources. No doubt this is to take a limited view; one could equally argue that the quality of the society of the future will depend on what solutions are achieved to the family problems of today. To address our efforts to the total scene, however, is not only impractical; it would also entail much more interference with the rights of parents and children than would be justified by our libertarian feelings, our restricted resources, and our extremely limited knowledge of successful rehabilitative techniques.

Thus we start at the point where the problem bursts through the walls of the family and begins to affect others, either because the family itself asks for help or because harm is done to someone else. The amount of stress that can be contained within the family unit varies greatly from family to family, but there is always a threshold that may eventually be crossed. In general, we tend to feel that when someone else has been harmed it is a matter of public concern upon which some public agency should act. This may be the court, and must be where a considerable degree of compulsion is necessary, because of the threat to civil liberties. Compulsion is, however, undesirable and should be avoided wherever possible.

At the moment we organize our aiding systems rather badly. It is often pure chance whether a child who has stolen is dealt with by teacher and school psychological service or by policeman and court: it depends who complains and to whom. If the person who has suffered the loss reports the matter to the police, and he is almost certain to do so if the culprit is unknown or the amount is large, then the judicial system takes over. If, on the other hand, the matter is reported to the school, it may well be that the child concerned will merely be referred to the child guidance clinic.

I do not say that the results are necessarily bad, but they tend to be haphazard and to turn too much on the extent of the damage done to property, which may be quite irrelevant to the extent of the damage already done to the child by the circumstances of his life. Much will depend, also, upon whether the parent is sufficiently concerned to take the action demanded of him by the school psychological service – e.g. to attend a clinic; and furthermore, unfortunately, a critical factor in the current situation is whether treatment facilities are available, no matter how willing the parent may be.

Children's departments intervene on a different principle. They are concerned with whether the child is being properly cared for (within the legal definitions of the Children Act, 1948, the Children and Young Persons (Amendment) Act, 1952, and the Children and Young Persons Act, 1963. The question here is not what type of treatment the child needs or what he himself has done, but who is looking after him and how adequately. The child care service is backed by the courts in a number of ways: directly, as for instance in determining a disputed resolution to assume parental rights under section 2 of the Act, or through the courts' powers in care, protection, or control cases. The power to take into care is wide, but is limited by practice, judicial decision, and economic considerations, and the tendency is to avoid children who are likely to be difficult – i.e. those who will steal or be violent, or who are severely maladjusted – if this is possible. It is obviously not possible where homes split up and parents disappear, but it may well be possible where the matter is one of dispute between parent and child, or of delinquency. Thus, in terms of types of children actually dealt with there is some degree of overlap between those in care and those in approved schools (indeed, a number of children in care are sent to approved schools); what matters, again, is the initial situation and the presenting symptoms.

A number of factors, then, determine which procedure will be followed in any particular case:

1. The extent to which the problem can be dealt with by the family.
2. The extent to which it can be dealt with by the (normal) school.
3. The presenting symptoms and how far they affect others.
4. The actual occasion of a report of difficult behaviour and how it is reported.

5. The physical presence of parents, i.e. whether the child can be treated as deprived.

6. How far the parents are prepared to accept, and are capable of operating, an agreed course of action, and how far this must be imposed.

7. The extent of the available facilities for carrying out agreed courses of action.

Whether or not a child appears before a court will depend upon a combination of these circumstances, and it is far more likely that he will appear if his parents are rejecting and unco-operative, and if the actual occasion is a delinquency involving considerable harm to others. There is thus only a partial overlap between the types of case dealt with by the school psychological service and those dealt with by the courts. Similar considerations govern the overlap between the children's departments and the courts, particularly the actual occasion of a report concerning a child who may also be regarded legally as deprived.

It should not be overlooked that the form that the difficult behaviour takes is itself a critical factor with regard to the choice of remedial measure. Both inturning withdrawal and outgoing violence may be expressions of maladjustment and may equally demonstrate that there is a problem to be solved; but the second is likely to involve others – which brings us to consideration of the difficult concept of punishment.

We are all full of superficial philosophical ideas on this subject. There were prolonged arguments at the time of the Committee on Social Services in Courts of Summary Jurisdiction (which reported in 1936), and subsequently during the second Criminal Justice Bill in 1947, about whether it was wrong to proceed to conviction before making a probation order. The result was a somewhat involved clause in the Criminal Justice Act of 1948, aimed at mitigating the possible effects of stigma (section 12). Similarly, it is sometimes said that committal to an approved school is not a punishment, because it is done by order.

The truth of the matter is that to what extent something is a punishment depends upon how it is seen by the individual child. Punishment is unpleasant, and it is done to you against your will. Thus, for some children, being taken to a child guidance clinic may be just as frightening as being escorted to an approved school. Furthermore, it will depend upon the staff of the clinic or school whether or not the experience goes on being a punishment. There is a difference between school and clinic in that the child can withdraw, if he is old enough, from the clinic, but not from the school; but whether he regards his experience as a punishment remains an open question. He is much more likely to do so,

M

however, if he is forcibly kept away from his home. Nor will the fact that
his removal is by agreement between his parents and a family council
make very much difference to him, if the result is the same. Indeed, he
may see the situation in much darker colours, as a betrayal and rejection
by his parents – and often enough he will be right.

If some of the recommendations of the Ingleby Committee (Home
Office, 1960) had been accepted, they would have modified some of the
procedural alternatives applicable to children. It was argued before the
committee that the compulsory powers of the court should not be used
in dealing with juveniles, and that there might be a hearing before an
informal committee in the first instance in order to elicit what could be
done without them. The committee rejected this proposal on various
grounds: the danger of a lack of proper procedure for establishing
guilt; the fact that juvenile court justices are the same sort of people who
might well sit on a child welfare council on the Scandinavian model
(which would seem a good reason for using them in this way!); and the
problem of what would happen if the measures taken failed (paras. 72–5).
In its place the committee suggested that the juvenile court should 'move
still further away from its origin as a criminal court' in respect of the
younger children. This would involve raising the age of criminal
responsibility to 12, and possibly 13 or 14 (the age was, in fact, raised
to 10 in the 1963 Act), and instituting a new procedure (described in
Appendix IV of the report) for those under that age.

One of the objectives of the new procedure was to give children's
departments a somewhat wider jurisdiction than before in care, protection, or control cases, presumably on the assumption that they might be
prepared to take action not requiring appearance before the court.
Where an offence had been committed there would be a procedure of
consultation between the police and the children's department before
proceedings were taken, which might, in some cases, result similarly
in avoiding a court appearance. The implication was that preventive
social work would be done by the children's department, and the child
might be taken into care. It would not be impossible for him to be sent
later to a child guidance clinic or a special school, if these seemed
appropriate. To effect these recommendations, children's departments
would have to be prepared to take responsibility over a rather wider
range than hitherto. Section 1 of the 1963 Act gives them such preventive powers.

The Home Office in 1965 issued a statement of policy (*The child, the
family and the young offender*) strongly supporting this trend of thought.
It appears to dismiss as unimportant, or at least as not worth discussing,
the Ingleby Committee's major objections, stated above, to the idea of

an informal committee hearing prior to the court appearance; and it advocates the setting-up by children's departments of 'family councils', to consist of child care officers and outside people specially appointed. Their role would be to try to effect an agreement with the parent to take some course of action, and the measures open to them would be compensation (not fines), attendance and detention centres, supervision by the children's department, and longer-term residence in a home or school or in a foster home. These arrangements would apply to children under 16 years of age, and approved schools for this age-group would be merged into the range of homes available. The juvenile court (renamed the family court and again dealing with the under 16s) would then take cases that the family council could not or would not deal with. There are already powers to bring to court those who break down under supervision and in children's homes, and these would presumably continue.

The evidence suggests that some redistribution between ESN schools, schools for the maladjusted, children's homes, and approved schools could usefully be effected (and the 1965 White Paper deals only with the last two), but it is not clear upon what basis this should take place. There are bound to be a number of children who are disruptive in a residential situation, who abscond and defy authority and incite others to do so. What is likely to happen with regard to the under 16s if the 1965 proposals are carried out is that the 'better' children will be removed from the present approved schools, which will become special schools for the most troublesome children. Similar developments have taken place in a number of other countries. There is no reason to believe that children's departments will be any more adventurous and experimental in dealing with such children than are the Home Office, the Department of Education, or local education authorities.

REGIONAL OR LOCAL ORGANIZATION

As an organized system, approved schools seem to have some advantages over other special schools. There is a considerable gulf between the conceptions of classification as held by the educationist and by the penal administrator. The latter thinks of it as an organized system of institutions with a central 'processing' place where individuals are studied and allocations made. The reason for this is that classification developed historically within a system owned by the State, which meant that there was no need to be concerned with problems of local control. The educationist, however, would hardly recognize the term in this sense. He has always worked through locally controlled bodies and sees the sorting-out process for special schools as diagnosis by a clinic or by the school psychological service of a local authority (generally only the larger authorities), followed by allocation to schools or places available within that authority; plus whatever arrangements can be made for places elsewhere.

Classification in the penal administrator's sense implies the ability to provide a planned range of institutions which are deliberately specialized to some degree. In a system run by local authorities it is very difficult to make specialized provision except where the authority is very large, and probably undesirably so. Where it has been attempted, as with ESNs in Hampshire, the range of places to which the children can be sent is limited by the county's provision and the availability of places elsewhere. There are two ways of attempting to extend the range.

It is possible to have regional arrangements under a joint committee. Such a system operates for technical colleges, but it is largely concerned to prevent duplication of courses, and it is not easy to envisage a joint committee running a system for sorting out students for allocation to specialized colleges. Also, the committee can draw upon the knowledge and experience of the Department of Education's inspectors, and consult them upon the merits and demerits of particular schools; in their turn, the inspectors may attempt to produce a balance in the area by advising authorities which are setting up new schools where there are gaps in the provision. It is unlikely that such an approach would improve the special school situation to any great effect.

An alternative approach would be advocated by the educationist. Many people feel that the need for residential establishments is very limited and that day schools, in conjunction with advice and help in the home, constitute appropriate and adequate provision for the majority of cases. Efficient organization of special classes might well reduce the need for special schools altogether, and, if special schools are required for a minority, then small classes and thus individualized teaching are the real answer. In the present context, the need for residential schools is not in question, since there obviously will continue to be a need for a long time to come. It may be that a wide range of provision of both day and residential schools is required to match the range of cases to be dealt with. The point at issue is whether to have specialized schools, each catering for a particular range of pupils, or every school taking the whole range, and relying upon small classes, high staffing, and internal classification to meet the variety of needs. It can be argued, on the one hand, that residential schools ought to be organized on the principle of the family group, thus encompassing the whole range, but having individualized teaching as far as possible; on the other hand, it can be said that the special needs of these children are such that there must be some limitation in terms of age and personality factors, so that the energy of the staff is not dispersed over a variety of types of provision and approach.

This kind of question is not easily settled because there are certain imponderable elements. The new form of classification in approved schools has moved towards dependence on small houses rather than on external classification. It seems unlikely, however, that any system based upon heavy staffing with trained personnel will be able to operate successfully, and an effective all-age family group system would have to be heavily staffed. Moreover, one cannot help feeling that the concentrated special treatment that is envisaged, both scholastic and therapeutic, would be more easily provided in a school with a limited age range and some degree of specialization. In addition, the residential school, even more than the day school, is imbued with the attitudes and methods of its head. In order to ensure a variety of approach, my inclination is towards a number of small establishments, with easy transfer between them.

There is no doubt that a planned system offering specialized facilities to a wider area is much more likely to deal with the range of problems presented than is a locally based system. I would maintain, therefore, that the regional classification system of the approved schools is much more appropriate for children whose difficulties are such that they need specially adapted residential treatment. It might well be that this regional system should be run by the Department of Education, but the chances of this happening are so remote that it need hardly concern us, whereas the approved school system is there, already offering these advantages. It would be a great pity, having got this far, to go backwards, especially since the dominating factor at the moment is the shortage of places in special schools that could accommodate the approved school type of child.

TEACHING OR SOCIAL WORK

Most people think of schools as places where 'subjects' are taught – arithmetic, history, geography, and the like. Most educationists would conceive of education in much broader terms: 'education for living', 'education of the whole man', 'character training', and so on. Definitions of education, like definitions of social work, mental health, or social medicine, tend to be vague and all-embracing and are equally good candidates for Baroness Wootton's elegant butchery. There is, however, an area in teaching that is, in a wide sense, social training, and overlaps a good deal with what we tend to think of as social work.

So far as approved schools are concerned, it is obvious that straight-forward teaching in the narrow sense must always occupy a central place in the curriculum if for no other reasons than that some 45 per cent of the boys who are admitted and some 25 per cent of the girls are under 15, and that most of those who are over 15 are academically backward, and sometimes intellectually backward also. This is not to say that the teaching has to be confined to 'subjects', or even that it need be confined to the classroom, but obviously the children must acquire some knowledge and develop some basic skills.

On the other hand, it is equally true that to impart knowledge or skills is a secondary aim in approved schools. The very large majority of the children who go to them need help with problems of adjustment to living. They have been presented, only too often, with family situations that would strain the patience and adaptability of the most mature of adults. They are full of fears, worries, pugnacity, resentment, hatred, revenge. And what is more, they did not want to come to the school.

The provision of a stable and sympathetic environment goes some way to help, as, indeed, does removal from a difficult emotional situation at home, much as it may be resented. Those who can cope with their own problems are given time to grow in the school, and to grow armour. A very great many, however, cannot cope by themselves and need a great deal of help. Whoever may be doing the helping, it is much more social work than teaching. For this side of the work, classroom skills are less relevant, whereas the ability to understand and handle emotional difficulties is essential; that is to say, the emphasis is upon the kinds of skill that are the core of what is taught to social workers rather than upon skills that are primarily imparted to teachers.

In saying this I do not mean to imply that teachers cannot do social work, nor, indeed, that social workers cannot be teachers. It is not so much a matter of sharp differentiation as of emphasis. As Rodgers and Dixon have pointed out (1960), there are some people who are naturally good at dealing with the problems of others, whatever their own basic training, if any, might be. Nevertheless, the majority of people need a greatly increased awareness both of other people and, even more important, of themselves, which is the central feature of social work training.

Working in an approved school, or in any institution for that matter, gives rise to problems not encountered by the ordinary caseworker. Fundamentally, it is group work, not casework, and the continuing and pervading presence of others, and the ethos of the particular school, delimit what can and what cannot be done. Even so, one senses a reaction of passivity, almost of apprehension, when one talks to approved school staffs about the social work aspects of their job. It is very common to be told, for instance, that a child's offence, or even his whole past history, is never, or only exceptionally, mentioned, the assumption being that when the boy or girl comes into the school he or she is making a fresh start; the slate is wiped clean, and the child must look to the future. Sometimes one suspects that this policy is a protective device evolved by heads to prevent unsuitable staff, of whom they have far too many, from causing damage by unskilful questioning. Other heads seem to believe in it themselves, although it is difficult for the outsider to credit that anyone should think that from ten to sixteen years of a child's life can be quietly dismissed as irrelevant, or that any child, let alone one with problems, could acquiesce. Such an attitude can only be the first step in a process that, similarly, sets what happens in the school upon one side as an irrelevant incident in the child's real life.

Equally, there seems to be a great reluctance to raise a child's problems unless he himself comes forward with them. Perhaps in some schools children are seen individually at fairly regular intervals, but in all the ones I have visited, some of them with excellent reputations, it appears to be assumed that the right way to deal with the social work side is to have little chats on the football field, during walks, or elsewhere, when the occasion arises, and if nothing else happens to distract attention. It must be remembered, nevertheless, that the situation presents very real difficulties. In an enclosed community, such as a school, there is no immunity from observation and everything that goes on is known by other people. To single out a boy is to invite comment from his fellows, and he must later on find a defence to their questions and to an allegation that he is 'sucking up' or 'crawling'. If one respects one's children, one must have regard to this; but it is only half the picture. One must also be aware that the boy is there for a purpose – to be given something he could not get at home, or elsewhere. The time available for helping him is comparatively short, and the opportunity may never recur, which seems sufficient justification for crowding on the pace and for a much more positive approach. If every child is seen regularly, an interview will no longer be regarded as unusual. It is not only in the larger school that the individual approach is needed; it is equally valuable in the smallest schools, where chance opportunities for talking with one child are likely to be few, because every activity is carried out by everyone together, or in twos and threes.

One cannot avoid the feeling that with most teachers it is activities that count. They are taught to believe that the way to reach children is to do things with them. This is true, but it is also essential, having reached them, to know how to use the relationship. Making contact by doing is a beginning, not an end; it is not the only way of establishing contact, nor is it necessarily the right way in every case. Some children cannot respond to this kind of approach; others may be highly impressed by the fact that the master can stand on his hands on the backs of two chairs (an opening gambit used very successfully by a borstal house-master of my acquaintance), but merely want to be able to do the same. The skill lies in utilizing the opportunity when one has made it, and one does not do that by waiting passively for the next opportunity. Nor is it true that those with the most serious problems will create opportunities for talking and counselling through their aberrant behaviour. It may well be the case that those who behave badly are those whose difficulties have gone beyond the point at which the school can help without pro-fessional aid; it is those who can more or less conform to the school regulations who can be helped most by the techniques within the powers of the staff.

Implications for training

Few people would deny that approved school work involves more than formal teaching, but not everyone would agree that the practice of individual casework demands an additional set of skills that need to be acquired. It is now accepted that teachers in special schools require an extra year's training, and courses are being provided for them. Although the Reynolds Committee's recommendation to this effect was made in 1946 (para. 45) in relation to approved schools, it is only recently that it has begun to be implemented, and the present courses are designed primarily to produce housemasters. It is extremely unfortunate that so little has been done in the training sphere, apart from refresher courses, because there is a gap to be bridged between the approach of the teacher and that of the social worker. A long period of shortage of staff, and the tradition, now dying, of the autocratic headmaster and headmistress, have made it difficult for heads to give staff the freedoms of professional status, and the difficulty is exacerbated where there is not a common basic training, and where the social worker's initial training is not as relevant as it might be to work in residential establishments, as is the case. Professional casework training is much too individualized for approved school staff, and group work training in universities hardly exists, but this does not excuse those concerned from organizing a course to meet their requirements, and this is gradually happening. The Prison Com-mission has its own training establishments (although it still believes that anyone seconded from the service for a few years can be a successful tutor). Various courses for residential staffs devised by the Central Training Council for Child Care have been mentioned in the section on training (pp. 103–5 above).

A certain amount of experience is available from the United States, where a good many group workers have been trained and are working in institutions of various kinds. Konopka's *Group work in the institution* (1954) throws some light on this field. In general, the key to social work training lies in carefully supervised training on the job, and this is not as easy to carry out as it might seem. It is not enough for the supervisor merely to be around or to be available, and exercise a kindly and informative sympathy towards the student. Practical training from which the student is really going to benefit demands carefully thought-out situations, preferably discussed with the course tutor, frequent seminars, good recording of cases and situations, and analysis of them in training sessions. A good deal has been done in a small way by John Gittins at Aycliffe (cf. p. 104 above), where about six housemasters a year have been going through a course; but the way this was organized was largely determined by Gittins's personal links with the Institute of Education of the University of Durham. It may be that particular colleges of further education or teacher training colleges should specialize in courses of this type in various spheres, just as some are going to produce Young-husband caseworkers and may well eventually produce other types of caseworker. We have started so late that the courses have not yet had time to settle down. A great deal remains to be done in the way of training, and the Central Training Council for Child Care ought to devote a lot of time and money to the needs of approved schools.

I have dealt with training at this point because its key role has been underlined as a result of the difficulties that have arisen with the introduction of increasing numbers of staff trained in the social sciences. The future picture of the school as a collection of comparatively small 'houses', probably physically separate units, each with its own house-master and houseparents, has several points in its favour, not least of which is the fact that considerable numbers of extra staff will be required. There are bound to be problems, however, in trying to develop methods of work that will please both the teaching element (which usually includes the headmaster) and the house staff. Many schools are being rebuilt to a pattern that will provide a housemaster and his wife for every thirty boys, and a housemother and the part-time services of a housefather for every fifteen. This will mean an addition of two or three housemasters and their wives, and four or more full-time housemothers, with part-time, or possibly full-time, assistance from their husbands. The larger staff will be a welcome relief, but it will also bring problems in methods of working.

We shall come back to these difficulties. What seems clear is that the present concern should be to place emphasis upon acquiring and elaborating skills more appropriate to the social worker than to the teacher. In a number of Continental countries there are trained teachers who, by taking additional courses, become social pedagogues (cf. p. 105 above), and it is they who staff the special schools, including, very often, the ones that take the equivalent of our approved school children. My impression is that the extra training they are given is generally poor, and no doubt we can do better, but we can certainly do with a class of social pedagogues not only for special and approved schools but also, as was mentioned earlier, for some primary and secondary modern schools. In effect, we create a separate class by giving extra increments and other payments, and we must now gradually add training.[1]

---

[1] Since this was written, courses have been devised in some teacher training colleges which contain considerable elements of social work training. These are not a substitute, however, for a post-qualification course.

9

The training process
I: general considerations

It is now appropriate to consider in detail the process of training that approved schools offer, and its operation. The focus of this chapter is the school itself and what goes on in it. First, however, we must look at some problems related to classification.

Classification and remand

For a long time there has been dispute about whether the remand home could or should do the job of the classifying school. It was recommended in the Report of the Departmental Committee on the Treatment of Young Offenders (Home Office, 1927) that there should be, in addition to the ordinary remand homes, central remand homes, which would be very much better staffed and would be used for more difficult diagnoses. The Howard League for Penal Reform had been instrumental in getting the members of this committee to see the Belgian observation centre at Moll, which impressed them considerably, and it tried hard to get central remand homes included in the Children and Young Persons Act, 1932, but they were excluded on the grounds of economy. If they had been set up at that time it is likely that the remand and classifying system would look very different today.

It is obvious that there is little point in collecting information and testing a boy both at a remand home and at a classifying school; although, it must be emphasized, the function of allocation does require expert knowledge. If there is to be a full report upon a boy, the court ought to see it first. There is also the question of an extra move for the boy. The problem that immediately arises, however, is one of location. If remand homes are to be used as 'places of safety' to which a child can be quickly and conveniently removed, and where he can await an appearance before the local court, or spend a period of up to three weeks on remand before disposal, they must be situated in convenient places. This will allow police, parents, lawyers, the children's department, and anyone else who is concerned with a particular child's welfare or with his appearance before the magistrate to see him easily, and will not involve a lot of travelling (and therefore added calls on staff time) when he has to appear in court. The solution proposed is to use most remand homes as holding centres with some diagnostic facilities, and to specify others as combined remand and classifying centres (i.e. central remand homes). If the latter were suitably sited their staff could get to know the schools as well as the staff of any classifying school in the area.

As the Ingleby Committee pointed out, however, this system would still mean that the children had an additional move. This consideration, together with the fact that the classifying schools are already well established, led the committee to recommend that things should be left as they are. In addition, the report commented upon the experience of Stamford House, London, and recommended the extension of this experiment to other populous areas (para. 401). The two new remand homes for girls in Manchester and Sheffield also classify, thus replacing the former classifying school for the north.

Stamford House

It is worth while taking a closer look at what does happen at Stamford House. This is the London area remand home for boys of all ages. It accommodates 104 boys (excluding the secure block) plus twenty-five in an annexe, and is the largest remand home in the country. The office accommodation is an old workhouse, but this has been supplemented by a new building and is itself to be rebuilt. There are four houses: two of these are in the old block and take new receptions of older boys (about 14 upwards); the other two are in the new block. The blocks are locked only at night, and the main gate is always open. Remand and approved school boys are mixed without obvious ill effect.

In 1964 the staff consisted of: a superintendent, his deputy, a senior housemaster and six housemasters, thirty-two full-time housefathers, six (part-time) housemothers, and two supervisors; the third in charge, who is head of the education department, his deputy, eight teachers, and various part-time instructors; a matron, her assistant, and domestic staff; and four full-time clerks. The professional staff in attendance comprised three educational psychologists, two psychiatric social workers, a consulting psychiatrist and several registrars, two full-time nurses, and a part-time medical officer. This may appear to be pretty heavy staffing, but Stamford House deals with much larger numbers than almost any other remand home and most of the other classifying schools. Admissions in 1963 were 1,933; 400–450 boys a year are transferred to approved schools. Nevertheless, although the staff are hard-worked, the facilities are much better than at most of the other establishments.

There has been in addition, since July 1961, a closed block accommodating seven boys; it can be used instead of committal to prison for boys aged 14 and 15 on remand, who are considered to be unruly (by the remand home staff, not the courts). It is not normally used for approved school boys, but may be in the case of difficult boys returned for reclassification. It consists of a day room and a dormitory entirely closed off from the rest of the building, and the boys stay within these premises most of the time.

The reporting system works as follows. Courts specify what types of report are required on a boy, usually general conduct reports (signed by the superintendent) and psychiatric reports, but he will in fact be reported on by everyone who comes into contact with him, and a file of information is amassed as a matter of routine. In 1959 a new report form, a comprehensive report, was introduced; it is very like a classification report, comprising conduct and education, and psychological and psychiatric reports, with conclusions added by the superintendent after a meeting of all those concerned. Even without this, however, if any information is lacking when a boy is sent to an approved school, it can usually be supplied. Subsequently, an assessment meeting is held, at which everyone who has made a report on the boy is present, with the superintendent in the chair; at this meeting the main points of the assessment and the main recommendations are decided. It is followed by an allocation meeting, which consists only of the superintendent, his deputy, the head of the education department, and the senior housemaster, who have all made special efforts to visit as many schools as possible. The whole process can be completed in a fortnight at the outside.

The experience of Stamford House shows that remand reports and classification can easily be combined in practice. The main problems lie in the need for specialized staff to ensure that remand home reports are full enough and of a sufficiently high standard to facilitate the preparation of classification reports; and, second, in the system of classification areas. On the first point, the staff required are simply not available at present in most places; but the problem may be overcome eventually. It is evident that highly skilled staff must be economically used, which points to the need to concentrate assessment in comparatively few centres. We are already failing to co-ordinate observation centres for adult offenders and for psychopaths, and it would be a pity if we failed equally to co-ordinate the assessment process in respect of children going to approved schools.

The question of classifying areas is more complex. Stamford House uses the same schools as the main classifying school for the south-east at Redhill, but it also allocates to other schools elsewhere as necessary. Thus it duplicates the classifying area of Redhill to a degree that must require a good deal of co-operation to make it workable. If most of the big towns were to take lumps out of, or to operate systems coexistent with, other classifying areas the position would become extremely confused. It is not so much that it matters whether a boy comes through a remand home/classifying school in Manchester or a classifying school at Red Bank some twenty miles away. It is rather that the present classifying system implies planning and specialization – indeed, it can induce a school to specialize in a particular field by allocating to it only certain types of boy – and a multiplicity of authorities with such powers would create a chaotic situation, unless there was very strong regional or central direction.

An interesting new venture is that at St Mary's Bay, annexe to Stamford House, which is located at a seaside resort. It started on 7 October 1961 and, except for one or two brief periods, has been continued without interruption. Initially, it was an effort to cope with the very serious overcrowding. The premises used have long been established as a children's holiday camp, and are well known to many children's departments and some approved schools. When the camp as a whole operates in its role of holiday camp from the beginning of May until early in September, the Stamford House party there remains self-contained, but the main camp provides the basic equipment and feeds the Stamford House party.

Use of the annexe is confined to boys who have been committed to approved school training. At first, it was further restricted to boys who had been assessed and allocated, and were merely waiting until vacancies were available in the chosen approved schools. It was soon discovered, however, as was anticipated in the beginning, that the rather different nature of the camp (as compared with Stamford House) and the different routine could be valuable as a further diagnostic tool. Consequently, it is now quite usual for a boy to spend a week at the annexe immediately after his approved school order has been made, and then return to Stamford House for the assessment process, so that a report from the annexe staff can be incorporated in his assessment report. He may, of course, then go back to the camp if there is no immediate vacancy in the approved school to which he has been allocated. The staff at the annexe comprises a housemaster, who has a special responsibility allowance, a housefather (Class I), who acts as the housemaster's deputy, two other housefathers, and a part-time housemother.

A new approach

As was noted in Chapter 3, there has recently been a move in the approved school world to reinterpret the objectives of classification. The intention in the past was to place each boy in the school that was most appropriate for him, taking into account the various factors mentioned in the earlier chapter. The new scheme reflects the general feeling that has arisen that a primary task of the schools should be to keep in touch with the homes; hence the emphasis on placement near home. The classification process is therefore limited to division into age-groups and the identification of certain categories of children who need special handling. As far as possible, then, it is the schools that will ensure that the home environment has been changed during the child's period of training – an expression of mistrust in the present system of aftercare ('aftercare begins when the boy comes in').

It can well be argued that classification is only a rough sorting-out and that, from the point of view of the school, the results are a mixed bag of problems and temperaments. A small school that is well staffed, or a school divided into small houses, can use internal classification and offer individual attention. Only one or two schools with these facilities would be required for each age-group, according to the demand for places, serving a catchment area sufficiently limited to allow for home visiting, with a number of special schools for the whole classifying area. As we have seen (Chapter 3 above), analyses showed that the present schools could be regrouped and most of the special units provided for without much change in the existing schools. Separate provision is required for boys in need of intensive psychiatric treatment; for very dull boys in the intermediate and senior ranges; for boys of high intelligence who need appropriate schooling; and for persistent absconders and very disruptive boys (who will be dealt with in the closed blocks attached to classifying schools).

This system returns, to some extent, to the pre-classification situation where courts sent boys to local schools, but it does ensure that each boy will be the subject of a comprehensive report (since they will all go to a classifying school), that special problems are catered for, and that the age-groups are separated. It should be noted that there is already some degree of local classification due to the differing characteristics of boys from different areas. The new approach implies, however, that the allocating function of the classifying school, relying as it does upon knowledge of individual schools, will be much less important, and one wonders if it will make the classifying school redundant in the long run, each catchment area having its own specially staffed, diagnostic remand home, at which classification reports would be either wholly carried out, or completed after an initial period in a less well-equipped place. It might also mean abandoning the wide choice of different types of work that a range of schools provided – though this was never quite as wide as one might think, owing to problems of vacancies.

Much depends upon the assumptions underlying the new proposals. If the object is to change the home in parallel with changes in the boy engendered by his stay in the school, there must be some considerable doubt how far it will succeed. Visiting from up to fifty miles away, even by a full-time officer, is not likely to be more effective or more frequent than visiting by the over-worked probation service. In any case, courts are reluctant to send to approved schools, but bad homes are one of the major reasons for doing so. It would seem, therefore, that the proportion of very difficult home situations needing a lot of attention is high.[1] Moreover, how far do the difficulties of these mid-adolescent boys derive from the home and how far from their peer-oriented attitudes and adverse neighbourhood influences?

On the other hand, if the major intention is not so much to change the home as to test the boy's adaptation to it, different conclusions follow. It would then be more appropriate to regard the school as an episode, probably of fairly short duration, in the offender's total scheme of rehabilitation, just as periods in a mental hospital may form only a part of the depressive's total treatment. The boy could then be tried out at home, under fairly close supervision, and returned to the school in case of breakdown, probably several times; and it would be advantageous not to hand him over from one person to another on several occasions. Such an aim, however, would involve a somewhat different conception of approved school training than exists at present.

It is, of course, only too easy for approved school staffs to believe that improvements they feel they achieve in boys are offset on their return to an adverse home environment. It may be that the schools are simply not succeeding in effectively changing a large enough number of boys. Or it may be that at least the latter part of the period of institutional training should be spent in day schools rather than boarding schools, situated much nearer the home, from which social work could be com-

---

[1] It is also possible that the declining success rate is not due to worse homes, but to worse boys – boys with more serious personality problems – or to an increase in the number of homeless boys. There is some indication of this in studies made of the intake of borstal boys (see Report of the Commissioners of Prisons for the year 1960, Cmnd. 1467, page 46).

bined with strict control over the boy. For the real trouble is the lack of intermediate provision between school, with comparatively little home visiting, and home visiting without any control and support of the kind that the school environment provides.

Another point is that the ability of the classifying school to sort boys is limited. The staff concerned cannot know, upon the basis of a short acquaintance, how a boy is likely to develop, and there is a strong case for the view that allocation of this kind can never be more than negative, i.e. sorting out the difficult cases, and dividing by age-groups. On this view there is much to be said for the new scheme, but it will certainly give added weight to internal systems of classification. It is thought that the new house system will make individualization possible and that this will obviate problems of classification, but it will have to work extremely well to do this, even if the more difficult boys are excluded, as they will be. There is also the danger of trying to force into a house system based on small groups and individualized supervision the boy who cannot really take the emotional demands of such an environment. There is no doubt, however, that approved schools are on the threshold of a great experiment which might radically change their character.

SYSTEMS OF INSTITUTIONAL TRAINING

We may now turn to the training process. A useful survey of some of the current systems of institutional training for young offenders is given by Dr D. Q. R. Mulock Houwer, Secretary-General of the International Union for Child Welfare, and previously director of an institution for children in Holland (Mulock Houwer, 1955).

The disciplinary system. Strict instructions and a set daily routine, based on a philosophy of rewarding good behaviour and punishing bad. This system can be found even in a small group setting, and there may be no outward show of uniformity or regimentation. However, there is little recognition of the importance of internal relationships between children, and this means that the child has two sets of values, one for the staff and the other for his friends, and the latter is likely to be the more significant.

The progressive, 'staircase', 'section', or 'degree' system. A more flexible variation of the disciplinary system, in which the reward for good behaviour is increased privileges. An example was the Belgian section system, consisting of a trial group, a merit group, an honour group, and an open group. The borstal system, with beginners, trainers, and leavers,

N

is another. This type of approach was strongly supported between the wars but has lost ground since; it has been dropped in Belgium and France, for instance. It has a tendency to force an unnatural adjustment which is followed by a falling-off after discharge because it is really beyond the powers of the offender. The theory is that the offender is like a worn piece of elastic: if you stretch him hard enough some of the threads will break and he will not spring back exactly to the original length when one lets go. Under such a system, strenuously applied, the more maladjusted tend to be very troublesome because they cannot make the grades. Both this and the disciplinary system place a great deal of emphasis upon work, which is one of the keys to progress and discharge. The norms laid down to measure progress tend, however, to be superficial and to be too influenced by the need to push everyone up the 'staircase'.

The homogeneous system. This is a reaction against the progressive system, and is based on the idea of a strong and continuing relationship with a single person. Thus the child remains in one small group of limited age range, and everything is concentrated upon changing his individual personality. There is much more variety in the work, and less emphasis is given to what can be done in an institutional setting.

The heterogeneous system. Very similar to the homogeneous system, but the groups are diversified and an attempt is made to turn them into substitute families by mixing ages and sexes. It also represents a reaction against those who insist on a homogeneity based upon some special analysis of the children's characteristics; e.g. Zetten, in Holland, where the division is upon the basis of an anthropological classification of temperaments.

   Both the homogeneous and the heterogeneous systems suffer from the limitations of who can in practice be received into a group, given the staff available; this usually means selection of cases and the exclusion of the most difficult, who thus, if these are voluntary institutions, find themselves in State institutions. The vertical age-grouping is of doubtful value for boys, and institutions are usually afraid of keeping older boys and girls together. On the other hand, these systems offer more scope for individual and group treatment.

The socio-pedagogical system. This is based upon the idea that the institution ought to reproduce as far as possible the structure of the community outside, with emphasis upon its constructive aspects. Examples are W. R. George's *The junior republic* (1910) and Makerenko's Gorki colonies. The child is faced with the same conditions as prevail outside: i.e. he gets nothing without working for it; he can also achieve a leading position in the community. The rationale is that what one does for oneself and for one's own society is of great value, and that to learn to work voluntarily and for the good of all is to take the first steps in citizenship. The difficulty is that such communities, like other small communities, are unable to cope with a high proportion of deviants who cannot be got to accept the basic tenets because they are too mentally handicapped or maladjusted.

The individual-pedagogical system. A system that puts the entire emphasis on the child; it has been much influenced by Aichhorn. As developed, it allows a good deal of freedom of action, but compulsion is not entirely absent. The staff attempt, by sustained tolerant understanding, to draw from the child his own solution to his problems, and thus attention is centred on interviews, play and expression therapy, group therapy, sociodrama, and so on. There is also a strong feeling that the parent must be brought in as much as possible to work through the whole matter as a family problem. A sound relation with the community emanates from a sound relation with individuals, especially those with whom one has strong emotional ties. Vocational training and work are not very important, since good work relationships stem from the same source. Thus the system is the direct opposite of the disciplinary system: everything comes from within the child and very little from outside.

Unfortunately this system, widely used with maladjusted children, depends largely upon the child's ability to deal with his own problems. A dull-witted child may be unable to formulate his problems to himself, and the majority of children in correctional schools are to some degree retarded.

The eclectic or differentiated pedagogical system. This system picks out various aspects of the above and tries to put them together. For instance, institutional care for young children (up to the age of 8, 9, 10?) is generally held to be completely undesirable. For those above this age-group and up to about 12 or 14, life in an all-age, co-educational family group with houseparents is a possibility. What is needed most is variety between and within institutions, to match the variety of problems presented.

On the whole, approved schools tend to have a strong leaning towards the disciplinary system, although some distinct elements of the homogeneous system are also being developed. Against the background of the history of residential establishments for children in England, some of which even in recent times have practised unpleasant repressive régimes, and in the light of the history of the approved school system, which did not shed uniforms and rules of silence until the 1920s, the term 'disciplinary' has overtones which may not be intended by Mulock Houwer. Perhaps 'the law and order system' is a less offensive title, for a characteristic feature of the approved school régime, as it is of the borstal system, is to put considerable emphasis upon keeping the rules. It is not that the personal element is missing; it is very much there, especially in the smaller institutions; but there is a very strong feeling in all approved schools that there are rules and one must abide by them, otherwise the community would not be viable.

It is clear even from the brief outline of systems given above that the real difference of opinion concerns not so much the existence of rules as their source. There are, as it were, two polarities. On the one hand, there is a continuum from rules imposed strictly by the staff to rules derived from the children; and, on the other, the range is from insistence upon the needs of the community to insistence upon those of the individual. These concepts are represented diagrammatically in *Figure 1* (remembering that diagrams are no more than analogies and tend to be misleading if pressed too far).

If we conceive of each spoke of the wheel as able to be shifted independently, it will be seen that A and C pushed closer together tend

Figure 1 The Institutional Wheel

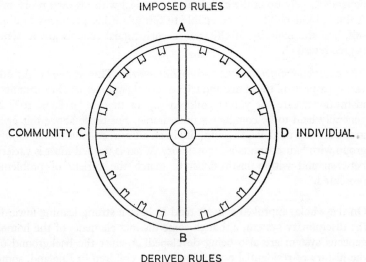

IMPOSED RULES

A

COMMUNITY C   O   D INDIVIDUAL

B

DERIVED RULES

towards what Mulock Houwer calls the disciplinary system, B and C towards the socio-pedagogical system ('community-centred' is a better term), and B and D towards the individual-pedagogical ('child-centred') system. In any combination some children will be carried and some broken on the wheel; there is no perfect answer, but a diversified system based upon classification can minimize the damage done and, we hope, maximize the good.

To represent the approved school system, both C and D would be pushed nearer to A. This is because the idea of the system is, in general, that what is needed is a strong basis of law and order in which to operate. Both self-government and individualized attention are subordinated to the belief that security is the first requirement, and that security derives from the staff. ('Security' here means 'making the child feel secure', but the idea of 'safety' is also present.) On the other hand, a consciousness remains, and is much clearer in some schools than others, that security, in both senses, derives ultimately from the children; this limits the extent to which rules can be imposed and prevents 'law and order' from becoming 'disciplinary' in its strongest sense.

It would be possible to play with the diagram further (e.g. Proposition: the size of the wheel to some extent determines the position of the spokes), but a visual aid can too easily lead to blindness. There is, however, a very real problem in balancing the needs of the individual against those of the community, and both sets of needs against the objectives of training. Its solution is governed by the type of people who form the community (including the staff), how big it is, how it is organized, what the therapeutic objectives are thought to be, and what resources are available for carrying them out. Nobody trains children without some theoretical basis, but most people either do not formulate the underlying assumptions or, if they try to do so, are satisfied with superficial answers to their questions.

Something has already been said in Chapter 4 about the nature of the residential community, and it will be clear from this that there are three aspects to be taken into account. First of all, there is the individual himself: a complexity of warring temperamental traits held together perilously by a balance of internal and external forces. Second, there is the group situation, a balance of individuals, which affects the external pressures on each. Third, there are the lines of communication, particularly those between staff and children, which might be summed up in the word 'knowledge', because nothing can be done without a good deal of knowledge of the individual, the group, and the relation between them.

POLICY FORMATION

Let us now consider the objectives of approved school training and how these can be achieved. Previously it was pointed out that there are two problems: to get close enough to the boy to find out what he wants of life and what he could get from the school; and to arrange the stream of institutional living so that there is the maximum possibility of giving him substantially what he wants as an individual without damage to the interests of other individuals, or to the permanent structure of the community. It is common ground that the aim of the training process is to achieve a permanent change of a particular kind in individual behaviour. It is now also common ground, after many years of trial and failure, that this cannot be done only by inducing fear, nor can it be accomplished merely by exhortation or religious precept. It cannot be imposed without acceptance; it is a voluntary change, even if the person changed will not admit it to himself.

It is agreed, furthermore, that the aim of classification is not so much to produce a truly homogeneous community in each school as to limit the range of heterogeneity, so that every school community will continue to encompass a wide range of personalities and problems, albeit clustered around one particular age-group. Classification is the frame, not the picture. Nevertheless, the fact of pre-selection does imply a certain degree of grouping according to the range of problems presented and the corresponding range of solutions required.

We may now put a number of propositions that are relevant to the construction of a training situation:

1. Imposed authority has the advantage that it provides a strong framework from which a child might, but not necessarily will, derive a sense of security; it is easier to operate, especially with low or ineffective staffing; it can more readily be explained and justified to outsiders, especially those who think that delinquents 'need a firm hand'. On the other hand, it is self-perpetuating, and is very liable to become imperceptibly shifted towards the convenience of the staff; it provides a ready-made framework which may not be appropriate for the child, and will almost certainly subtly distort his reactions; it tends to imply objectives (good work, good behaviour) which are not always ends in themselves.

2. Knowledge is increased by anything that brings an observer into contact with a child and anything that increases the child's confidence in him; by any system of centralizing information from a number of observers, and by increasing the variety of situations in

which the observations are made; in particular, by the deliberate organization of test situations, of discussions among those who know the child, and of careful recording of previous knowledge. It is correspondingly reduced when these things are not carried out. Authoritarianism is one of the major sources of ignorance – the more you see of the rules the less you perceive the people they apply to. In general, knowledge has to be gained by planning to gain it; casual knowledge may be misleading and harmful.

3. Knowledge gained is not knowledge used. It is often impossible to do what really ought to be done to solve the problem. One cannot provide fathers, mothers, wives, or husbands. It may, however, be possible to provide a solution, or at least to ameliorate the situation so that the child comes to terms with his trouble. The chances of doing this rise with the skill of the staff; but it may not be practicable to do anything at all except hold on and wait. It is, however, important to assess jointly what can and should be done in each case, and to make constant reassessments; even eighteen months is a very short period for wait-and-see policies. If the policy is wait and see it is vital that it should be a deliberate decision. If everyone is stumped it is as well to admit it, and decide what to do next, or to do nothing.

4. Grouping is one way of gaining knowledge, and it is also a way of gaining confidence; but it works well only if the adult centre of the group is reasonably constant and can handle the range of personalities concerned, and if they fit in with each other reasonably well. The smaller the group the more dangerous the active dissident, unless he can be controlled. Grouping is no good for people who cannot stand close emotional ties, since emotional stresses are likely to be more intense the more effective the group (there is nobody one loves or hates so much as one's own family). Grouping also reduces the range of adults available to the child. Because the stresses are greater it is much more tiring and difficult for staff who themselves need help and reassurance. (Perhaps one should add that family groups are not families, however much one tries to balance them or restrict their size.) Using grouping effectively entails increased understanding and knowledge of the child, and a readiness to apply these if necessary to offset the effects of the group. It may also entail a narrowing of the situations in which knowledge is gained, and this needs to be guarded against.

5. In any institution there are three major classes of children: those who are strong enough to cope with their own problems and need little

help but sufficient protection to allow them to get on with it; those who need help in varying quantities and can benefit by it; and those who cannot be helped at this particular institution, although it does not follow at all that they cannot be helped elsewhere. The first group need stability; the second, individual or group attention, ranging from an occasional word of encouragement to psychiatric treatment; and the third need to be shifted out as quickly as possible. The classification is easy to lay down on paper, but difficult to make in practice; this is one reason why one needs so much knowledge, so much discussion, and so much skill and experience.

These are by no means all the considerations that need to be taken into account in framing an approach to training, but they are the most important. They imply the following requirements:

(a) A stable environment. It does not follow that this must derive from imposed authority but it is much easier to achieve it this way; moreover, the deficiencies of the type of children who are committed to correctional institutions, the comparatively short time they remain there, and the limitations of the staff, make such a system almost inevitable. The rest of the requirements, however, indicate considerable restriction on the scope and degree of the authority imposed.

(b) A variety of situations which can be used for unobtrusive investigation and as testing group situations; work and house situations are the most obvious.

(c) Freedom, within limits, to move children into these situations without obvious favouritism or breaking one's own rules.

(d) Opportunity for the children to make close contact with staff members of their choice.

(e) The deliberate offering of relationships with staff to children who appear to need them.

(f) Constant collection, collation, and discussion of knowledge about the child and his relationships to his peers, to particular situations, and to particular staff members.

(g) Maximum opportunity for the child to express himself freely, to take his own decisions, and to follow his own interests without let or hindrance. This derives from the need for knowledge, and helps to produce the variety of situations.

These recommendations may not appear to pay as much attention as might be thought necessary to what the child wants to do. In different circumstances letting him follow his own interests might be more valuable, but he is in an approved school because following his own line has brought him into conflict with society. What he wants has to be subordinated to what he needs. This does not, however, mean that he should be debarred from pursuing his own interests when they do not conflict with these overriding principles.

10

The training process
II: approved school training

In the light of the general principles set out in the previous chapter, we can now look at approved school training as it is at present. All that has been said so far is in very broad terms. In practice, many of these principles conflict; there are all sorts of problems of space, money, and people, and one can never quite do what one would like. As guidelines, however, the considerations put forward would seem to indicate one or more areas of intensive small group experience, one or more areas of less intensive experience, opportunity for developing individual attachments, and deliberate and conscious staff planning of progress and methods of treatment.

REAPPRAISAL OF STAFF ATTITUDES

What is missing in very many approved schools is the idea of a responsible, professional training team offering a variety of relationships to a comparatively small group of boys. Most schools of any size are not organized in small units either physically or administratively, and where houses exist they tend to be without real relation to training problems, or much too large. Plans have now been made for the rebuilding or conversion of many schools to facilitate the introduction of the small group system. This system will not prosper, however, unless there is a general change in attitudes. Often, too much is in the hands of the head, who does not allow anyone else to correspond directly with parents, and sometimes does not let the rest of the staff see the boys' records.

Many of the shortcomings are the result of staff shortage and of untrained staff. It is only recently that approved schools have begun to realize quite how short of staff they are. When I asked one deputy headmaster what opportunity was taken to get to know boys during the evening activities, he replied by showing me the duty rosters and pointing out that most of the people on duty were likely to be very tired in the evening through having been on their feet too long. And he added

192

that if any of the staff fell ill or went on leave there were no reliefs, and everyone would be even more tired. There has never been any provision in approved schools, as there is in borstals for historical reasons, of a second grade of officer to carry out routine duties and supervise work parties in the daytime, and assist with evening duties at night. Thus a borstal house of forty has a housemaster and two or three officers on duty in rotation; in addition, other supervision activities during the day or in the evening are carried out by other officers, or by 'civilian instructors', or teachers or voluntary workers from outside. There are, therefore, at least six people on duty in the houses alone every evening in an institution of 120 boys, in addition to those who are running special activities. In a similar-sized approved school there would be fewer staff on duty, they would be responsible for everything, and one or more of them might well be the school clerk, the general handyman, or the gardener (paid 'extraneous duty' rates, which makes it profitable for them even if they are not particularly suitable for the job).

Shortage of staff is not the only trouble; there is also a widespread attitude that conceives of training as the creation of a sound, activity-full background against which, with some help when difficulties arise, the child should be left to solve his own problems. In the past this kind of approach was probably effective in the majority of cases, as the success figures testify; but the character of the approved school population is probably changing, and the success rate is certainly falling. More changes are to be expected in approved school work, for it cannot but be affected by the improvements made in allied services. The schools are already beginning to react to current trends, but they entail fundamental changes in staff relationships. The head can no longer be the centre of all individual casework, and the only link with parents. It was a boast of the older type of headmaster that he 'knew every boy in the school'; and no doubt he did know all their names, and something about a good many of them. This is no longer enough. The future organization of the schools is already fairly clear. It will be based upon a small group system rather like the family group home, and probably two groups will be combined to make a 'house'. Thus the main features of what is now thought of as 'social training' will be carried out in the house, and the major burden will rest on the house staff. In this situation, the headmaster and his deputy will become much more co-ordinators and general administrators and the real responsibility for training will rest upon the housemaster, on the one hand, and upon whoever runs the school side (in junior schools and to a lesser extent in intermediate schools), on the other.

Now this prospect need not strike terror into anyone's heart. All sorts of variations are possible, and there is nothing to stop the head and deputy from collecting round themselves groups of boys for whom they have special responsibility. Systems of this kind must always be worked with great flexibility, because the material upon which one is operating, the child, is itself infinitely flexible. The house is both liberating and limiting. It is liberating because it offers opportunities to the boy for close contact, and to the rest of the staff for freedom from overwork; it is limiting because the range of personalities it offers to the boy is limited. Almost everyone is better with some types of boy than others, and there is no reason why any member of the staff should not acquire particularly close contacts with an individual boy, so long as he works in conjunction with the house staff.

Furthermore, there is no reason why the housemaster should be a social-science trained, officially designated housemaster, drawing the scales of pay laid down by the National Joint Council, and not the Joint Negotiating Committee. He might equally be a suitably experienced qualified teacher, with or without extra training and qualifications, if they should become available. It is very much a question of who can do the job, and it would be unfortunate if there grew up in the schools a distinction between those who officially do social work and those who do not. On the other hand, it must be unequivocally accepted that extra people are needed, and not merely a diversion of interest on the part of existing staff.

Basing the operation of the school upon training carried out by teams working with small groups has other consequences also. It means a revision of the way in which incentives are provided. The occasion might be taken to have a small Home Office working party on mark systems. Some of these seem unnecessarily complicated and, indeed, one cannot help wondering whether there is any need for them at all. Do they really act as an incentive? Are they really essential as a means of control? If one has sufficient staff for proper supervision throughout the day, is it really necessary to give good and bad marks for everything that happens? If they must exist surely no more is required than a good, average, or bad indication for each day. And is it wise to link mark systems with pocket money, especially if they are very complex? What boys do not really understand is likely to be regarded as unjust for that reason alone.

Second, it is essential to have a regular reporting process, in which everyone who knows the particular boy is involved. This is not mere paper work. As pointed out above, it is of fundamental importance to build up a picture of each boy's progress through the school. It is sometimes extremely difficult to guess upon what information a headmaster makes recommendations to the discharging committee. Is it the result of conversations with staff, or his own observations, and how much do these depend upon memory, or upon recent events?

As a corollary to the process of data collection it must follow that assessments of progress are made regularly at staff meetings, where the decision concerning release on aftercare should also be taken. There does not seem to be any tradition in approved schools of grades through which a boy must pass before he can be discharged and which to some extent govern privileges. Perhaps the nearest to this are the separate discharge 'houses' into which boys move before discharge, and where they get greater privileges. Grading systems can be overcomplicated, and even if they are very simple – of the type of beginners, trainers, leavers – they introduce an element of rigidity; but they have two advantages: they ensure that a general assessment is made of every boy at regular intervals, and they can be used for disciplinary purposes. A third advantage is often put forward – that they give the boy something to aim at. Unfortunately, there are few members of staff who are capable of explaining to a boy what exactly it is he is expected to do. Nobody will accept that conformity is all that is required. Keeping to the rules and working reasonably well in school or vocational department go a long way; but, in addition, a boy is usually expected to make some real effort to change himself. Conformity is, however, easy to understand and explain, whereas what 'making an effort' means is very difficult indeed to put into precise terms. Failure to attain a grade can therefore be frustrating, and it needs careful handling to ensure that it is a testing experience and not a discouragement.

Whether or not there is any place for grades in approved schools, it can hardly be doubted that it is the staff who really get to know the children, and that the decision concerning release must rest with them. It seems to be quite pointless to place this responsibility upon the managers; indeed, it hardly amounts to more than hiding behind their skirts, since they cannot possibly actually make the decision. It may be a good idea to invite suitable managers, or other outside people, or staff from other schools, to sit in as advisers – and there is nothing to stop parents approaching the managers, who would then make inquiries – but the decision rests squarely upon the staff and, in the last resort, upon the headmaster. Similarly, whether a child should be recalled is a decision to be taken by the staff, in consultation with the aftercare agent.

It may be thought superfluous to have staff meetings in a small school. It is a great mistake to believe that this is so. Discussing matters, even routine matters, singly, with individual members of staff, is never the same as having all the staff sitting together and arguing the point out. Furthermore, a great deal depends upon good staff relations, and vital information has an odd way of getting lost, even when the staff is very small; the result is that every now and again quite important things happen about which some member of the staff knows nothing at all, or has gleaned only a hint, possibly an erroneous one, indirectly. This is asking for staff trouble, and inviting staff losses. There is very little point in being secretive, as long as there is mutual trust and respect among the staff – and if there is not, being secretive certainly will not help matters. It may be a difficult policy to pursue when staff shortages are acute but, as one headmistress said, 'If you can't trust your staff you shouldn't appoint them'.

SIZE AND LOCATION

Consideration must be given to the size of a school. It has been thought in the past that what was most needed was, for boys, a stable atmosphere and trade training; for girls, individual care in small groups. It is doubtful whether either of these theories was valid, and it is even more doubtful now. Given the conception of a range of environments, of testing situations, and of people, the indications are that what is needed is units of varying sizes as part of a larger institution. Such a framework provides opportunities, on the one hand, for small and closely defined groups and, on the other, for larger groups, more loosely defined. It also gives opportunity for a range of staff, and for a wide variety of work situations. The argument is akin to that for the comprehensive school: that, as long as the whole is not so large that it falls apart from sheer weight of numbers, the increased size can be combined with small group work to provide greater variety. Only in this case we are not thinking in terms of a variety of courses, but of a variety of possibilities for individual and group training.

Where special facilities are required for physical or psychological treatment it is necessary for the school to be sited near a town. In general, the principle of variety applies to work, leisure, and outside contacts as well as to what happens in the school. Outside situations are equally good for testing-out, but much less controllable. Outside work is useful for some boys, and very valuable for girls, who tend to be limited to the domestic arts (girls' schools are considered separately in the final chapter). Outside youth clubs and other community activities offer a wide range of additional contacts. Most schools already have extensive links of this kind with the local community.

WORK AND LEISURE

A special word needs to be said about work. Work takes up the majority of the time in intermediate and senior schools (although the schoolroom remains a key factor in the training), just as schooling does in junior schools. Some 75 per cent of the approved school population is in intermediate and senior schools, so that preparation for work is desirable. For some boys, work undertaken in the schools is primarily to train them for a trade or to teach them skills which might subsequently be useful. For most, however, the real point is the type of social situation work provides, where demands are made and instructions must be carried out in order to produce something. One often hears staff members say that a boy has been put with a particular instructor because it is good for him, but one never feels that the work available has been planned with the training situations it produces as a primary factor. Some jobs involve teams working together; others, individual work; some entail constant contact with an instructor; others, very little. It would no doubt be considered spendthrift to have two small woodwork shops, sharing machinery, under two instructors, rather than one big one under one instructor, but the former arrangement would provide an opportunity for an extra and different group experience. The literature on the social psychology of industry is full of examples of different social situations produced by the type of work, the size of the working group, and the attitude of the foreman, but it does not seem to have penetrated to approved schools, or indeed to any correctional institution known to me.

Work is a traditional article of faith in the credo of those who run reformative institutions. Idleness is obviously bad, and work has the advantage of introducing a boy to a trade. Apprenticeships can be found for some approved school leavers, particularly in the building trades. Some work there must be, but care must be taken not to elevate it into a fetish. There is a strange belief abroad that somehow or other good work habits are inculcated in a boy by means of regular hard work. For an uncomplicated, but lazily brought-up boy this might be so; but the average approved school boy is by no means uncomplicated, and his failure to work, either in school or in industry, is symptomatic of his difficulties. Boys work wonderfully well in the carrot-and-stick atmosphere of the institution, but this is no indication that they will do the same once the incentives it provides are removed.

The discipline of work is not to be despised, but in an institutional atmosphere it is an opportunity for testing progress rather than a training for what may happen outside, much as one needs to provide this in suitable cases. Attitudes to work and behaviour at work are part of a boy's reactions to the general institutional situation, and from them are to be deduced something about his personality, bearing in mind always the pressures generated by the institution. There is no particular virtue to be derived from spectacular finished products – pedigree herds, new buildings, ornamental gates, and beautifully executed bits of painting – though they may be valuable if they have given a sense of achievement to the boys concerned. It does not necessarily follow, however, that they will be valuable in this way and, in many respects, badly organized work, which permits low standards within the boy's range of achievement, and gives him the opportunity to take his own line and make his peace with working standards and objectives, fulfils a much more useful function than the production of the kinds of objects that impress visitors – and, sad to say, boards of managers. In a very real sense in approved schools, the approach to work is educational, and, though it is not necessary to go all the way with those reformers who believe in passivity until the boy himself chooses work in preference to chaos, there is much to be learned from them about devising means of making work worth while to the boy himself. What is a botched job to the craftsman can be an introduction to the satisfactions of labour to his pupil.

Much the same kind of comment can be made about leisure activities as about work. The mechanics of sport and sportsmanship in an approved school are more significant than the achievements. Who picks a team, how it is picked, and who does not get on it are often as indicative of the lines of influence in the community of boys as of prowess in the field. Similarly, good and bad sportsmanship should be seen in the context of the individual boy and his needs. Club activities may often stimulate interests which needed to be stimulated, or create interests where none existed; but the awakening of interests is not in itself an end: it is a further means to knowledge of a boy or in a process of persuasion. The possession of a variety of talents among the staff is essential to create links through common interests, but someone must be able to work with and through the links from a knowledge of the whole boy.

PUNISHMENT

Another issue needing special attention is that of punishment. Punishment is one way of solving a problem, that of the disruptive influence of the rule-breaker. One of the essential points to remember about small residential communities is that everything is public, and in this type of community particularly, and in all communities to a greater or lesser extent, the question of how rules are to be maintained is of primary concern. There appears to be very little question in most schools that authority must, in the last resort, be imposed by the staff, but it is equally well understood by both staff and pupils that it is sanctioned by public opinion, as indeed it is outside. There is a necessary basis of security in the maintenance of law and order, and an understanding of this is implicit in the actions of most boys and girls in the schools. When this tacit agreement does not exist, and there are some small senior girls' schools where it is imperfectly and intermittently accepted by the girls, life becomes exceptionally difficult and unpredictable for everybody.

A certain amount of punishment, therefore, is implicit in the fact that the school is an organized community. It does not follow that the punishment should be applied by the staff, and there are some progressive schools outside the approved school system in which it is administered by a school council. The nature of the approved school population would make this a difficult operation, however; and fear of untoward consequences which might redound upon the system as a whole makes it an impossible proposition. Thus the staff are left in the position of sole arbiters and dispensers of punishments of all kinds. It is therefore most desirable that the great majority of the boys and girls in the school should have at least a feeling that the staff are honest and impartial, and at best a real degree of trust in them.

Punishment implies both rejection and acceptance: rejection of the transgression and continued acceptance of the boy. It is easy to put this concept over in one's own family where the emotional bonds are strong, but much more difficult to do so in any kind of institution – especially one for people who have, in most cases, been committed to it because they have been in conflict with authority, and many of whom have, in addition, distorted attitudes towards authority derived from unusual and stressful situations in childhood.

It is for this reason that formal punishment is best avoided wherever possible in institutions – by adroit handling of the situation in some other way. The real issue is whether the behaviour concerned is intended as a challenge that needs to be met for the sake of maintaining the law and the security that derives from it, for the sake of the boy himself, or for both these reasons. The expertise lies in the ability to make a rapid appraisal of the whole situation, and to side-step the direct challenge without losing face. The boy who refuses to work can be heavily punished; alternatively, he can be told to stand by himself doing nothing until he joins in, without anything being said, from sheer boredom. The boy who is untidy can be coerced by manipulation of the pressures of either

o

competition or ridicule. Anyone who works in an approved school could produce strings of examples of how to do this sort of thing in different situations.

Thus, to a considerable extent, the nature and amount of punishment in a school reflect the skill of the staff in handling the incidents that tend to give rise to punishment. To have recourse to punishment is not disastrous, since one cannot avoid using it altogether, but it is in a real sense a defeat, for it means that the situation has been dealt with by force. This may have been the only feasible course to take, for a calculated use of force is often unavoidable in a society where there are disturbing elements, but to employ force is easy, whereas its effects are difficult to predict, and by no means always what one hopes. There are more ways of 'standing up' to the boys and making it clear that they must 'toe the line' than by walloping them, and most of the other ways are preferable in a closed community where every action has widespread, and often distorted, repercussions.

Observations of this kind would be generally accepted, though rarely clearly formulated, in the schools. There is less agreement about what should be done when serious threats are made to the stability of the community. These are sometimes the result of bad handling on the part of the staff (which seems to have been largely the case at Carlton[1]), and sometimes a particularly difficult boy or girl may be the source of the trouble. There is a very strong feeling among heads of schools that they ought to be able to deal with any situation that arises in their school, or with any boy or girl assigned to them, with the minimum of recourse to the cane or to the detention room. It is basically sound to feel that the schools ought to be entirely open and without the trappings of punitive detention, even on a small scale, but it is a pity that this sentiment is carried to the extent of believing that *every* school should *always* be able to cope, no matter what happens, and that it is a defeat and a criticism if it cannot. This really derives from failing to see one's own school as part of an organized system of schools, operating as a whole.

It is one of the dangers of the new classification scheme that it may help to foster such attitudes, which are at the basis of the resistance to closed blocks in any shape or form. It is understandable that there should be a feeling that a closed block in a particular school would greatly change the nature of that school, but it is difficult to see why there should be any objection to consigning a boy or girl to a closed block attached to a classifying school for a cooling-off period, followed by reallocation or return – now apparently the official policy. This is

[1] See the report of the inquiry into disturbances at Carlton approved school (Home Office, 1959).

done in the borstal system with excellent effect. It is, indeed, a corollary of small institutions and intensive individual work that things can go wrong – not on the scale of the Carlton disturbances, but to a degree that makes it necessary to take a breather and start again. In fact, the more positive and more searching the type of work done, the greater the danger of occasionally stirring up critical situations that are best handled by temporarily removing someone from the scene. If one takes into account in addition the tendency, already discussed, to consign to approved schools those who cannot be held elsewhere, it is hardly surprising that serious difficulties may sometimes arise.

The Carlton report recommended heroic measures, which were subsequently incorporated in the Criminal Justice Act, 1961, as summarized on p. 20 above. The power to send to borstal is probably useful; previously it was necessary to prove an offence before a court had power to send to borstal an offender of the appropriate age. It remains much more difficult, however, to transfer an offender *to* borstal than to transfer him *from* borstal (or prison) to approved school, which can be done by the Home Secretary under section 58 of the Children and Young Persons Act, 1933. The reason is, no doubt, that committal to borstal is regarded as a much more severe punishment than committal to approved school, although in practice there is little to choose between an open borstal at the lower end of the age scale and a senior approved school.

The power to remove a boy is obviously a panic measure, and just as obviously ought not to be used. It derives from the attitudes criticized above, that heads cannot see themselves as units in a system and cannot accept removal through a closed reclassification unit. It is now settled policy that such units should be provided at boys' classifying schools, and this provision will facilitate the removal of individual boys before the unrest they are causing has reached a critical point. If their departure does no more, it gives time for some regrouping of alliances among the children at the school, and for a general period of recuperation; it may also lead to another placing where the boy has a further chance to start again. It is a common experience in borstals that boys thus reclassified often do very well elsewhere. There are no figures available, but it is my strong impression that transfers between schools are very few, and returns to the classifying centre are certainly low.

There does not seem to be any prospect, at the time of writing, of similar facilities for girls. There is a greater danger here of clogging, owing to the large number of difficult senior girls; on the other hand, girls' senior schools are mainly very small, so that a troublesome girl can be highly disruptive. Periods of removal are therefore more necessary for girls than for boys. Under the 1961 Act, the school must agree to take the girl back if required.

If this system works as it should, section 15 of the Act will be a dead letter, as indeed it should be. It is silly in the extreme that an approved school boy or girl should be liable to be removed by the police to a police cell for misconduct, when this cannot be done to a borstal boy or a prisoner. The fact that it has happened is a measure of the insularity of approved school heads and managers, and of failure on the part of the Home Office.

THE LINK WITH THE FAMILY

An unfortunate aspect of classification is that many boys are placed in schools some distance away from their homes. Even under the new system, this will continue to happen with a number of boys. It increases the difficulties of visiting, even though help towards fares is often available and special arrangements are made for parents who come a long distance. In some ways approved schools are better off than some other correctional institutions, for although the children do not get school holidays, they get thirty-three days a year, of which not more than sixteen are normally to be taken at one time, and it is common to have home leave three times a year. (A school 'holiday', in which the whole school goes away, is also usually arranged.) There is no restriction on letters either way, except that they are read to prevent misinformation likely to upset parents and to cushion the shocks sometimes contained in parents' letters. The Rules state that boys must be encouraged to write to their parents at least once a month and that stamps must be provided; in fact, letter-writing is generally more frequent than this. There is no control, either, apart from considerations of convenience and of what is best for a boy, as regards the number of visits or the person who visits. Usually a school has regulations about what may be sent in, but these again are a question of what can sensibly be accepted and the limitations are few. There is therefore plenty of opportunity for keeping in touch with home and family.

Classification may also make it difficult for the school staff to visit the boys' homes, and the visiting often has to be carried out by an aftercare officer; a few schools in built-up areas employ their own social workers.

The main difficulties here concern to what extent and in what ways it is possible to work with the family. Removing a child from home may or may not relieve a difficult situation – in most beyond control cases it obviously does. It may be the best course to work with the home and to keep the child right out of it, but unless the worker concerned already has a good relationship with the home it is rather difficult to see what motivation there might be for the family to work with him. Where losing the child has been a shock to the parents and there is some feeling of guilt, perhaps it can be used as a lever; but, for many families, losing the child for a period is to a greater or lesser degree a relief and his return is not necessarily welcomed. It is very doubtful whether we have thought about this problem at all clearly or made a real attempt to tackle it. Lip service has been paid to the phrase 'aftercare begins when the child goes in' but nobody has ever had time to do it properly; as long as aftercare remains an additional burden upon people otherwise occupied, and is the responsibility of heavily understaffed services, it will never be carried out adequately. The best that can be done is to keep in touch with the family, allay any fears they may have about the school, and assess whether the child ought to go back home.

The aftercare period is dealt with in the next section, but it is perhaps appropriate to say here that there is some doubt, at least in my mind, whether we have a sufficient range of methods of dealing with child-family relationships. In particular, there is no way of partially relieving a family of the care of a child, with the object of lightening the load, while keeping the problem sufficiently on the boil to try to solve it. When one takes a child right away from home one changes the situation radically. If relationships between child and family have reached breaking-point, then removal is the proper action. But there are cases where things are by no means so bad, yet they are bad enough to need some relief. We have tried to solve this problem with probation homes and hostels, but these still involve complete removal of the child, usually a long distance away, for a period. It may not be out of place, therefore, to suggest another possible solution: the day approved school.

It may surprise some people to know that the last day industrial school did not close until 1934. During most of the nineteenth century there were a variety of day schools, sometimes called truant schools, sometimes day industrial schools. They began to decline at the end of that century because their functions had been very largely those of feeding children in need and of dealing with truancy cases which were usually a consequence of poverty. The Departmental Committee of 1896 commended these schools, but the Committee of 1913 noted that they had declined in number from twenty in 1896 to twelve, with an average attendance of about 2,000.

The tasks that these schools undertook are no longer current, but we might consider the idea of a special form of day school for another purpose. If there are day schools for the educationally subnormal and for the maladjusted, why not similarly for approved school children? It is true that the latter would be unlikely to attend them for most of their school life, as ESN children generally do, but there is considerable variation in the period of attendance among children at schools for the maladjusted. A day school for approved school children would need to be linked either with a hostel or with an ordinary type of residential approved school, so that if necessary a child could be withdrawn from home entirely for a longer or shorter time. It would also need to have its own social worker, or some special link with a social worker in another service. In this way the school could work with the boy in his family setting, removing him when things got too difficult and putting him back when they were more favourable. It would provide distinct advantages in the case of a fit person order, in that the boy would be throughout in an institution specially adapted to his needs. A day school of this kind might be set up experimentally in one of the big towns, and the relevant courts could then, when committing a boy to an approved school, express the wish that he be tried out at the day school. It is at least worth trying.

AFTERCARE

The organization and problems of aftercare have been discussed above (Chapter 4) in a general way, and they must now be examined in more detail. It has already been pointed out that there are some advantages in having a variety of agencies available for aftercare services, and in any case most of the criticism has been directed at the welfare officer system, which entailed very heavy caseloads. Alternative solutions were to expand the welfare officer system to a large degree so that it provided a proper coverage of trained workers with caseloads of reasonable size in the main centres of population, or to let this system run down and transfer the responsibility for aftercare to other agencies, primarily the probation service. The approved schools – both managers and staff – urged the Ingleby Committee to take the former course, pointing to the excessive loads currently carried by the probation service and the shortage of probation officers, and the shortage of staff in children's departments also. The Committee, however, was impressed by the difficulties of providing an overall service of welfare officers, and argued, furthermore, that the officers were isolated from the other social services and that it was difficult to supervise their work. It therefore concluded that the system ought to be run down.

Neither of these arguments seems very convincing. Both, in fact, derive from the reluctance of the Home Office to run anything itself.

Welfare officers were attached to particular schools and they worked in almost complete isolation, with no attempt by anyone to bring them together. Had they been sited in large towns they would have had easy contact with other social workers in the same fields, and their companionship and support. It is difficult to understand why the Home Office could not pay for office space, but perhaps this is merely a reflection of the fifteen years of hesitation about what to do with this service. If the service were expanded and there were several officers in each large centre, it would be easy to appoint seniors and a chief officer. Thus the criticisms about isolation and supervision could have been as easily met by expanding the service as by running it down. Furthermore, the very high caseloads could have been avoided: the number of cases referred is entirely up to the schools, and if they had used other services more they could have reduced the load on the welfare officers.

As noted in Chapter 4, the Advisory Council on the Treatment of Offenders confirmed the recommendation that the service should be run down (Home Office, 1963a), and this recommendation has been implemented, much as the schools dislike it. Since, however, there will be increasing concentrations of boys in schools near their homes, it may well be that the welfare officers will be replaced by school social workers, a number of whom exist already in schools in or near large towns.

We are here concerned with the job itself, rather than with its staffing. The most obvious aspect of the work is that of the transition from the institution to the outside world. The shock of release is cushioned by home leave and frequent parental visiting, whenever these are appropriate; nevertheless, the residential school is not home, however much it may be run on family group lines. Several schools have put up discharge houses, or have a detached house in the grounds where a small number of boys and girls can live prior to their release, comparatively free from the restrictions that must be the accompaniment of school life and close supervision. This experience provides something of a test of whether the child is responsible enough to be discharged, but it is not a very satisfactory one, with the carrot of discharge so near to the end of his nose. However, this approach seems generally very sensible and will, no doubt, be more widely developed.

Perhaps pre-discharge houses will also contribute in some degree towards what is undoubtedly the most difficult problem in all aftercare, the problem of the homeless. It is thought that 10–20 per cent of all discharges are homeless, and they constitute a tremendous task. Briefly, there are four possible solutions: foster homes, hostels, lodgings, residential work. Which is appropriate is a matter for decision in the individual case, but availability of facilities will also affect the issue.

Approved schools have a long history of fostering, probably longer than that of the poor law guardians, who preceded the children's departments in many of their functions, and whose powers in respect of boarding-out were very limited until the end of the nineteenth century. We are beginning to appreciate that fostering is a difficult art requiring a lot of skill, and it seems advisable that it should be left to children's departments except where it can and should be done near the school. The arrangements under section 6 (4) of the Children Act, by which an approved school discharge can be taken into care, are difficult to operate because of the clash of responsibilities, but informal arrangements may work equally well.

Fostering is likely to be more appropriate for the younger child. Those above school age are more capable of standing on their own feet, given a certain amount of help and supervision. Lodgings need to have some element of care and mothering about them, and careful selection and close supervision are required. Similarly, residential employment – a common solution for girls who have illegitimate babies and wish to keep them – is fraught with danger and can very easily fail. A certain number of boys are placed out from schools in the country on near-by farms: this can be a very good solution, especially for those who are of low intelligence, provided, of course, that exploitation can be avoided.

The village of Sabden in Lancashire offers an interesting example of what can be done in this way. In the First World War the owners of the cotton mill with which the village is associated were persuaded to take in some boys from an approved school, and it gradually became a tradition that the mill would employ and find lodgings for such boys. A number of them settled there and have married into the community, and there is thus a strong basis for accepting the scheme in the village. Nowadays the boys are accommodated in what can be regarded as either an extension of lodgings or a small hostel. There are two houses with a communicating door, in one of which lives the 'landlady' or 'warden', whichever one prefers, and in the other, five or six boys. The boys are carefully selected by the approved school welfare officer, who supervises the arrangements and visits regularly. They appear to be good prospects who, nevertheless, have been rejected by their homes for some reason or other. Inevitably, difficulties do arise and have to be dealt with by the welfare officer. About half of the boys go home eventually, and the rest set up on their own, a few staying on in Sabden. The success of this scheme seems to derive from a long tradition of acceptance on the part of the local community and the school management and from the special situation of the industrial village. Selection is also a vital factor.

The experience of Sabden sheds some light on the question of hostel provision. It is virtually impossible to find suitable lodgings for numbers of children, owing to enuresis and other difficulties. The alternative is to put them into hostels, but such hostels as have been tried have been found particularly difficult to run. Of hostels solely for ex-approved school children, the following problems have been reported: despite all efforts, there is a great deal of trouble with bad timekeeping, irregular work, stealing, absconding, and so on; the stay in the hostel tends to be regarded as an extension of the approved school 'sentence' and is therefore resented; the local police and sometimes the people in the neighbourhood regard the children with suspicion; the children resent the limitation on their pocket money in that it puts them at a disadvantage with their friends (most hostels insist that they save money as well as pay for their board). Those who go to hostels tend to be, of course, a severely maladjusted group who find it as difficult to settle in a hostel as anywhere else; a high staff ratio is therefore essential.

The Association of Headmasters, Headmistresses and Matrons of Approved Schools, from whose pamphlet the above information is drawn,[1] recommend an increased number of hostels run by children's committees (the necessary powers exist under the Children Act, 1948), which could take a variety of children, including those discharged from approved schools. This would hardly solve the problem facing the approved schools, however, in view of its size, and also because it is likely that only a small proportion in any hostel could be ex-approved school, or, indeed, seriously disturbed children from any source. An extension of the hostel system by children's departments would need to be supplemented by a system of special hostels for the backward and for the maladjusted (or for both together) run by health departments. The National Association for Mental Health, for instance, has two hostels for ESN school-leavers, one for boys and one for girls, both in London, and one could envisage a considerable extension of specialized hostels of this kind. The basic problem is, again, that of cost and staffing, and one is impelled to suggest that more could be done in the way of finding suitable lodgings. We have not really addressed ourselves fully to the need to give support and backing to both the landlady and the foster mother. Somerset children's department, for instance, produces a magazine especially for its foster mothers and arranges tea-parties and talks for them. In a world of professional social workers it would be a pity if we lost sight of the professional duty of cheering and arming the good-hearted.

One could describe at length the tasks of the individual aftercare

[1] Technical Sub-committee Monograph No. 2, *Aftercare in approved schools*, 1952, p. 20.

worker: completing forms, reporting, handling cases, and so on; but these have to be seen in the context of a total system. It would be otiose, and possibly even misleading, to try to put forward detailed procedures until a viable system is established, with built-in supervision, and has time to develop a life of its own and to examine its own problems. The real need is for well-trained workers who can solve their own problems; not for advice.

I I

A planned system?

Is there really anything that could be called an organized system of schools? On the face of it, the 'system' consists of a large number of separate units, each owned and operated by its managers, whoever they are; and the Home Office has no hesitation in making use of this concept, when it suits it to do so. At one point in the debates on the Criminal Justice Bill, Mr Renton, the Parliamentary Under-Secretary to the Home Office, justified a proposal (subsequently passed) to produce an annual statistical report and a general report every four years (as against reports from six to ten years apart) by saying that the Home Office does not run its own institutions as the Prison Department does (the latter issues an extremely detailed annual report). He failed to comment upon the point made by a previous speaker that the Ministry of Education, which does not run the schools, nevertheless produces a very full annual report. The argument is, of course, nonsensical. Under the Rules very little can happen without reference to the inspectorate, and the Home Office could easily issue a monthly report if it wanted to. The decisive factors are time, staff, and the amount of information the Home Office is prepared to publish. It is reluctant, for instance, to publish details of punishments, though these appear regularly in the Prison Department reports.

There are clearly strong elements of organization, of which the most obvious is the system of classification. Once an approved school ceases to be a local centre taking all the cases in one area, as ESN schools tend to be, and its intake, like that of other schools, is determined according to a wider agreed scheme of distribution, then it begins to be seen as a unit in a general plan. And if there is to be an overall plan of organization and it is to work successfully, someone must operate it, or it will fall apart. Thus we have Home Office inspectors acting as middle management, the children's department of the Home Office acting as top management, and politicians appearing occasionally in the role of directors of the company.

Yet the analogy is not a good one, for the separate units are in fact owned and, if in a restricted way, managed by independent bodies, and the staff are not employed by and cannot be directed by the central body.

Thus the organization has some features of a centralized system, and some of a locally managed system. Indeed, it is reminiscent of the relation between the Department of Education and the local education authorities: independent local entities firmly 'guided' by a central body which provides a substantial part of their income on current account and controls their capital outlay. Local education authorities, however, are elected bodies, controlling large numbers of schools and employing large staffs. They are not small individual units, run by a variety of committees, mostly non-elected, and employing very few people.

Any assessment of the approved school system must not start from a series of *a priori* ideas. There is no particular virtue in either central or local control as such. Nor is the question of local democratic control relevant. For great authorities controlling the lives of thousands it is very pertinent, but it is of little consequence for an individual school so long as there are some safeguards built into the system, as there are in approved schools. Furthermore, there does not seem to be much point, so far as local representation is concerned, in an elected body from one district running a school to which boys and girls are sent from a wide area. It happens in other cases, of course, but incidentally, and there is clearly no particular connexion with the local electors. When an authority deals with a wider area, the tendency is for it to be appointed, as in the health service or the nationalized industries. A joint board for an approved school, based upon the areas from which the pupils come, would be an unwieldy instrument indeed.

In attempting to determine the best balance of relationships for the running of the schools, two preliminary considerations must be kept in mind. In the first place, the system is there, and, whatever its deficiencies, it is a going concern with a long tradition. If anything is to be done, it must be upon the basis of what has already been done. Second, any changes must, on the one hand, enhance the general efficiency and freedom of action of the individual school and, at the same time, ensure the greatest benefits from regional and central administration. As general propositions these are eminently general, but they serve as a starting-point. And at least they demonstrate that the crucial question is not so much who is to control the schools, locally or centrally; but what the balance of local-central control ought to be.

The range of possibilities is wide. At one end is the example of the Prison Department, our first nationalized industry (if one excludes the poor law on the grounds of the elected Boards of Guardians), dating from 1877 and, until 1964, despite its great growth, as centralized as ever. Perhaps the nearest analogy to the approved school system is the borstal system, which, though smaller, is likewise based upon differentiated units welded together by classification. At the other end are the approved schools as they used to be – independent entities controlled only by regulation and by infrequent inspection by an inadequately staffed inspectorate. And in the middle are a variety of possibilities, including the current arrangement, which is untidy, and dependent upon that peculiarly British (and Dutch) facility for operating illogical administrative compromises with a reasonable degree of efficiency and without any wish to make them tidier and more logical. It is not necessarily to be condemned or praised on this account.

What are the advantages of central direction? The obvious one is the possibility of the creation of some sort of 'system'. It was argued previously that there are virtues in classification, and that these grow in proportion to the difficulty of the problems of treatment and training with which one is faced. Furthermore, a centralized organization can facilitate the movement of staff, to give them broader experience, to solve difficult staff problems, and to meet emergencies; it can more easily alter the tone of an institution, and more efficiently decide on the opening and closing of institutions (there is no reason why a central body should have any more trouble than anyone else in convincing local residents of the relative harmlessness of a correctional institution). One cannot conceive, for instance, of a central body allowing the girls' classifying school for half of England to close down, as has in fact happened. A centralized organization is usually also better placed to cope with staff recruitment and training, and to ensure reasonably high salary scales. (Consider what the Prison Department pays completely unqualified assistant governors and governors!)

On the other hand, there is always the danger of excessive centralization. One can move staff around too frequently, to their disadvantage and that of the institution. One can insist too rigidly upon conformity to a pattern either in the organization of training or in administrative arrangements, and in so doing deter initiative and originality in devising new methods.

In general, though, these disadvantages are outweighed by the deficiencies of an unorganized collection of individual units. The latter is simply not appropriate to the nature and complexity of the work, which demands a staff of high quality sustained by careful training and a plentiful supply of information. The advantage of the local institution is that links with the parental home may more easily be maintained, but this is often offset in practice by inadequacy of staffing and by the size of institution required for a large community. Good local contacts can as easily be achieved by a centrally operated as by a locally operated institution.

It might, then, be concluded that the best solution would be some form of decentralized administration, whatever the position in regard to the ownership of the schools. Thus we might have:

1. Central ownership and control with regional administration under
   (a) an Approved Schools' Department, or
   (b) a Young Offenders' Department, assuming combination of all or some part of the borstal and approved school systems, or
   (c) the present Prison Department.

2. An improved version of the current system, in which the present inspectors' regions would be recognized as decentralized management units and suitable powers delegated to them. There would be no change of ownership under this alternative.

Central ownership and control with regional administration

There is much to be said for centralizing the approved school system in one of the ways suggested above, and the 1965 White Paper advocates development along these lines. There is no reason at all why a central body should be in a worse position in relation to the possibility of interchange between approved schools and special schools. Such a move would, of course, be the natural extension of increased Home Office control, and it would be comparatively simple to run the system in a decentralized way, if necessary, basing much of the administration on the existing regions. This would turn the managers into advisory bodies, which they already are to a large extent, and release the inspectors from the pretence that they are inspecting. It would also greatly facilitate the handling of staff problems, the carrying-out of policies concerned with classification, whatever form they may take, and the raising of standards generally.

The Prison Department already has what is in effect a Youth Section, headed by the director of borstal training, who also deals with young prisoners and detention centres. It might well be considered advisable, however, if most of the approved school system is merged with the borstal system (junior approved schools would presumably become part of the special school system), to have a separate Young Offenders' Department, not necessarily with the same upper age limits. If this is too large a pill to swallow, there could just as easily be an Approved Schools' Department dealing with the present schools. The advantage of combining borstal and most of the approved school system would be the increased range of institutions for the middle range of the age-groups covered, and thus the possibility of running the whole system on a regional classifying and administrative basis similar to that of the present approved school system, under a separate Youth Authority. This would not prevent some distinction between age-groupings, as there is formally at present in approved schools, and informally in borstals. It would greatly improve the range of classification facilities, would reduce the chances of over-centralized control in borstals, and increase the efficiency of operation of the schools.

Now that the minimum age for sentence to borstal has gone down to 15, there is considerable overlap with the age-groups sent to senior approved schools. There is no way of determining whether younger boys committed to borstal are substantially different from those of the same age sent to senior approved schools. On the whole, the courts tend to feel that a borstal sentence is a more severe punishment, and, of course, it is imposed by a higher court, not by a magistrates' court; but there may be little relation between the problem presented by the offender when he gets into the institution and the seriousness of his offence.

It is generally believed that a stigma attaches to borstal as compared with approved schools. It is extremely difficult to say how true this is, and how far it is a question of age. People are inclined to be more sympathetic towards young people of school age than towards those above it, and the fact that approved schools are called 'schools' may well be a help here. (I am, incidentally, very much against the name 'borstal', which, like 'convict', tends to stick in the mind. The term 'youth training centre' put forward in the 1965 White Paper is much better.) Even so, senior approved schools certainly, and intermediate schools to a considerable extent, are hardly 'schools' as we usually think of them, but much more training centres. On the other hand, it was suggested in the Carlton report (Home Office, 1959) that the term 'school' caused resentment in older boys. The alternatives proposed by Mr Durand, however – 'registered residential training centre' or 'registered training institute' – are not very suitable.

Less radical solutions would be either to transfer the younger age-group in borstal to the Approved Schools' Department or to merge the senior approved schools with the borstal system. The former would affect perhaps 10 per cent of borstal boys and very few girls, but there seems no advantage in terms of organization. The latter would seriously affect the approved school system since the senior schools contain about a third of the boys and half of the girls. If the 1965 White Paper proposals are followed and the junior and intermediate schools go to local authorities, this would, of course, be the end of the present system.

The Carlton report recommended committal to 'residential training' of those aged 15–17, without specifying approved school, borstal, or detention centre. This entails a difficulty so far as detention centres are concerned because the delay in classifying would materially add to the sentence (an extra three weeks, plus any waiting-time in the remand home or elsewhere, on a sentence lasting ten or twenty weeks), but it might be an appropriate procedure for some cases. There would be considerable advantages if such a system could be worked out, but the administrative problem of keeping staff in one type of classifying centre abreast of the situation in the other is formidable, especially since one side is organized regionally and the other nationally.

Against central ownership is the whole tradition of approved schools as independent units, and the fact that they are very largely staffed by teachers who think in terms of the education service. These are not insuperable objections if there are strong enough reasons for making a radical change. The poor law was centralized because of the spread of indiscriminate giving of outdoor relief, the prisons because of complaints that the local ratepayer was paying for a national responsibility, the hospitals because the voluntary hospital system was in great difficulties, the coal industry because it was in a mess, and electricity, gas, and transport partly from utilitarian and partly from doctrinaire motives. Similarly, the National Assistance Board came into existence in 1934 as the Unemployment Assistance Board because there did not seem to be any other satisfactory way of paying out government funds to help the unemployed who were not entitled to benefit. Whether there is a compelling case for radical changes in the approved school system on the grounds of increasing efficiency is highly debatable. However great the attraction of a tidily organized system, there are bound to be strongly held views on the other side.

Improved regional control, with or without change of ownership

We must therefore consider a structure involving both central and local control, with ownership of the schools retained by an authority other than a central body or a government department. Local control does not necessarily mean local authority control, but counties and county boroughs are the obvious authorities to consider first; moreover, since many approved schools do in fact deal with children of school age and all are staffed largely by teachers, it is inevitable that one should think in terms of the education system.

No one was more likely to think in terms of the Education Act, 1944, than its author R. A. Butler, Home Secretary at the time of the passing of the Criminal Justice Act, 1961, or Chuter Ede, who was his second-in-command on the earlier occasion and one of the leading opposition members in 1961. In fact, Butler said explicitly during the report stage in the Commons that he had contemplated reform on the lines of the Education Act, but that it was not practicable 'in view of the nature of approved schools'. It is doubtful if he meant that the schools might be taken over by the local education authority, but his line of thought could not have been far off that expressed in the major opposition amendment, which wanted local authority representation of one-third upon all local committees (except in schools run by large-scale voluntary bodies) and all schools to be brought under local authority supervision. This proposal is clearly based upon the provisions of the Education Act, 1944, in respect of voluntary schools, which has the same effect, although presumably it would be children's committees and not education committees that would exercise the supervision over approved schools. The exclusion of the national voluntary bodies was probably to avoid being accused of attacking institutions run by religious communities, especially Roman Catholic organizations.

This idea could hardly be more misconceived. In the first place, the situation is radically different from that of the voluntary schools at the time of the Education Act. There the problem was how to provide the voluntary schools with enough money to bring them up to standard, without taking them over completely, and local authority representation was partly a matter of bringing them under the aegis of the local education authority whose job it was to plan school provision, and partly a means of ensuring some measure of control in the usual way over the money to be spent by that authority. There is no financial problem of this kind in approved schools, but in any case, if an equivalent system were to be tried, representatives should be appointed by the Home Office and by the County Councils Association and the Association of Municipal Corporations, representing the joint interests of the local authorities who provide the money. At one point in the debate it was suggested that the appointment of local authority representatives would bring the schools into closer relation with other local authority facilities. This is a doubtful advantage, however, since the development of such a relationship depends upon the siting of the school and upon the availability of suitable facilities. It does not seem very likely, for instance, that a boy will be transferred more easily from an approved school to an ESN school which has a long waiting list because there are some local authority representatives on the board of managers; and if it is more likely it certainly ought not to be!

But there is a much more important principle involved. If there is any value in operating approved schools as an integrated system upon a regional basis, the last people one wants to introduce are the local authorities. Not only are local authorities notoriously bad at operating

P

regional arrangements, but they are extremely resistant to direction from above. There is a clause in the 1961 Act under which the Secretary of State may give directions to the managers of approved schools upon any matters relating to premises and equipment; the number and grades of staff; and the education, training, and welfare of persons under the care of the managers (section 18). This led to an outburst of violent indignation in the *County councils gazette*, organ of the County Councils Association, which put up an M.P. to move an amendment, unsuccessfully, to exclude local authorities. The central organizations are more tender in this respect than the authorities they represent, and the County Councils Association than the Association of Municipal Corporations, but local authorities would obviously be less easy to integrate into a general system than the present managing bodies. It is all right while there are few local authority schools, but a lot might create considerable problems for the Home Office. One has only to look at the persistent difficulties with regard to the provision and standard of remand home accommodation, and at the failure of the smaller authorities to provide properly staffed special reception centres for children, to see what problems could occur. Even if the Home Office were to hold on tightly to classification facilities, the need for flexibility would remain, and flexibility is essential in a system which must take those committed to it, without delay, yet has no control whatsoever over the committing authorities.

Local authority operation might well confer some advantages: in terms of efficiency, of greater use of other services, and even of obtaining more money; but one cannot really believe that these would outweigh the loss of the conception of the schools operating together as an interlocked system. Nor can it be argued that putting the schools under local authority control would integrate them into the special school system or with children's homes, and thus greatly enlarge the area over which classification could operate. This is unlikely to happen if the schools remain under the children's department, but it would be equally unlikely to happen if they were under education authorities owing to the restricted amount of overlap between the types of children taken, which would greatly limit the actual area of choice – not to mention the shortage of places in special schools. Indeed, the process ought to be the reverse of this as far as residential schools for the ESN and the maladjusted are concerned. In these spheres the range of choice is much too limited, and as it increases these schools ought to be operated upon a regional classifying basis. They are, in fact, at the present time where approved schools were before the Second World War, with too many separate authorities allocating children to various schools without sufficient knowledge of the schools – though they probably have greater knowledge of the children. As long as only one or two schools are used, or the situation is obscured by an immense shortage of places, which was never the case with the approved schools, the need for classification is hidden, but it undoubtedly exists. One simply cannot provide adequately for a wide range of maladjusted children, for instance, in a limited number of schools unless the schools themselves are highly selective in their intake, or offer only superficial training.

The analogy with the voluntary schools under the Education Act must therefore be rejected; likewise the idea of increased control by local authorities. The 1933 Act laid on local authorities the responsibility for providing new approved school places where necessary, and it seems that the Home Office is currently using this fact to persuade them to establish new schools. One, for girls, has recently been opened, and others are promised. This policy has probably been adopted owing to the difficulty of securing suitable local support, or support from national voluntary bodies, and owing to reluctance upon the part of the Home Office to open a school itself and find local managers. It is, however, a mistaken policy which ought to be changed.

The case for a regional system

The approved school system is large and complex. It is true that it deals only with some 8,000–9,000 children at any one time, but it must embrace the whole country, and they are by definition difficult children, and likely to get more difficult. Furthermore, the system may well become more complex and at the same time more interdependent and integrated, and for the same reason – the need to provide more varied facilities to deal with the range of problems presented; this means, in effect, smaller schools where there are at present large ones, and closed facilities for holding and reallocating disruptive boys and possibly girls.

Because of the geographical and other complexities, approved schools have already developed a regional classification system, although this does not cover every school. The inspectorate, mainly for reasons from the sphere of child care, but partly for approved school reasons, is also regionalized. It would seem sensible to utilize these facts, and they would appear to lead to the following conclusions:

1. Structurally, the present approved school classification and inspectorate systems should be merged, so that there would be regional inspectors for each classifying region, which would then become an administrative area. This would not obviate changes in the type of classification, such as smaller groupings within the area.

The implementation of this proposal would raise some problems, especially if the inspectors are to continue to be employed on child care duties. There is now a strong case for the separation of the two duties, even if this means more inspectors or a new range of officers. The argument for keeping them together is that the approved schools have much to learn from the operation of the residential child care services. These lessons have already produced the idea of the school as a collection of family units, and there is no doubt that a continuing link between the two services would be essential. The initial impetus has, however, been given, and the type of inspector likely to be appointed, and the overall responsibility of the Home Office, are likely to keep it going. It does not necessarily follow that the change suggested above would mean that the staff concerned would work from different places, though sub-offices might be needed. What does seem essential is that each region should have a number of inspectors who are primarily or only concerned with approved schools, under their own regional superintending inspector.

2. In addition to the inspectors there should be in each region a regional officer, with the rank of civil service principal or above, and an appropriate staff. He would be the local representative of the administrative side. There is a similar organization in regional offices of the Ministry of Health, although the functions are different.

3. The regional office should be responsible for the day-to-day operation of the schools, and should have delegated powers. In particular, it should have power, without reference to the central office, to:

    (a) approve dietary scales, daily routine, the schoolroom timetable, and similar detailed provisions under the Rules, and changes in them – in so far as these continue to exist, and they should certainly be pruned;

    (b) organize regional training schemes for all types of staff;

    (c) exercise general control over the flow of boys through the classifying system into the schools (the vacancies pool would be best left to operate centrally), and make recommendations about the types of places required;

    (d) approve transfers between heads of estimates, distribute extra grants, approve capital expenditure up to an agreed figure, and generally consult on the submission of estimates.

4. The regional office should be responsible for forward planning in the light of future needs, and for submitting such plans to the centre.

Presumably there would be other functions also, but the main aim is to put the day-to-day running of the region, and general responsibility for looking at its problems as a whole, into the hands of the regional office, thus removing from the Home Office the immense burden of routine operation. More staff would undoubtedly be required, but I welcome this since I think that the whole system is acutely understaffed from top to bottom. There might be some delays with regard to matters that must go through the regional office to the Home Office, but they could be limited by using a 'copy to the regional office' system where something has to go direct to the centre without requiring any action in the region; on the other hand, many minor things could be dealt with much more speedily.

The primary need is for people with time – and the capacity – to think about the problems of each region as such; and, similarly, for people to think about the problems of the whole system at the centre. The regional superintending inspectors fulfil this duty already to some extent, but their work needs some reorientation and supplementation, as does that of the chief inspector at the centre.

I have left aside the delicate question of who should employ the staff. It would be a major change, and a considerable reduction of the powers of the managers, if the staff were to be employed by the Home Office and directed by the regional office. It is difficult to say how far the staff themselves would object to such an arrangement; there would be some disadvantages, but essentially they would gain.

Failing this very desirable change, however, it would be possible to carry out some improvements without going so far. The Home Office should have power to direct staff to undertake particular work in exceptional circumstances and in the interests of the service – or with some such qualifying phrase. The object of this would be to prevent breakdowns in vital parts of the system, like the closing of the classifying school for girls in the north, and to help to solve any serious staff problems that may arise, as, for instance, when a man has come into conflict with authority in his school and really ought to move. The sisterhood of the National Children's Home can be used in this way and, though this is an unusual body, the principle is good. Directed labour, unless it is drawn from an order of this kind, tends not to be very good labour, and one would hope this would be a reserve power; but it needs to be there in order to be effective. The central and regional offices should do all they can to facilitate a reasonable amount of movement in the system, especially among headmasters and headmistresses, who tend to stay in one place far too long.

One of the somewhat surprising features of the present approved school situation is the reluctance of the Home Office to operate schools. The difference between a school sponsored by the Home Office, and operated and owned by a managing committee got together by it, and a school owned and run by the Home Office is comparatively small, although the latter arrangement is no doubt safer for the Home Office when something goes wrong. Though nominally separate schools under local committees, the classifying schools are as near as could be Home Office schools because of the key role they perform. Yet it seems a great pity that the Home Office is not prepared to try upon its own account to provide special facilities. The result is that badly needed types of school must wait until a body like the National Association for Mental Health (which runs two schools for girls needing psychiatric treatment, one near London and one in the north) or a local authority is interested enough to experiment, or until an existing school changes direction. The Home Office finds premises and organizes the opening of a new school, but it obviously feels that this is not in accord with its image of itself as an inspecting body. Yet surely the overriding consideration is whether a school is needed, not whether the Home Office can continue to pretend that it does not manage the schools. It has been possible to argue in the past that capital considerations prevented the opening of new schools; it is less easy to argue this now.

A regional system along the lines suggested would be equally necessary if the present borstals and some part of the approved school system were merged. The 1965 White Paper mentions only senior approved schools in this connexion, but for the reasons set out previously it is unwise to increase local authority control, and some, if not all, of the intermediate schools ought also to be transferred on the assumption that the creation of family councils will reduce the demand. It would be a retrograde step to hand over a large proportion of the schools to local authorities who are mainly too small to be able to offer a sufficiently diversified range of residential centres. There will, in any case, be at least fifty 'youth training centres' for boys and probably more, and it should be possible to re-gionalize the system either by basing it upon the present classifying schools or by merging the latter with the remand centres.

THE ROLE OF THE MANAGERS

Critical appraisal

It was suggested in Chapter 6 that the position of the managers is one of some difficulty. On the one hand, they are legally responsible for the running of the school and for the care *in loco parentis* of the children committed to it. On the other, they are to a considerable extent in the hands of the headmaster, as the man who really does the job, and of the Home Office, which controls everything that goes on. Thus, looked at in one way they are a governing body, in another way a judicial body (the final arbiters concerning discipline in difficult cases), and in a third way an advisory body peripheral to the line of control from Home Office to headmaster.

The delicacy of the managers' position emerged strongly from the Carlton case. The school correspondent (secretary to the managers) was quoted in *The Times* as saying in evidence: 'It is not the managers' function to interfere with the headmaster in his work'; and although he had seen the boys regularly and asked them questions, he clearly felt that he must accept the headmaster's recommendation for discharge without question. Indeed, the managers of this school had written to the Home Office in November 1954 pointing out that they could not be in direct touch with individual boys and therefore could not assess their progress from their own knowledge. They simply had no means of contesting the headmaster's recommendation from independent knowledge.

One might well ask, therefore, why the managers have the power to authorize discharge. Indeed, when one considers the other functions of the managers, there does not appear to be anything that could not be handled perfectly competently by the headmaster in consultation with the Home Office inspectors. In a similar situation in the prison and borstal services these things are handled directly, and practically the only real function of the visiting committees and boards of visitors is the disciplinary function. To all intents and purposes, the governing committee as a body with real power died in 1877 when the prisons were centralized. A similar process of attrition has practically eliminated the boards of governors in State schools as bodies of any significance.

Yet these attenuated management committees survive and presumably have some purpose. The one that is perhaps most often put forward concerns individual liberty: the board exists as a check; it is a body to which an aggrieved person, either boy or parent, can appeal over the heads of the staff. One finds boards of State schools coming into prominence in certain circumstances – where a child has been heavily caned, for instance, or a girl is sent to school in slacks against the headmistress's wish. It would be interesting to know what proportions of boys in approved schools, or of their parents, in fact complain to boards of managers, and what happens when they do complain. Is the complaint normally handed to the headmaster and the reply drafted by him? For the managing body is not really the best place to go to obtain an

impartial consideration of a case, and this is recognized in many spheres:
consumers' councils in the nationalized industries, tribunals and referees
for income tax and social insurance, mental health review tribunals,
service committees for doctors and dentists. They do not all work very
well, and perhaps we really need an ombudsman in addition to councillors, M.P.s, and tribunals, but at least they indicate recognition of a
problem, and of the need to provide an *independent* body to deal with
complaints. It can be held that the Home Office itself, approached
directly through an M.P., is a more appropriate, though inadequate,
body for coping in these circumstances, since it is at least sufficiently
remote not to be identified with a particular school. And if it is argued
that there are few Archer–Shee cases in public schools, and very
few cases for complaint in State schools or in approved schools, it is
equally arguable that the child in the approved school, since he is so
often there because he has been rejected or neglected by his parents,
needs all the more the watchful eye of some protective but independent
authority.

It is not without relevance, however much it may be claimed that
these were exceptional cases, that both the Standon Farm and the
Carlton reports (Home Office, 1947, 1959) found evidence of irregular
punishments, and the secretary of the National Association of Approved
School Staffs, a deputy at another school, when asked at the Carlton
inquiry if members of his staff cuffed boys, replied: 'I am not going to
say my boys are not sometimes cuffed.' It may be that irregular minor
punishments of this kind do not in practice matter very much; in fact,
it is difficult to believe that they do not occur quite often in ordinary
schools; but there is obviously a danger here of excesses, particularly
with staff as inexperienced and untrained as those often working in
approved schools.

Of the other hand, in the long run the control of this kind of problem
rests with the senior staff of the school and there is no reason to suggest
that the great majority are not perfectly competent, and anxious, to
stand between a boy and any injustice perpetrated by another member of
staff. And it would be quite wrong to infer that serious improprieties are
of frequent occurrence, or that they are glossed over by boards of
managers. The implication here is simply that, while the existence of
the managers is a safeguard against injustice, it is so only to a limited
degree. If the headmaster is prepared to countenance irregularities, or
does not know that they occur, it is unlikely that the managers will
know; and it is doubtful if they would accept the word of a boy or a
parent against that of the headmaster unless there was strong sub-
stantiation; moreover, they are less likely than an independent body to

press a case strongly. Despite these limitations, there remains some safeguard in having in existence a body of persons other than the staff.

A second reason often put forward to justify the managers' existence is that they represent a link with the community. A similar case is made out in respect of boards of visitors of borstals or training prisons. Why do approved schools need links with the community? Nowadays boys and girls go out from most schools at weekends into towns and villages, and are often seen about the countryside in ones and twos or larger groups. They belong to outside clubs of various kinds, attend classes, sometimes attend ordinary schools, go to church, and sometimes help with church and village activities. It may be a help in the organizing of such activities if local people of standing are on the school board, but it hardly seems an important consideration.

As far as the problem of absconding is concerned, much can be done to increase the tolerance of the area by having good contacts, and the wider these are the better. Absconders are sometimes a great nuisance to local people: they tend to steal clothes, bicycles, money, and food. Local people will put up with a lot, however, if they feel that the school is doing a worth-while job; many a bitterly complaining householder has been turned into a staunch supporter after being shown round a school and told what it is trying to do, and something about the kind of boys it has to deal with. An additional advantage of local contacts is acceptance of the staff and their families into the community, a necessity if they are to be happy in their work. Some schools are connected through their boards with a particular community – the Jewish community, or the Roman Catholics – and this also can be very valuable. All the same, most of these links and relationships can well be established, and usually are, by the staff by direct contact, and it is doubtful whether any special committee is required. The local conditions must be taken into account, however, and they may well justify a committee in some areas, although not one with the legal powers of the managers.

Let us now take a closer look at the functions at present exercised by the managers. That of release has already been mentioned and it seems virtually impossible for the managers to carry out their powers adequately. Indeed, this is true of all questions concerning individual boys and their treatment. Headmasters look upon the managers' role as a protective one, for it relieves them of the final responsibility which rests, not with them, but with the managers, who base their decisions upon headmasters' recommendations. This is a pleasant situation for the headmaster, since the managers have no grounds upon which to question his recommendation. It may be argued that the headmaster ought to have to justify himself to an individual or a group of people who have the right to question him, but unless they have a certain amount of expertise, it is extremely difficult for them to ask sensible questions or to disagree except on the basis of personal foible. It may be good for the headmaster for someone to say to him, 'Why do you do that?', but only if that person is not fobbed off with an inadequate explanation or a rationalization, however sincerely adhered to by the headmaster. Obviously the best people to put such a question are the inspectors, and they can also add that the same thing is done differently elsewhere.

This brings up the general problem of expertise among the managers. Headmasters vary enormously, as do chief officers of local authorities with their committees, in what they like to see in their managers. It is only natural that most would like a manageable committee, giving little trouble. But some would welcome social workers or teachers, others would not; some appreciate business experience, whereas others feel it is not relevant; some want a cross-section of the community, others do not. It is not necessarily the worst headmaster who wants, or obtains, a rubber-stamp board, nor the best who has one that is active and interested.

On the whole, however, it is my impression, after questioning a number of heads on this point, that they really do not want people who are sufficiently expert to advise them either upon teaching matters or upon social work practice, though they are less averse to expertise on the business side. If they want advice there are proper channels through which it can be obtained. Nevertheless, a number of teachers, often retired, and a few social workers are members of boards; they presumably use their knowledge with tact, and there seems to be no reason why there should not be a lot more of them. One cannot avoid the impression, however, that the ex-military type, like the Carlton managers, or the local philanthropists and public figures predominate. Some of these may be sensible and helpful, some are not. There is simply no way of telling how capable boards of managers are of addressing themselves to the point and discussing it with good sense – but committees in general are not notably efficient in these respects.

To return to the question of individual treatment, it is difficult to believe that the managers have anything to contribute in this field. Some boards, especially in the more progressive schools, have small case sub-committees which carry out the three-monthly reviews and decide upon release. They are undoubtedly a good institution, and ought to be general if these functions are to continue with managers. One school has an even better procedure, whereby all those concerned in the immediate care of a boy sit with two of the managers as a case subcommittee. In this school the boys are divided among various members of the staff who act as 'parents', and, since they also attend, the managers are very much outnumbered. Indeed, this is really an internal school board, with the addition of two outsiders; a useful arrangement, which reflects the realities of the situation.

In my view, the responsibility for assessing progress, for saying when a boy or girl can be discharged, and for deciding upon recall, can rest only with the staff, and I do not believe that in these issues the headmaster can or should hide behind the petticoats of the managers. If there is need for an appeal it should be to someone who really has the ability to assess the situation and to probe the reasons for the decision, namely the inspector, not to the managers. If it is necessary to maintain the fiction of a legal parent this function should rest in the Home Secretary and be delegated to the headmaster.

When a child is under supervision, control remains legally with the school. Here again the actual functions are exercised by the headmaster, upon the statements of the aftercare agent. Nobody seems to have considered whether there might be advantages in recalling some boys to a different establishment where the pace is adjusted to the short time they are likely to remain there, but if this were the case it might be better for the power of supervision to rest with the central authority.

As a disciplinary body the managers have always had a very limited role, although under the 1933 Rules they can award extra corporal punishment. In practice, it is rarely that the managers exercise judicial powers at all, but they are likely to be consulted in cases of difficulty. Occasionally, boys are brought before the managers for one reason or another, but it is undoubtedly better to avoid anything resembling a judicial procedure. Where a boy has to be removed to another school this can be done by the headmaster, in consultation with the inspectorate, and any question of bringing a boy before a court under the 1961 Act would also be dealt with in this way.

The real justification for the managers is that they own the school, and their central function might be taken to be that of managing its general affairs. Ownership and operation do not necessarily go together, however, and whether each school should be separately owned is itself a matter for argument. But any change in these arrangements must be part of a general pattern, and we have already discussed possible alternatives.

Before summing up on the question of functions of boards of managers we need to take into account the special position of local authority schools. Much of what has been said about the limitations upon the effectiveness of the managers' role applies more forcibly to local authority schools which are under the general eye of the children's officer as well as the inspectors. There is a special reason why a local authority committee acts as managers, and it is the same as for any other local authority committee: that the authority's money is spent under the surveillance of democratically elected councillors who personify public responsibility for running public services. It would be impossible to run a local authority school without being responsible to some council committee, though it need not be direct responsibility as it is at the moment.

All in all, it seems on the face of it that there is not much justification for boards of managers with their present powers. It seems hardly conceivable that any English institution could be run without a committee, though some are. Nor are the problems set out above peculiar to approved schools. Many of the criticisms raised could be levelled against hospital management committees or regional hospital boards, or indeed against government by committee in general. There are, however, interesting differences. Regional hospital boards are appointed by the Minister of Health, and hospital management committees are appointed by the boards; thus the possibility of selection by the hospital itself is limited, though not excluded since someone has to make recommendations. Furthermore, appointments are for a three-year term, although members are eligible for reappointment. Also, there is a requirement for prior consultation with various bodies, which tends to produce a sizeable proportion of nominees. In hospitals, however, unlike approved schools, very large sums of money and the interests of a number of important bodies and professional groups are at stake.

Managers of approved schools sometimes do more or less represent interests, e.g. the vicar in the Anglican school and the priest in the Roman Catholic school, but this is not a significant aspect. For the most part, managers tend to be a somewhat fortuitous collection of people, as when, in the case of some local authority schools, the preference or suitability of the councillor may not be the main consideration for putting him on a particular committee, and co-option may or may not be favoured for reasons unconnected with the needs of the school. Or they may be a self-perpetuating body, the selection of which is influenced partially by the headmaster and largely by the members themselves, with a varying degree of reference to the capabilities of those selected. Indeed, since their role is so equivocal it is difficult to know what their capabilities should be. The impression remains, nevertheless, that, on the whole and with many individual exceptions, managers are not the sort of people who have a great deal to offer to approved schools, and some of them find it difficult to understand their aims and methods; some, indeed, even if they do understand them, are opposed to them as being too soft.

Suggested measures

There are two courses open. One is to take measures to improve the quality of boards of managers; the other is to increase the directness and ubiquity of Home Office control and, gently or roughly, elbow the managers aside by reducing their powers and using them in a largely advisory capacity. The former is being approached by strengthening Home Office control over appointments, limiting the period of appointment, and introducing a retiring age; the latter could be done by redistributing powers and responsibilities so that a greater share would fall upon headmasters and inspectors.

Are we then to continue with the present untidy system? If the 1965 White Paper proposals are accepted, the managers will probably disappear completely in the holocaust. In any case, it seems likely that some of the anomalies will be removed in the near future. Under the 1961 Act the Home Office has power to regulate the constitution and proceedings of the managers (section 19 (1)), other than in a local authority school, and if the 'Secretary of State is satisfied that by reason of special circumstances it is necessary to do so in the interests of the efficient management of the school, he may appoint one or more persons as additional members of the body constituting the managers of the school' (section 19 (3)) although, again, not in a local authority school. It is unfortunate that this latter power does not apply in the case of local authorities, who may refuse to co-opt members on to their committees as a matter of (political) principle. This is another example of the difficulty of operating through local authorities.

In the Commons, on report, Chuter Ede read part of a letter sent him by the Home Secretary, as follows:

> 'I intend that we shall examine the constitution of each committee of management and that in the exercise of powers under Clause 19 (1) we shall provide for the addition of one or more local authority members unless it is clear that the constitution of the Committee already provides a sufficiently broad representation. I must reserve my judgement in exceptional cases, but I should expect the result would be that it will become the normal practice for local authority members to be on the committees of management' (*Hansard*, 12 April 1961, col. 362).

R. A. Butler agreed that this should have read local authority 'representatives' rather than 'members', to make it easier to put children's officers or chief education officers on the committees. Presumably section 19 (3), which gives the same powers 'in special circumstances', will be used only when it is necessary to dismiss a board of managers which has deteriorated badly, despite the review, or in order to avoid a direction under section 18 (1) (which, however, does apply to local authority schools).

There is an even more subtle way of controlling the constitution of the management committee. The Ingleby Committee recommended that every school should have an Instrument of Management laying down 'such things as the composition of the board of management, the procedure for the election of the chairman and other officers, the appointment of subcommittees, arrangements for filling vacancies, the frequency of meetings and the recording of proceedings' (para. 437). This is quite obviously inspired by the arrangements under sections 17–22 of the Education Act, 1944, which lay down that every county and voluntary school must have an instrument providing for the constitution of the body of managers (in primary schools) or governors (in secondary schools). For county schools it is made by order of the local education authority, and for voluntary schools by order of the Minister. In addition, every county and voluntary primary school must have 'rules of management' made by order of the local education authority; and every county and voluntary secondary school must have articles of government, made by the local education authority and approved by the Minister in the case of a county school, or made by order of the Minister in the case of a voluntary school, and these articles must 'determine the functions to be exercised in relation to the school by the local education authority, the body of governors, and the head teacher respectively' (section 17 (3) (b)). These provisions are very similar to some parts of the approved school Rules. The Act goes on to lay down what the proportions of voluntary and education authority governors should be in various types of voluntary school. A typical instrument lays down the constitution and period of appointment of the managers, how often they must meet, what a quorum consists of, how the chairman is to be appointed, and what their powers and duties are both in respect of the general surveillance of the school and in respect of the appointment and dismissal of staff.

These instruments are capable of considerable variation but it is usual for the Ministry to provide models, even for non-maintained schools.[1] Thus a general pattern runs through them. It would be possible, and it seems as if it will be done, to make similar arrangements for approved schools, using, as a general basis, the sections of the Rules that are akin to those in the Education Act, and achieving local variations

[1] Various examples can be found in Alexander and Barraclough (1947).

through Instruments of Management or, where appropriate, trust deeds. It seems very likely that voluntary schools will in this way receive much better constitutions in future.

At the same time, something should be done about the duration of appointment and about retirement. On the latter point the Ingleby Committee has already recommended a retiring age of 75. There is no indication why it did not choose 65, the age of retirement from the juvenile panel, which would seem to be more appropriate on the grounds that managers under the present powers have to make key decisions about individual children. The assumption must be that the Committee thought that the major role of the managers was just general management, in which case 75 is understandable, though hardly logical, being the age at which a magistrate is thought to be past adjudicating at all, presumably owing to loss of faculty. In an ageing population it is perhaps right not to set the retiring age too low, but the decision must be determined by the role the managers are supposed to play. It seems advisable to absolve them of decision-taking upon individual cases and to keep a higher limit (70 rather than 75), provided that some other conditions are fulfilled. There should also be some limitation on the period served by managers, and especially on the term of office of the chairman, to give opportunity for the introduction of new blood.

The question of what the managers or governors are, and whether they are necessary at all, is as valid in respect of ordinary schools as it is with approved schools. Section 20 of the Education Act, 1944, gives local education authorities power to arrange for a single governing body to cover a number of schools, and county, voluntary, primary, and secondary schools can be put together under one such body. Probably against the intentions of the section, and certainly against the wish of the Department of Education, some local authorities have simply made the education committee the governing body of all schools, arguing that there is no real function for local management to perform. In Manchester attempts have been made to get away from this system, which has been in operation since the Act was passed, by grouping schools and appointing governing bodies as was presumably originally intended, but it is extremely difficult to see what useful function they serve. Even if they appoint a headmaster they have to have an inspector of the authority sitting in, really because they can hardly be expected to be able to assess the merits and demerits of applicants for a particular school without advice. Perhaps, however, like other such committees they perform the function of making officials state a case, and this in itself is enough to justify their existence.

This brings us back to the question of whether we want revitalized management committees for approved schools. If they are not going to be allowed to manage without the Home Office dogging their every step, what is the point of them?

PROVISION FOR GIRLS

Girls represent a considerable problem for approved schools, as they do for many institutional systems. The problem is threefold. In the first place, the older girls are often extremely difficult to handle, although to what extent this is inevitable is not very clear; second, the numbers concerned are quite small, which usually means that there cannot be the same variety of institutional provision as is available for boys; third, it is, if anything, even more difficult to obtain and keep suitable staff in girls' schools than in boys'.

Approved schools for girls are in some ways quite well off. There were in 1966 seven schools for juniors (two RC), seven for intermediates (two RC), and nineteen for seniors (three RC). This gives a reasonable spread, especially since one of the junior schools, Princess Mary Village Homes, although it takes eighty girls, in fact consists of eight separate houses with ten girls in each, and the Northumberland Village Homes, the other major junior school, which accommodates ninety, is organized on a similar basis. Most of the senior schools take only twenty-five to thirty girls, and are thus small enough for individual work, although the staffing position rarely allows this. The reason for their size is that they were largely developed out of 'rescue' homes and orphanages – it is not a matter of planning, except in the newer schools.

As can be seen from the figures in Chapter 3, the majority of girls are care, protection, or control cases; furthermore, a good many of those who commit offences are of much the same calibre. The younger girls, even more than the younger boys, are sad rather than bad, and they present few problems. Indeed, it seems a pity that more of them are not dealt with as deprived children by children's departments; presumably this will happen if the 1965 White Paper proposals are carried out.

It is the older girls who constitute the major problem, and there seem to be two main sorts of difficulty. On the one hand, a number of them are prostitutes or near-prostitutes; they like prostitution as a way of life, and they can get more money and more satisfaction out of it than can be offered to them by the school in any shape or form. They have broken completely through the strong social controls that surround and support the lives of most women, and they have found in doing so that they can live in a community which, whatever its drawbacks, accepts them, even if 'respectable' people reject them, as do their families.

In the second place, there are the girls, and they may be the same people, who are highly maladjusted, near psychotic or frankly psychotic, usually with aggressive tendencies, which have made all sorts of other institutions, including mental hospitals, reluctant to deal with them, so that they end up compulsorily committed to an approved school. Such girls are unpredictable and subject to fits of violence when they can become fairly dangerous; they literally do not know what they are doing and may find it difficult or impossible to remember afterwards what has happened. They are almost impervious to lasting emotional relationships, and entirely egocentric.

It is widely held that difficult girls are more difficult than difficult boys, and it is certainly true that the atmosphere in some senior girls' schools appears highly charged even to the casual visitor. However:

'It is commonly said that women are more conscientious than men. The Heads of the boys' schools would say that their feminine colleagues are, at any rate, more prone to worry. It has always been pointed out that, although the girls coming to approved schools are probably a more highly selected (and therefore more difficult) group than the boys, the rates of success are good. Apart from any possible differences between masculine and feminine attitudes, it is obvious that Headmistresses are more emotionally bound up in the situation with which they are dealing. They are for the most part unmarried and both the geographical situation of their schools and the nature of their work preclude adequate alternative interests or relaxation. They bear the brunt of any public complaint in their neighbourhood. The Head of any approved school is in an invidious position in this respect. Something may go wrong in his or her school from inefficiency of himself or his staff, because he or she is off colour or has attention diverted by private worries, or simply by accident. The consequences may be serious and one can rely on official or unofficial inquiry or comment being profoundly wise after the event. If the girls' schools are indeed dealing with more inflammable material, the potential risk is more obvious.'[1]

Perhaps this is the right way of looking at it; there is no way of comparing degrees of difficulty of behaviour since punishment rates, even if available, are very much governed by the ethos of the school. All we know is that there are a sufficient number of girls of this type to provide

[1] Association of Headmasters, Headmistresses and Matrons of Approved Schools, Technical Sub-committee Monograph No. 6, *Girls in approved schools*, 1954, p. 8.

a highly disruptive element in a wide range of senior and intermediate schools. It is pretty clear that the present methods of dealing with them are inadequate – we do not even know how inadequate, since the assessment of subsequent success or failure cannot be related to subsequent court appearances. Perhaps there are no ways of dealing with them, or no ways that could be devised or sanctioned within the straitjacket of a publicly financed and publicly accountable system.

There are two further problems. A proportion of girls are suffering from VD on committal and require treatment, and precautions have to be taken against infection. Also, a proportion are pregnant and may have their babies while at the school, which means that special arrangements have to be made for them and their infants.

As they are at present organized, girls' approved schools and girls' borstals are in no position to do whatever can be done, or to devise new ways of dealing with the problems that confront them. The basic requirements that spring to mind in considering how to tackle the situation are highly trained staffs in ample numbers, with plenty of psychiatric aid and strong links with adolescent units in mental hospitals. The present institutions for girls have none of these facilities and do not look as if they ever will have. There is little or nothing to be said for a collection of small, isolated units scattered all over the place in a haphazard way, some of them miles away from everywhere, without even the facilities for an adequate range of daily occupations, and without any way of disembarrassing themselves, even temporarily, of difficult or dangerous girls. Residential establishments staffed by women must inevitably suffer as a result of the current high marriage- and birth-rates. How can they operate if they continue to depend very largely on the services of unencumbered women, when these are in increasingly short supply?

Whatever may be the right and wrong ways of handling the girls, everything seems to point in this case to a strong and vigorous central organization, and to a long-term programme for concentrating the schools in areas where they are likely to be able to get and hold staff, and can find and use economically professional resources. They need to develop ways of using part-time staff which do not seriously damage the running of the schools, and to have large relief staffs.

The ideal system would surely be to group a loose federation of units under a single headmistress, within the area of a large town, with a good, co-operative psychiatric hospital available, and maternity and VD services at hand. Such an arrangement would improve the chances of getting and keeping staff; it would solve the problem of finding suitable employment for the girls and increase the range of work available in the schools (a workshop or a vocational training course could be fed from several schools); it would offer professional help and opportunity for experimentation; and it would permit a wide range of schools with different degrees of discipline, and easy transfer from one type of school to another, and if necessary in and out of mental hospital.

Perhaps this is day-dreaming, given the present situation, and perhaps it merely results from the general lack of knowledge about the girls' side; it is certainly true that it is here, most urgently, that new thinking and resolute action are required. The key to good training in women's establishments even more than in men's is in providing the right atmosphere to attract responsible and mature staff. Whether the heads of boys' schools are right in suggesting that women are more prone to worry, it is probably true that single women are more likely to be heavily involved in the job without a great deal of outside support in the form of strong personal relationships. It is necessary, therefore, to minimize the strain by giving the staff plenty of opportunity to make such relationships, male or female, in the vicinity, or to retain them if they already exist in the form of husband and family; and to organize things so that they can escape to them as often as possible. Married women are not necessarily better than single women in this kind of work, but it is absurd to narrow down the pool of possible candidates by making it difficult for suitable married women to undertake it. The authorities ought to regard housing provision and facilities for looking after children as part of the price to be paid for scarce labour.

These general principles might well be extended to cover all staff. It is trite and axiomatic to say that the kernel of all problems of residential training is staff. We do not know as much as we should about the reasons why staff come and why they leave, but if the findings of studies of the nursing profession are anything to go by, pay is only one of the factors. Of the others, by far the most critical is likely to be whether those immediately in charge have the ability to impart a sense of confidence in new staff, to assure them that they are trusted and reliable colleagues, carrying out their work within their own spheres. In a service with a long tradition of difficulties in this area it is not easy to create such an atmosphere – impossible, of course, if the only staff obtainable are not of a calibre to warrant it. Nevertheless, it remains as true of public service as of industry that a sound personnel policy is the basis of high productivity. Where the product is human happiness, the value of this approach is immeasurably increased.

Bibliography

ADAMS, A. E. (1945). A study of the conditions related to the delinquency of a group of boys in an approved school. Unpublished M.A. thesis, University of London.

AICHHORN, A. (1935). *Wayward youth*. New York: Viking.

ALEXANDER, W. P. and BARRACLOUGH, F. (1947). *Establishment, maintenance, and management of county and voluntary schools under the Education Acts 1944 and 1946*. London: Councils & Education Press. (Subsequently revised.)

ASSOCIATION OF HEADMASTERS, HEADMISTRESSES AND MATRONS OF APPROVED SCHOOLS Technical Sub-committee Monographs:

1. *Misfits in approved schools* (March, 1952).
2. *Aftercare in approved schools* (April, 1952).
3. *Aftercare in approved schools* (Report of a conference held in May, 1952, and statement of the Association's policy) (October, 1952).
6. *Girls in approved schools* (March, 1954).
7. *Approved schools and the future* (March, 1955).
8. Evidence to the Ingleby Committee.

BAKER, T. B. L. (1889). *War with crime*. London: Longmans.

BARNETT, MARY G. (1913). *Young delinquents*. London: Methuen.

BASELEY, ELSIE T. (1928). *Homer Lane and the Little Commonwealth*. London: Allen & Unwin.

BETTELHEIM, B. (1950). *Love is not enough*. Glencoe, Ill.: The Free Press.

BLACKER, C. P. (1946). *Neurosis and the mental health services*. London: Oxford University Press.

BRIGGS, I. G. (1924). *Reformatory reform*. London: Longmans.

BURT, C. (1925). *The young delinquent*. London: University of London Press. (4th edition, 1944.)

CARPENTER, MARY (1851). *Reformatory schools for the children of the perishing and dangerous classes and for juvenile offenders*. London: Gilpin.

CARPENTER, MARY (1853). *Juvenile delinquents, their condition and treatment*. London: Cash.

CARPENTER, MARY (1864). Suggestions on the management of reformatories and certified industrial schools. (Pamphlet.)

CHERNUCHIN, P. (1957). A study of boy absconders from approved schools. Unpublished Ph.D. thesis, University of London.

CHILDREN'S DEPARTMENT. Reports. First, 1923; Second, 1924; Third, 1925; Fourth, 1928; Fifth, 1938; Sixth, 1951; Seventh, 1955; Eighth, 1961; Ninth, 1964; and every four years subsequently. London: HMSO.

CLEUGH, M. F. (1957). *The slow learner*. London: Methuen.

Conference on preventive and reformatory schools, Birmingham (1857). (Pamphlet.)

COYLE, GRACE L. (1948). *Group work with American youth*. New York: Harper.

DEUTSCH, A. (1950). *Our rejected children*. Boston: Little, Brown.

EDUCATION, MINISTRY OF (1946). Pamphlet No. 5, *Special educational treatment*. (Reprinted 1951.) London: HMSO.

EDUCATION, MINISTRY OF (1954). *Training and supply of teachers*. Fourth Report of the National Advisory Council. London: HMSO.

EDUCATION, MINISTRY OF (1955a). Pamphlet No. 30, *Education of the handicapped pupil*. London: HMSO.

EDUCATION, MINISTRY OF (1955b). Report of the Committee on Maladjusted Children (Underwood Committee). London: HMSO.

FRIEDLANDER, K. (1947). *The psycho-analytic approach to juvenile delinquency*. London: Routledge & Kegan Paul.

GEORGE, W. R. (1910). *The junior republic*. New York: Appleton.

GITTINS, J. (1952). *Approved school boys*. London: HMSO.

GLUECK, S. and E. T. (1950). *Unraveling juvenile delinquency*. New York: Commonwealth Fund.

GRÜNHUT, M. (1956). *Juvenile offenders before the courts*. London: Oxford University Press.

GUNASEKARA, M. G. S. (1963). The problem of absconding in boys' approved schools in England and Wales. *Brit. J. Crim.* 4, 145–9.

HALL, SIR WILLIAM CLARKE (1917). *The state and the child*. London: New Commonwealth.

HEALTH, MINISTRY OF (1929). Report of the Mental Deficiency Committee (Wood Committee). London: HMSO.

HEALTH, MINISTRY OF (1959). Report of the Working Party on Social Workers in the Local Authority Health and Welfare Services (Chairman: Miss E. L. Younghusband). London: HMSO.

HEALY, W. (1915). *The individual delinquent*. Boston: Little.

HENDERSON, SIR V. L. (1946). Approved schools. In L. Radzinowicz and J. W. C. Turner (eds.), *Penal reform in England*. English Studies in Criminal Science. London: Cambridge University Press.

HILL, M. D. (1848). Report of a charge delivered to the Grand Jury of the borough of Birmingham at the Michaelmas Quarter Sessions for 1848.

HODGE, R. SESSIONS, WALTER, V. J. and WALTER, W. GREY (1953). Juvenile delinquency: an electrophysiological, psychological and social study. *Brit. J. Delinq.* 3, 155–72, January.

HOME OFFICE (1852–53). Report of the Select Committee on Criminal and Destitute Children (with minutes of evidence) (XXIII). London: HMSO.

HOME OFFICE (1868–1916). Annual Reports of the Inspectors of Reformatory and Industrial Schools. London: HMSO.

HOME OFFICE (1884). Report of the Commission on Reformatories and Industrial Schools, 1882–84 (with minutes of evidence) (C. 3876). London: HMSO.

HOME OFFICE (1896). Report of the Committee on Reformatories and Industrial Schools, 1895 (with minutes of evidence) (C. 8204, 8290). London: HMSO.

HOME OFFICE (1913). Report of the Committee on Reformatories and Industrial Schools, 1911–13 (with minutes of evidence) (Cd. 6838–9). London: HMSO.

HOME OFFICE (1927). Report of the Departmental Committee on Young Offenders. London: HMSO.

HOME OFFICE (1936). Report of the Committee on Conditions of Service of Approved School Staff (Henderson Committee). London: HMSO.

HOME OFFICE (1946). Report of the Committee on Remuneration and Conditions of Service in Approved Schools and Remand Homes (Reynolds Committee). London: HMSO.

HOME OFFICE (1947). Report of the Committee of Enquiry into the Conduct of Standon Farm Approved School and the circumstances connected with the murder of a master at the school on 15th February 1947 (Cmd. 7150). London: HMSO.

HOME OFFICE (1951). Report of a Committee to Review Punishments in Prisons, Borstal Institutions, Approved Schools and Remand Homes (Franklin Committee). Parts III and IV, Approved Schools and Remand Homes (Cmd. 8429). London: HMSO.

HOME OFFICE (1959). Disturbances at the Carlton Approved School on August 29 and 30, 1959. Report of Inquiry by Mr Victor Durand, Q.C. (Cmnd. 937). London: HMSO.

HOME OFFICE (1960). Report of the Committee on Children and Young Persons (Ingleby Committee) (Cmnd. 1191). London: HMSO.

HOME OFFICE (1961). Directory of Approved Schools, Remand Homes and Special Reception Centres in England and Wales. (This has a useful descriptive foreword.) London: HMSO.

HOME OFFICE (1963a). *The organization of aftercare*. Report of the Advisory Council on the Treatment of Offenders. London: HMSO.

HOME OFFICE (1963b). Statistics relating to approved schools, remand homes and attendance centres in England and Wales for the year 1961 (Cmnd. 2051). (The first of an annual series.) London: HMSO.

HOME OFFICE (1964). *The sentence of the court*. A handbook for courts on the treatment of offenders. London: HMSO.

HOME OFFICE (1965). *The child, the family and the young offender* (Cmnd. 2742). London: HMSO.

HOME OFFICE. *Making citizens*. (Various editions.) London: HMSO.

JONES, H. (1960). *Reluctant rebels*. London: Tavistock Publications.

KONOPKA, E. (1954). *Group work in the institution*. New York: Whiteside & Morrow.

LEVINE, S. (1962). Runaways and research in the training school. *Crime and Delinq.* 8, 40–45.

MANNHEIM, H. and WILKINS, L. T. (1955). *Prediction methods in relation to borstal training*. London: HMSO.

MULOCK HOUWER, D. Q. R. (1955). The institutional treatment of juvenile offenders from the point of view of the director of an institution. In Report of the European Exchange Seminar on the International Treatment of Offenders, 1954. UN Series IV, ST/TAA/5CR.C/23.

PEARCE, S. B. P. (1958). *An ideal in the working : the story of the Magdalen hospital 1758–1958*. London: Magdalen hospital.

RED LODGE REFORMATORY SCHOOL, BRISTOL (1956). Principles, rules and regulations, with the first report. (Pamphlet.)

REDL, F. and WINEMAN, D. (1957). *The aggressive child*. A twin volume containing *Children who hate* and *Controls from within*. Glencoe, Ill.: The Free Press.

RODGERS, B. N. and DIXON, J. (1960). *Portrait of social work*. London: Oxford University Press.

SCOTT, P. D. (1951). The residential treatment of juvenile delinquents in approved and other special schools. *Brit. J. Delinq.* **2**, 5–24, July.

SCOTT, P. D. (1964). Approved school success rates. *Brit. J. Criminol.* **4**, 525–6.

SCOTTISH HOME DEPARTMENT (1947). *Approved schools*. Scottish Advisory Council on the Treatment of Offenders.

SELECT COMMITTEE ON ESTIMATES (1949). 18th report 1948–49: Approved schools.

SELLIN, T. and WOLFGANG, M. E. (1964). *The measurement of delinquency*. New York: Wiley.

STEIN, Z. A. and SUSSER, M. W. (1965). A socio-medical study of enuresis among delinquent boys. *Brit. J. prev. soc. Med.* **19**, 174–81.

STOTT, D. H. (1950). *Delinquency and human nature*. Dunfermline, Fife: Carnegie United Kingdom Trust.

TAPPAN, P. W. (1949). *Juvenile delinquency*. New York: McGraw-Hill.

TAYLOR, S. H. (1954). Some clinical types in an approved school. *Brit. J. Delinq.* **6**, 189–98, January.

TEETERS, N. K. and REINEMANN, J. O. (1950). *Challenge of delinquency*. New York: Prentice-Hall.

THOMSON, MARY HORNER (1912). *Environment and efficiency*. Birmingham: University of Birmingham.

UNESCO (1960). *Statistics on special education*. Paris.

UNITED NATIONS. Department of economic and social affairs. *Comparative survey of juvenile delinquency*.

    Part 1. *North America*, 1958 (ST/SOA/SD/1/Rev.1).

    Part 2. *Europe* (in French), 1952 (ST/SOA/SD/1/Add. 1).

    Part 3. *Latin America* (ST/SOA/SD/1/Add. 2).

    Part 4. *Asia and the Far East* (ST/SOA/SD/1/Add. 3).

    Part 5. *Middle East* (ST/SOA/SD/1/Add. 4).

    An English summary of Part 2 of the *Comparative survey of juvenile delinquency* appears in *International review of criminal policy No. 5* (United Nations, January, 1954).

WILLS, W. D. (1941). *The Hawkspur experiment*. London: Allen & Unwin.

WILLS, W. D. (1945). *The Barns experiment*. London: Allen & Unwin.

WILSON, G. and RYLAND, G. (1949). *Social group work practice*. Boston: Houghton Mifflin.

WINTER, A. (1891). *The New York State Reformatory at Elmira*. London: Sonnenshein.

WOODWARD, M. (1955a). The role of low intelligence in delinquency. *Brit. J. Delinq.* **5**, 281–303, April.

WOODWARD, M. (1955b). Low intelligence and delinquency. London: Institute for the Study and Treatment of Delinquency. (Pamphlet.)

Index